House of the Turquoise Roof

House of the Turquoise Roof

Dorje Yudon Yuthok

Preface by Tenzin N. Tethong
Foreword by Heinrich Harrer

Translated and edited by Michael Harlin

Snow Lion Publications
Ithaca, New York USA

Snow Lion Publications
P.O. Box 6483
Ithaca, NY 14851
USA

Printed in the USA

ISBN 1-55939-035-2

Library of Congress Cataloging-in-Publication Data

Yuthok, Dorje Yudon, 1912-
   House of the turquoise roof / Dorje Yudon Yuthok ; preface by
Tenzin Tethong ; foreword by Heinrich Harrer ; edited by Michael
Harlin.
      p. cm.
   Includes bibliographical references.
   ISBN 1-55939-035-2
   1. Yuthok, Dorje Yudon, 1912-   . 2. Tibet (China)—Social life
and customs. 3. Tibet (China)—Biography. I. Title.
   DS786.Y87   1990
951'.5—dc20   90-41455
                                                          CIP

Contents

To
The People of Tibet
My Late Parents
My Late Daughter, Thubten Choden

Preface

It is my distinct pleasure to write a few introductory remarks to the autobiography of Mrs. Dorje Yudon Yuthok, whom I have known since childhood.

This is one of those rare books that will shed insight into a whole culture and a historical period of great importance to the Tibetan people. As you read through this unique life story, you will understand the way of life in Tibet before the Chinese occupation and the tide of events that swept through her life bringing her all the way to the United States: a story of changes and events beyond one's control, happiness and tragedy, and the spiritual beliefs that constantly anchored her life.

Tibetans have generally shied away from writing their own autobiographies except in the rare case of a distinguished lama or scholar. However, this book comes at a time when the life story of any Tibetan is an important human document, at a time when Chinese propagandists and Western scholars debate the status of Tibet and Tibetan culture. Mrs. Yuthok's autobiography is a frank and open account by any standard. It is not the story of a woman's liberation, but her life does shed light into the status of women in Tibet, their position in society and the rights they enjoyed.

Those who know Mrs. Yuthok will agree that this book does what she has always done so successfully: to quietly, diplomatically and gently present herself with dignity and straightforwardness.

I hope that *House of the Turquoise Roof* will be on every "must read" list on Tibet.

Tenzin N. Tethong
Special Representative of
His Holiness the Dalai Lama
Washington, D.C.

July 10, 1988

Foreword

by Heinrich Harrer

During the winter of 1946, when Peter Aufschnaiter and I reached the "forbidden city" of Lhasa, we were at the end of our strength and run-down like beggars. Our hands and feet were crippled by frostbite. Since we had fled the prisoner-of-war camp in India two years earlier, we had crossed more than fifty mountain passes of between 15,000 and 20,000 feet in temperatures much below freezing. Our deplorable condition raised much commotion and caused the compassionate Tibetans to shower us with presents. Soon we were to become closely acquainted not only with the highly respected family of the Dalai Lama but also with the aristocratic houses of Tsarong and Surkhang. Our affection for these families has never ceased. In those days during the winter of 1946, we came as refugees into a prosperous land and were welcomed with typical Tibetan hospitality. Today, as the roles are reversed, it is my deeply felt desire and duty to show my gratitude in whatever way possible.

Quite apart from my feelings of affection and gratitude for the author, this book deserves to be widely read. Yuthok Lhacham Kusho (as I used to address the author in Tibetan) describes with great candor and knowledge the complicated, and to us almost incomprehensible, family ties which resulted from legalized polygamy and polyandry. In addition she lets us experience the very deeply rooted family sense which enables Tibetans—in a manner often puzzling to us—to stay close to each other while separated by continents.

The book fascinated me from beginning to end since I knew not only the environment but also each of the persons referred to. Details are what makes a good book so interesting, and Mrs. Yuthok explains in great detail many of the customs and traditions. Although I knew these customs and had observed them, I could not always comprehend them. During our flight from prison I had faithfully kept a diary, updating it even during temperatures of minus twenty degrees. But later in Lhasa where Aufschnaiter and I eventually became government officials, our daily routine included numerous receptions such as that for the Tibetan New Year, the birth of a child, a marriage or an official appointment, as well as religious processions and festivals. I then stopped keeping my diary as I felt that I would be able to remember it all by heart. That was a mistake. Thankfully now I am able to read in this fascinating account how the nomads braid their hair, what the different pieces of traditional jewelry are called and how old families are related by marriage. Many of my questions have been answered.

Since I knew the parents, brothers and sisters of Mrs. Yuthok very well, I should like to add my own observations of her family to those of the author.

Her father Surkhang Dzasa was Foreign Minister and as such my immediate superior in the government. He shared his office, which was housed in the big Central Temple (Tsuk Lhakhang), with Liushar Dzasa. All government functions were handled jointly by a monk and a lay official, with the monk having senior rank. I had managed to assemble a battery-operated wireless, and it was above all Surkhang Dzasa who took interest in the latest international news I received. Often he also dropped by just to chat. I can still picture him in front of me, taking off his dark, smeared eyeglasses and cleaning them with fingers stained brown by opium.

A half-brother of the author, Ngawang Jigme, had the reputation of being a collaborator with the Chinese; he was known as "go nyipa," a Tibetan expression meaning "double-headed." When I returned to Tibet as a tourist in 1982, thirty years later, a man clad in a leather jacket welcomed me with the words: "Don't you remember me? You saved my life!" It was Ngawang Jigme Surkhang. He acted rather pompously and told me that he was the head of a trekking operation. I was happy for him, but as it turned out, he could not make any decisions without asking his superior who was, of course, Chinese. Since I was persona non grata to the Chinese as well as to China and thus was not allowed to travel freely in Tibet, Jigme was no help at all.

Forty years earlier, when I had pulled an unconscious Jigme from a whirlpool in the Kyichu River and had managed to revive him through mouth-to-mouth resuscitation, his father Surkhang Dzasa had shown his gratitude by letting me live in one of his beautiful mansions. It was called "Po Lingka," had a huge garden and was actually much too big for me. But it was to remain my residence during my last two years in Lhasa. (My faithful servant Nyima would profit from it even after the invasion and occupation, as he could sell the vegetables which I had begun to plant to the Chinese).

I also stayed for some time at the beautiful Yuthok mansion. It had been constructed of granite blocks, was surrounded by a big garden and occupied a particularly advantageous site between Yuthok Bridge and the Potala. When I visited the site in 1982, I found nothing but charred ruins. In fact, I had great trouble finding the spot, as all those places I once knew as wide, open meadows with horses grazing on them are now occupied by buildings. Yuthok Bridge, once covered with turquoise-colored tiles, is now an ugly shed and so dwarfed by other buildings that one cannot recognize it as a bridge anymore.

I could say much more about other members of the family, about the brothers, the Minister, the General and above all about Mrs. Yuthok's Guru, Kyabje Trijang Rinpoche, who was my great benefactor at a time when many monks were less than enchanted with my regular visits to the Dalai Lama. However, I would just like to add a few sentences about the youngest brother, Wangchuk Dorje. The two of us had been especially close for a long time. When the Dalai Lama fled to Southern Tibet during the winter of 1951-52, I was allowed to accompany His Holiness. At that time Wangchuk was Governor of Gyantse and was responsible for the safety of the Dalai Lama's escape route. He used a very primitive field telephone. Together we cleaned a big area of stones so as to enable a small aircraft to make an emergency landing in case the Chinese were to cut off the Dalai Lama's escape route. Wangchuk later renounced the monkhood and married a pretty Bhutanese girl. Their son is now one of the high tulkus (reincarnated lamas) of Rumtek Monastery in Sikkim. During one of my visits with him I was able to give him many old photographs of his late father.

In 1959, when the Tibetan exodus from their homeland started, I traveled to Tezpur in Assam for *LIFE Magazine*. Here I saw many of my old Lhasa friends again: the Yuthoks, the Tsarongs and the Surkhangs. It was heart-breaking when Dekyi-la, the wife of Minister Surkhang and sister-in-law of the author, fell into my arms sobbing, and when the mother of the Dalai Lama, always a deeply caring lady, was overcome with sadness at the fate of her people and concern for the well-being of His Holiness.

During the three decades since that time there have been repeated uprisings against the foreign invaders of Tibet as well as attempts at reconciliation in order to allow the Dalai Lama to return to Tibet, for without him even the powerful Chinese could never manage to appease Tibet.

May this valuable and interesting account help ensure that the quest for freedom of the Tibetan people not be forgotten. When I asked a Tibetan oracle after the oppression and destruction of Tibet about the fate of the Tibetans and their religion, he jumped up in trance and shouted "*Lha gyelo!*"— "The Gods will win!"

Translated from the German by Gigi Lhalungpa

Introduction

My life tells, though indirectly, something about our peaceful country, Tibet. The book unfolds the events—often amusing and sometimes agonizing—that so sheltered and shaped the fate of myself and my family. It also reflects the place of women in a traditional society and the values and experiences shared by Tibetan women.

Tibet is an ancient country with a history of some two thousand years. For much of that time Tibet had little contact with other countries, so that in earlier times people in the rest of the world did not know about life in Tibet. Although a few missionaries from Europe arrived in Tibet in the seventeenth century, they did not stay long, and it was very difficult for them to understand the Tibetan social system and its culture.

A few educated persons of the West—English officials, Americans, Germans, and others—came to Tibet, but except for noting the history of political events, methods of formulating policy, and religious systems, they did not write much about everyday life. Later, although some Westerners wrote about conditions in Tibet, they seldom dealt with the life and customs of Tibetan women. As a matter of fact, even in our own literature, little can be found about women.

For this reason I dedicated myself to the writing of a book

about the women of Tibet, especially as I was encouraged to do so by my good friend, Mrs. Marge Ranney. I had great hope that if I could write about my life as a woman of Tibet many people around the world might read it with interest. At the same time, I hope it may give to the younger generation of Tibetan women some idea of how their mothers lived. I would like to take this opportunity to acknowledge here the many friends and family members whose kind assistance and encouragement have been essential to the completion of this book.

First of all I would like to thank two very special friends, Mrs. Marge Ranney and Mr. Michael Harlin, without whose help and kindness this book would never have been published. During my trips to India, Mrs. Marge Ranney has always shown me her kindness and generosity by putting me up at her house as if I were a member of the family. Likewise I must extend the same thanks to Michael regarding my visits to Philadelphia.

I must also thank Mr. Lobsang Lhalungpa for his kind assistance and perceptive advice. His vast knowledge of our culture, history and religion have been invaluable, and his generous advice in the translation is greatly appreciated. I must also add my nephew Nuchin Tinley Surkhang, and thank him for the countless hours he helped me in the translation and in keeping up with my correspondence. To my son Dondul Wangchuk I owe thanks for his support in compiling this book. To Bha Tulku Pema Tenzin Rinpoche and Dorje Kuntrup Yurwog who were the pioneer translators, I extend my gratitude and thanks. To Mrs. Ruth Ruttenberg I am especially indebted for the typing and the many changes she has had to make. She has also been an inspiring friend who stood by me for many years. I cannot forget Mrs. Nima Lingden, Mrs. Danielle Rouch, Mrs. May Williams and my cousin Dr. Kalsang Wangdu Sharchitsang, all of whom had a hand in the writing of this book through the kindness of their hearts. I also wish to thank Mr. Tenzin Chodrak and Dr. Paljor Tsarong, who have been most helpful. To my niece, Choden Dolkar, I extend thanks for giving me a home in Cleveland. I have lived here since 1982 during which time she has shown me nothing but kindness and care and will always be a very special person.

During the seventeen years I lived in New York my late daughter Thupten Choden helped me through the initial stages of this writing. She was a great source of inspiration. Her love and devotion allowed me to live in New York and write my story. Her untimely death was a tragedy that I can only overcome through my spiritual endeavors, and it made me more determined to finish this book. Without her love this book would never have come to completion.

I have tried to present, as best I can, life as it was in Tibet, in what now seems a bygone era. I have done so truthfully and to the best of my knowledge. For all the errors and omissions, I take full responsibility.

1 Drak: My Birthplace

I was born on one of our family's estates in a village called Drak (Boulder), which lay over a mountain pass, fifty rough and twisting miles southeast of Lhasa. Even though we all loved Drak so much, it was not expected that my birth would take place there. The family was not accustomed to staying very long in the peaceful village, because our main residence was in Lhasa. It was only due to serious political disturbances that the family had to flee the capital in 1912 shortly before heavy fighting erupted between the Manchu soldiers and Tibetan forces. Lhasa was becoming more dangerous day by day. The Chinese boldly showed disrespect to the Tibetan government and harrassed Tibetans in various ways. It was decided that my mother along with my grandmother, my uncle Sonam Wangdu and my older brother Wangchen Gelek together with a few servants would go to Drak before the fighting broke out in earnest. My mother was expecting my birth and could not help but worry about her brother and husband back in Lhasa. Messengers were sent often to bring back news of the happenings there.

Shortly after arriving in Drak, my mother heard that her brother Lhagyari Namgyal Wangchuk had been killed in Lhasa. When the trouble started, he had gone out on his own and raised a volunteer regiment of more than twelve hundred soldiers from Kongbo and Dakpo. He was killed by Chinese cannon fire during a battle.

For centuries the Chinese had maintained an *amban* or ambassador in Lhasa accompanied by a small detachment of Chinese troops to provide his escort to and from Peking. Through the amban the emperor of China exerted diplomatic pressure on the Tibetan government. When relations became strained for one reason or another, the number of Chinese troops in Lhasa would be increased enough to become threatening in the tiny capital. Such circumstances had once again come to pass. A political faction in Peking, eager to win glory for itself by subjugating Tibet, had gradually built up troops until they totaled about seven thousand. At the time the population of Lhasa was only twenty thousand, half of whom were monks at the three great monasteries. When another contingent of Chinese troops arrived in 1910, they marched into the city in a hostile and threatening manner, opening fire in front of the *Tsuglak Khang,* the great central cathedral built in the eighth century and the holiest temple in Tibet, and the Potala Palace, which was the residence of the Dalai Lama and seat of the government. Casual passers-by were killed, and among the dead were several Tibetan officials, civilians and a policeman.

In the ensuing widespread alarm His Holiness the Thirteenth Dalai Lama and his government decided that night to flee Tibet for India. The Tsemonling Hutuktu, a high-ranking lama from Tsemonling Monastery, was appointed regent with full powers to rule until His Holiness decided to return. The regent assigned our father special duties that required him to remain in Lhasa. Early the next morning the Dalai Lama, three prime ministers, three cabinet ministers and a number of other officials including our uncle Pema Wangchen left the palace accompanied by servants and thirty bodyguards. Upon arrival in India the Tibetans were warmly received by the British government, which offered them full protection. His Holiness established his exile headquarters in Darjeeling from where he could negotiate a truce with China.

Inside China the reigning dynasty was on the point of collapse as internal factions struggled for power. One group called by Tibetans Lu Chun Gyanag opposed the invasion of Tibet and prevented provisions for the invading troops from being forwarded to them. As a result the Chinese in Tibet were frustrated and insecure, and vented their anger on the local population. They pillaged the storehouses of the Potala and Norbu Lingka palaces looking for guns and ammunition. For nearly two years this state of affairs endured, while both the people and government of Tibet bore the humiliation with restraint. They did not have much choice.

This state of siege turned into full-scale armed combat when the Chinese troops attempted to take over Sera Monastery outside Lhasa. Since the monks had learned of these plans in advance, they were well prepared to meet their assailants, and were joined in the defense by warriors from Kham as well as the local populace. Forced back from their unsuccessful attack, the Chinese troops camped in the southern end of Lhasa, while the Tibetans held the more strategic northern part which included the Potala Palace and the Tsuglak Khang. The government headed by the regent and local community leaders met frequently to coordinate the defense of the city. The small standing Tibetan army was joined by monks from the three large monasteries of Sera, Drepung and Ganden, and the people of Lhasa.

The inhabitants barricaded their section of Lhasa with piles of stone and sandbags. The soldiers had guns and a few cannons but the monks and common people often only had swords and spears. Most of the fighting took place in hand to hand combat. Many Chinese met their end when the Tibetans dug tunnels under the houses they occupied and blasted them with gunpowder and dynamite. Since the Chinese were surrounded by the Tibetans, they ran out of food and had to rely on the carcasses of dead horses or anything else they could find.

At the next meeting of the Tibetan National Assembly the military chiefs and monks from the three big monasteries ordered the arrest of several important government officials. Cabinet Minister Tsarong, his son, another official named Tsagur Shakpa, and our father were rumored to be collaborating with the Chinese who were threatening Tibet. While the fate of these officials was being debated, a close family friend who was the treasurer of the Je College of Sera Monastery spoke up on behalf of our father, promising that Surkhang had never been a friend of the Chinese. Since this monk was a very powerful personage, the charges were dropped and nothing more was ever said. The others were dragged down the steps of the Potala and shot.

When these troubles broke out, Grandmother and Mother left Lhasa for Drak. Father stayed behind in Lhasa not at the Surkhang house, but instead with his maternal uncle's family Nara Kyishong (Narkyid for short) who lived at the foot of the Potala. Father's uncle Jigme Dorje Surkhang and six servants remained in the Surkhang house to look after it. The southern part of town, on the edge of which the Surkhang house was located, was occupied by the Chinese. One day twenty Chinese soldiers lead by an officer arrived at our house. While conducting a search, they demanded all of the locked storerooms be opened so they could supply themselves with food and bedding. Shortly afterwards the Chinese imprisoned about thirty Tibetans there along with our servants and uncle. Next to be put under arrest and placed in our house was the entire family of the Thirteenth Dalai Lama, consisting of His Holiness' maternal aunt, nephew, nieces,[1] and their mother, along with their servants. The little nine-year-old nephew Kunga Wangchuk later became a prime minister with the title of Silon. All of the Yabshi Langdun family, as they were known, stayed on the second floor in the best part of the house where each had his own room.

Now that seventy or eighty people both Chinese and Tibetan were camped throughout the house, they all had to be fed, so the Chinese organized a common prison-style mess with bad food which was doled out to each prisoner in tiny amounts. Because there was not enough, the Chinese allowed individual

prisoners to have a day pass to go to the side of Lhasa under
Tibetan control to get extra food or medicine. The Chinese
officer in charge said that if the prisoner on leave failed to return, others remaining behind would be killed in reprisal. Once
when an old couple's step-daughter named Kunzang failed to
return, they were shot the next day in their room. Everyone
became very afraid.

The fighting was fierce and brutal in the initial stages but
as the months went by gradually subsided. Upon the collapse
of the reigning dynasty in Peking and the rise of the Chinese
Nationalist Movement, the amban and several of his officials
approached the Nepalese Embassy to arrange their surrender
to Tibet. The regent accepted and ordered the Chinese to leave
for China via India. They were provided with food and expenses up to the Indian border. They departed in three groups
within the span of two months. His Holiness the Dalai Lama
returned to Lhasa early in 1913.

Even though we had been forced to flee the capital, the journey from Lhasa to Drak was the same, still memorable for
both its hardship and beauty. While other mountains in this
area had very little vegetation, the Drak side of the high mountain separating it from Lhasa was a sight to behold. But first
we had to climb the mountain from the Lhasa side. Horses
could not move fast on this trail and yaks were even slower.
The geography of the area made it difficult to ride on anything but yaks. Even then in some places the travelers had
to dismount and walk. Because there were no villages or people on this side, we had the choice of taking our own tents
for camping overnight in the open or finding shelter in one
of the caves along the way. Most travelers chose to stay in caves.
These difficulties, however, were more than made up for by
the natural beauty, peace and tranquility. Several small mountain streams splashed down providing water for the many varieties of wild animals: leopards, brown bears, wolves, rabbits
and a little animal similar to the guinea pig called *chiphi*, which
we saw now and then.

After we reached the summit and were ready to descend,

the picture changed radically. Rainfall was plentiful, so that in spring and summer the trees and bushes with their colorful sweet-scented flowers covered the mountainside. Wildflowers bloomed beside rare medicinal herbs, and spices such as caraway, thyme and tarragon abounded. On the upper reaches of this side of the mountain were white and gold mushrooms. Lower down were large patches of fine grass where both wild and domestic animals came in large numbers to feed. There were musk deer and red and black foxes in addition to the animals already mentioned. Although we did not see many herdsmen along the trail, they sometimes appeared with their yaks, sheep and goats. Occasionally we saw villagers who had come to harvest mushrooms, herbs or spices.

Drak itself was a very small village. There were only about fifteen households, which if included with those who worked on our estate, totaled about one hundred twenty persons living in this valley. Scattered here and there, their houses were surrounded by gardens filled with potatoes, radishes, spinach, turnips, and other vegetables. In addition, each family owned a few yaks, *zomos* (hybrid yaks), cattle, and sheep from which they could get enough dairy products for their own use. These dairy products included milk, butter, curd, and dry and wet cheeses. They also raised poultry only for eggs since Tibetans almost never ate chickens. The villagers kept sheep and goats for their wool and meat, and donkeys for carrying loads.

Fields for farming were allotted to them from my family's estate. These fields might be close to their homes or some distance away. The allotments were hereditary and recorded even before the estate had been awarded to the Surkhang family. Since the land was fertile, the harvest was good and the villagers could produce enough surplus food to trade for a profit. During the summer in whatever direction we looked we saw pastures and fields of emerald green. Life in this valley was peaceful. It was not difficult for the villagers to maintain their families in a comfortable manner.

It was the custom in Tibet for government officials to be assigned estates in places far away from Lhasa as a form of payment for their work. In the eighteenth century the Sur-khang family had been given Drak during the reign of the Seventh Dalai Lama. It was up to us to develop the estate into a prosperous business. The villagers living on these estates were required to work, for which they were compensated in two ways: first, their labor was considered as tax owed to the estate holder; and second, they were given for their private use a plot of land on which they grew the larger crops. Estate owners had in turn an obligation to the government, which varied from place to place. From Drak we were expected to send a special kind of wood cut in various sizes convenient for cooking use. This wood was tied together in bundles and sent to Lhasa for use in the kitchen of the Dalai Lama.

The villagers were truly co-owners of the estate. They were free to use our grazing pasture and to collect wood, herbs and spices from the mountainsides. They also harvested twigs for making baskets. They were expert weavers of beautiful baskets of all kinds and sizes. Some were for their own use and others for sale. Very large baskets were used for storing as much as three or four quintals[2] of grain; small ones might hold the rare herbs and spices. Each had geometric designs formed by dark twigs and lighter ones stripped of their bark. The sale of these baskets was very profitable for the villagers.

While about half of the land was reserved for the owner and the other half belonged to the peasants, each family had its own hereditary farm, house and animals reserved for its use that were listed in the records of the estate. The size of each family's lands varied considerably, and the whole was handed down from father to son. A hard working or clever farmer could save money and buy a neighbor's acreage if he wished.

The estate owner provided seed, tools, and plough animals. The peasants spent only about a quarter to a third of their time on the landlord's property. The amount of time owed depended on the extent of the peasant's own acreage. After having done his share of work for the landlord, he was free to come and go at any time for pilgrimage, trading trips or whatever. During the four coldest winter months, everyone stayed inside doing indoor work such as weaving, spinning thread, or just resting. There was no concept of being forced to do anything. Each peasant owned his own land and was usually reluctant to leave. Thus, both directly and indirectly the owners of estates were acting as overseers to guarantee the well-being of the villages.

There were also nomads on the mountainside in a little valley high above our house. They kept yaks and *dris* (female yaks). Every year the surplus products coming from these animals had to be carefully packed for the long journey to the market at Lhasa. Among the things sent were butter sealed in hides, hard dried cheese and powdered cheese. Together with the villagers' own crops, these products were transported to Lhasa by a team of pack animals arranged by our manager.

The journey for these goods was even more difficult than that for travelers. Until about 1953 there was no bridge over the river separating Lhasa from the mountain trail. We crossed in a ferry, but goods had to be unloaded on one side of the river, put into hide boats and rowed to the other side. Donkeys and mules had to be sent from our residence in Lhasa to wait for the loads to be taken out of the hide boats and transported the rest of the way. When it was time for the return journey to Drak, the transportation team never returned unladen. Salt, sugar, brick tea, cotton, cooking utensils, farming tools, and other necessities would be carried back to the village.

Although we had several other estates, some of which were much larger, the Drak estate remained a favorite with us all. Comparatively near Lhasa, it was also the residence of our great aunt Kalsang Choden. The Drak valley had a breathtaking beauty of its own; there was a ban on hunting in the area because it was considered sacred to Guru Padma Sambhava, the eighth-century saint.

Thus it was that in 1912 my birth took place in the house which my great-great-grandfather had built about 1870, and had named "Kunsang Choeling." This was a very charming two-storied building with a total of fifteen rooms, including a small chapel, a separate living room and a huge storeroom on the ground level. Not long after my birth in this peaceful valley, my father was able to come to Drak and to welcome me personally into the family. By this time the fighting had almost come to an end.

When we returned to Lhasa we discovered that the home in which our family had lived since the eighteenth century had been badly damaged in the fighting. After the hostages in our house had been released, it had been occupied by Chinese troops and officers. Tibetan resistance fighters tunnelled under the house and ignited quantities of gunpowder in order to destroy the garrison. Many Chinese were killed and the house was ruined. We had to rent another house for two years while our own was being rebuilt. Of course, I was too young to remember any of these things. The memory of my childhood really starts when we moved back into the Surkhang residence in Lhasa.

2 The Branched House of Surkhang

Tibet was ruled by a succession of kings from a single family since the second century B.C. Srongtsen Gampo the thirty-third king, Trisong Detsen the thirty-seventh, and Tri Ralpachen the fortieth were the most revered and powerful kings of Tibet. These kings were called *chogyals* or religious kings, because they introduced and supported Buddhism. It was in the seventh century A.D. during Srongtsen Gampo's rule that Buddhism became widespread. Even after thirteen centuries, the descendants of the chogyals continued to be remembered and respected for the part their ancestors played in spreading Buddhism in Tibet.

The Surkhangs descend from the king Lang Dharma, who was the forty-first king and the brother of Tri Ralpachen. Lang Dharma had two wives, Namdey Odsrung and Tridey Yumten. They each bore him a son. After the death of Lang Dharma, there was a power struggle between these two queens, each of whom wanted her son to assume the throne. However, this problem was resolved without bloodshed. Namdey Odsrung agreed to rule the Tod region in western Tibet while Tridey Yumten ruled U province in central Tibet. As a result, from that time until the Fifth Dalai Lama, Tibet was never ruled by a single king. During this interim period, the country was subdivided into many kingdoms, each with its own ruler.

In the eighteenth century during the reign of the Seventh Dalai Lama some of our ancestors moved to Lhasa from Maryul, Ladakh, in western Tibet. Since the seventh century Lhasa had been the most holy place in the country, and from the fifteenth century it was the seat of the Dalai Lamas who ruled a unified Tibet. Upon the arrival of my father's ancestors, the Dalai Lama ordered the government give them an estate and house in recognition of their royal lineage. Since ours was a *khang* (house) established as *sur* (branched) from a chogyal, we were called Surkhang, meaning "branched house." A second explanation of the origin of our name says that when our family came to Lhasa, they settled near the *sur* (southeast corner) of the great Tsuk Lhakhang, the central temple. People began to call our house Surkhang, meaning "corner house." In any case, the family name was Surkhang from then on.

When the Surkhang family was so honored with an estate, they were also appointed as *shungshab* or hereditary officials to serve the government under the authority of the Dalai Lama. The estates of lay officials were hereditary, and they derived their sole income from the management of these lands. There were two kinds of officials in the Tibetan government. One was the *kyawo* or layman group which included us, and the other was the *tsedrung* or monk officials who were celibate. Most monk officials received an income directly from the government, but three at that time had their own hereditary lands passing from uncle to nephew. When a family had more than one son, often one of them would enter the government service as a tsedrung. In our family, our youngest brother became a tsedrung since there were two older brothers who were already in the government service as lay officials. In the tsedrung's family one of the brother's sons would be chosen to succeed his uncle as head of the household with the duty of becoming the next official to serve the government. He would also inherit his family's land. Monk officials numbered about one hundred and fifty, and came from every social stratum of Tibetan society, including tradesmen or peasant families. Some were selected from monks already in monasteries, mostly Sera, Ganden, Drepung and some others. They ranged in age from fifteen to twenty years. After their selection by the Yigtsang office of the Potala Palace, they were sent to Yigtsang School where they were taught the essential principles of government.

As advancement was purely by merit, this represented a significant prospect for upward mobility in our society. Furthermore no parents could ever prevent their son from becoming a monk. Many ambitious and talented people were found in the religious communities. The highest leaders in Tibet were the incarnate lamas, chosen as infants usually from peasant families.

There were three groups at the top of the aristocracy in Lhasa: the depon, the yabshi and the midrak. The group of *depon* consisted of four families, all with enormous land holdings that had been awarded at some time in the past by a ruler of Tibet for long government service or some achievement leading to the betterment of the country. Along with the award came a letter bearing the seal of the Dalai Lama or his regent, depending on who was in power. These estates were hereditary. From this group, only the Lhagyaris were in direct male descent from a chogyal or early king.

The next group, the *yabshi*, held somewhat smaller but still sizeable estates. The name yabshi means "father estate." Only families into which a Dalai Lama was born had yabshi status and thus automatically were raised to become members of the hereditary nobility. These families had all been from the peasantry before their elevation. Older and younger brothers of the Dalai Lama were given the honorary ranks of *gung* or *chung*, which is equal in prestige to the rank of *shapey* or government minister. Gung is a high title like duke and chung is a Tibetan word for younger brother or sister. Therefore, the older brother was called gung and the younger brother chung. The yabshi families held the highest rank among the nobility.

The third group was that of the sixteen *midrak* families. The midrak had the same estate size as the yabshi but with the position of the depon. The midrak and depon both entered government service with the same rank, the fourth. The families of these three groups had large houses in Lhasa. Although the depon families had a lot of land, they held the same rank as the midrak families. The yabshi on the other hand, were of higher rank like cabinet ministers, even if they did not hold a powerful official position.

Below the midrak, the next and largest group was the *gerpa*, of whom there were one hundred thirty-seven families. They had much smaller estates (although a few gerpa families had fairly large holdings) and began government service in the seventh rank. Estate size in no way limited or delayed their rise to high positions. Advancement was based solely on merit and ability. Many great leaders in our history were from the gerpa class. Many of these families did not own homes in Lhasa but instead rented houses or apartments. They tended to be based more in the provinces.

Although the Surkhangs were midrak, in a special way they had at one time become similar to the yabshi. The Ninth Dalai Lama Lungtok Gyatso, who was born in 1805 in Dhencho Khorgon in Kham, was brought to Lhasa a few years after he was born. His father had died and his mother Dondrup Dolma lived with her brother-in-law and her three daughters. On their arrival in Lhasa the government decided to merge them with the family of Yabshi Samdrup Photrang, who were the descendants of the Seventh Dalai Lama's parents. However, after a short period of time there was a falling out between Dondrup Dolma and the Samdrup Photrangs. She decided she wanted to live with the Surkhangs. After deliberations between the government, Dondrup Dolma, and the Surkhangs, everyone agreed to this change. Not only were the Surkhangs from the midrak rank, but also they had sons who were eligible for their daughters. The eldest married Surkhang Tseten Dorje, who later became a *sawang* or cabinet minister. When Dondrup Dolma and her daughters joined the Surkhang family, the government awarded them the Kalung estate and its adjacent area, which became the largest estate the Surkhangs possessed. The brother-in-law remained with the Samdrup Photrang family.

As the Surkhang family was one of the eighteen midrak families, their position and property were hereditary. But if ever a generation produced no sons, then it was customary to adopt a husband from another family for one of the daughters. He was required to take the wife's family name, and upon inheriting the estates assume all the responsibilities involved. He was called a *makpa*.

This happened once in our family. Sawang Surkhang Tseten Dorje and his wife, the sister of the Ninth Dalai Lama, had three sons and one daughter, named Tseten Yudon. One son went as a bridegroom or makpa to Treshong, another to Shatra, and the third became a monk but lived at home. After the death of the father, because the family had no heir, Wangchen Norbu of the Changlo family from the city of Gyantse in Tsang Province was brought into the family as the bridegroom. The Changlo were also of the midrak rank. Their ancestry was traced from Dakchen Rabtan Kunzang Phak of Gyantse, who donated funds to establish a new monastery there called Palkhor Chode just before the Fifth Dalai Lama's time, and thereby enhanced his family's reputation. Wangchen Norbu came to Surkhang house as a makpa in 1850. This match was arranged by the mother of the bride along with the Surkhangs' good friend Shatra Kalon who was then prime minister.[1] The Surkhangs had a family connection with the Shatras since earlier a Surkhang son had gone to their house as a bridegroom or makpa. Matches were usually made by men, but since the Surkhang and Changlo fathers had died, in this case the women made the arrangements.

The Surkhang daughter Tseten Yudon had earlier married a son of the Trimon family of midrak rank and had one daughter. Since her husband died soon afterwards, she came back to Surkhang house with her daughter Tseten Gyalmo who was known as a Surkhang. Shortly after returning home, Tseten

Yudon married Changlo Wangchen Norbu who took the Surkhang name. When he came to the house, it was in a critical financial position. There was a threat of bankruptcy resulting from earlier poor management and large outstanding debts. Our great-grandfather must have been a good manager with sound judgement. In a short time he was able to restore the financial position of the Surkhang family both in wealth and reputation. However, Tseten Yudon's mother and her monk brother did not get along with Wangchen Norbu, and decided to leave Surkhang. They were given the estate Dechen Kharab Shenkha located about twenty miles east of Lhasa as their share. Later when the monk took off his robe and married, they became known as Kharab Shenkha and held the gerpa rank thereafter. Tseten Yudon's mother was evidently a bit difficult and resented her new son-in-law. Before her own marriage she had declined to remain with the Samdrup Photrangs. Her own youngest son with whom she lived was weak-minded.

Wangchen Norbu and his wife had six children in addition to the daughter of his wife by her earlier marriage, Tseten Gyalmo. There were three daughters, named Kalsang Choden, Dorje Yangkyi and Wangdu Dolma. The three sons were Sonam Wangchen, Norbu Tsering and Jigme Dorje. Sonam Wangchen, the eldest son, was our grandfather. He married Namgyal Dolma, the daughter of Rong Nara Kyishong (gerpa) from Rong in Tsang province.

Sonam Wangchen and his wife had three sons: Samdup Tseten, who was our father, Uncle Pema Wangchen and Uncle Sonam Wangdu. Several months after Uncle Sonam Wangdu was born, Grandfather died of a heart attack. He was only thirty-seven. Grandmother then became the head of the family. She took on the responsibility of managing the financial affairs of the estate as well as rearing the children. At first, Surkhang and Nara Kyishong relatives often had to advise her on the management of the property and the duties of the workmen, but she soon had everything operating smoothly. She held these responsibilities until her sons were old enough to assume the official duties of the family. It was during this crit-

ical time that our grand-aunt Kalsang Choden, who lived as
a nun at Kunsang Choeling, the house on our estate at Drak,
had to leave for the time being to help her sister-in-law manage the estate.

Although Kalsang Choden traveled extensively to visit
numerous lamas at different places, she spent most of the time
at Drak practicing what she had learned from them. She was
a very able woman both in religious and secular affairs. She
lived with a nun servant who did most of the work and another woman who took care of some cattle that contributed
to her support. When I was seven years of age, she came on
her last visit to Lhasa and stayed with us for some months.
I remember her as a religious person, tall and serene, and very
highly revered by all the family members.

The younger aunt Wangdu Dolma was also a nun, but she
stayed with the family in Lhasa until the death of her father.
Then she chose to stay in a nunnery called Tsering Jong in
Chongay about sixty miles to the south of Lhasa. Her brother
built a house for her near the nunnery where, like her sister,
she lived with a nun servant. When I was seventeen years old
my mother took me there on pilgrimage. We stayed with her
for seven days visiting the temples nearby and enjoying very
much the atmosphere of the nunnery.

The livelihood of both the nuns was taken care of by the
family. A long time before the death of their father it was
decided that they should be provided with money, grains, butter, tea, and other necessities—more than enough for their own
needs and those of their servants. Wangdu Dolma collected
these supplies from an estate near her nunnery while Kalsang
Choden used to get hers directly from the Drak estate. They
would always come to the aid of the family if any of the family members were sick or whenever there was an emergency.
In my day almost every family, high or low, would boast of
having at least one monk or one nun. There was a Tibetan
saying: When you need a master, make your son a monk, and
when you need a servant, make your daughter a nun.

The inner relationships and responsibilities in Tibetan families were extensive and involved. However strange these customs may appear to non-Tibetans, they served to provide for the safety and care of the various family members. They also served as the foundation and basis for providing a continuity to the social, economic and political aspects of Tibetan life. This is very well illustrated by my mother's case. My mother's name was Tseten Chozom. Her father's name was Sinon Wangchuk Lhagyari. His title was Trichen, "Enthroned One," in recognition of the fact that the Lhagyari family was directly descended from the original royal family of Tibet. Her mother's name was Tashi Gyalmo, daughter of the Tethongs of Karak. The Lhagyari family was the only one from among the four depon families not required to send sons into government service. They lived one hundred thirty miles outside of Lhasa in an ancient castle which they had occupied since the seventeenth century. On the rarer and more important public appearances of the Dalai Lama such as his first public enthronement, the Lhagyari Trichen would attend dressed in the ancient costume of his ancestors. This costume was easily recognizable to all Tibetans since it was identical to that worn by the famous life-sized statue of King Srongtsen Gampo in the Lhasa central cathedral, built by that king in the eighth century. The history and genealogy of the Lhagyari family was recorded by the Fifth Dalai Lama in his book, *History of Tibet (Dzokdan Shonul Gaton)*.

The Lhagyaris gave my mother to the Surkhang family in 1908 when she was seventeen years old. It was during a visit to Lhasa by my mother that our father's uncle, Norbu Tsering of the house of Yabshi Samdrup Photrang, arranged a small dinner so that my mother could meet my father. After this brief encounter my father expressed great desire to take my mother as a bride.

She was married to two brothers: our father Samdup Tseten who at that time was nineteen, and his younger brother Pema Wangchen who was only sixteen. Although at first she lived with two husbands, after a while our father insisted on keeping her for himself. From the first it had made him very jealous to share his wife with his younger brother. He had not at all liked the idea even before the marriage, but he never dared say anything to his mother. Afterwards there was no opportunity for Uncle to be with her again, because of my father's jealousy. There was no rivalry between the two brothers over this as Uncle Pema Wangchen was a very far-sighted person and agreed to the wishes of his elder brother. It is a typical Tibetan characteristic to try one's utmost to preserve family harmony and prosperity by avoiding feuds and open disputes.

At the time of the marriage, Uncle Pema Wangchen had been a *kadrung* or executive cabinet secretary, a fourth rank official in the government. Since he carried out all of his responsibilities with exceptional ability, the Dalai Lama asked that he be given a special title: *Kadrung Chemo*, Grand Secretary of the Cabinet, an unprecedented position and honor. Ordinarily a kadrung or secretary handled the administrative and legal documents under the direction of the cabinet ministers. Although he was a fourth rank official, Uncle was given a position inside the cabinet (which automatically conferred third rank status), charged with authority to participate in all discussions as an equal.

When Uncle came home at the end of the day, his habit was to stay in the library or sometimes remain alone in his small bedroom writing letters and reading to himself. He was an excellent scholar and knew how to read and write Chinese. He even created a Chinese study room and invited a Chinese scholar to be his tutor, paying him handsomely. Uncle was very famous in Lhasa for his outstanding qualities. During our Surkhang family dinners he would talk about both religious and secular topics. He knew these subjects well and his conversation was so witty and interesting that everyone was kept laughing. My mother used to tell me that when Uncle Pema Wangchen was not present everyone missed him terribly. He was said to be the incarnation of Jamyang Khentse Rinpoche, an important Nyingma lama. This had been indicated by a number of lamas but it was never established for sure. In any case he possessed outstanding and unusual knowledge about religious sects and always acted with wisdom and dignity.

Uncle Pema Wangchen had absolutely no desire to take a bride again but his mother and some of the older servants continued to urge him to marry until he finally agreed. Many families wanted their daughter to marry him. The Surkhangs chose a girl named Tsering Yangchen of the gerpa family Shakjang for the bride. The marriage between our uncle and Tsering Yangchen took place in 1915. At that time our father was working for the government as the Lhasa *Nyertsangpa* (lay head of the Lhasa Municipal Council). As was the custom, our grandmother was in complete charge of the household affairs, so did not allow our mother and Tsering Yangchen any special responsibilities, thus freeing them from doing any family work. Mother later told us that during these days she and Tsering Yangchen became very close friends.

A son was born to Uncle Pema Wangchen and Tsering Yangchen but died several days later. Soon afterwards Pema Wangchen himself became ill with a form of cancer. The medicine given to him was not effective. He continued to suffer ill-health for about nine months before he died in 1918, at the age of twenty-five. All of us grieved over his death, but our grandmother reacted by laughing all the time. At first everybody was of course shocked, but we soon discovered that she had become insane. She was so depressed that she often talked irrelevantly to herself and spoke her dead son's name as if he were still alive. Our parents asked Grandmother's younger sister Nawang Choden, a nun, to come from Kyishong to stay with her night and day. Our parents also stayed near her and tried never to upset her. They tried to please her by doing whatever she wanted. This was the Tibetan way to support people who are deeply disturbed or mentally ill. Two and a half years later she became sick with dysentery. In spite of the best medicine administered to her, she died. Since the family had lost both Pema Wangchen and Grandmother Namgyal Dolma within three years, everyone in the family felt the loss keenly. In their grief the surviving family members made many charitable offerings in the memory of their dear departed relatives.

While Uncle Pema Wangchen was still alive, his younger brother Sonam Wangdu went as a bridegroom to a family of the midrak rank named Kunsang Tse or Khemed to marry their daughter Dekyi Yangchen, thereby taking their family name. Our family had initially planned for Sonam Wangdu to become a monk. Although he was very reluctant, he had nevertheless assumed the attire and countenance of a monk. It was during this period that the Khemeds had asked the Surkhangs through a mutual friend, Tsarong Shapey, for Sonam Wangdu to come as bridegroom. The marriage proposal was accepted by Sonam Wangdu, who later was made *gosa* or commander-in-chief of the armed forces. After his marriage he was known as Sonam Wangdu Khemed.

From the time I was born and until the death of my grandmother, my elder brother Wangchen Gelek stayed in her room. Both Grandmother and Uncle Pema Wangchen loved him much more than any of the other children. Once when Wangchen Gelek went into Uncle's bedroom, he accidentally knocked down and broke one of the Chinese vases on the altar. When the servant told Uncle that my brother had broken the vase, he sent for him to explain how it happened. Wangchen Gelek went bravely into Uncle's room alone and made a salutation of respect. Then Uncle asked, "Why are you making salutation?" My brother replied, "I broke your vase. Please forgive me. It wasn't the fault of the servant."

Then Uncle told him please not to worry and that it didn't matter. After my brother left, Uncle Pema Wangchen called me into his room and gave me some money saying, "You broke my altar vase, didn't you?"

I very softly explained that I had not broken it, but my uncle replied, "It does not matter if you broke it or not; please say that you did it."

Then I put the money back on the table and escaped as fast as I could to my parents' room. Because Uncle loved my elder brother so much, he could not stand to have others think that the vase had been broken by him. At that time my brother was seven and I was only five years old. Much later when my uncle told the whole story to my mother, they both laughed. After I later heard this from her, I realized that I had been very obstinate even in my childhood.

Some months later our father was appointed as general or *depon* of the Dalai Lama's bodyguard unit. He spent three years in this capacity. During that time our family often went to the military camp and sometimes stayed there for two or three weeks at a time during the summer. The commanding general was given a large separate residence with about six or seven rooms, which was enough space for all of us. Since ordinary soldiers had to stay ten in one house or barrack, it was not practical for them to keep their wives with them. Officers, however, had their own private quarters where their families could stay. Since this camp was close to the Dalai Lama's summer palace, the Norbu Lingka, everything had to be kept immaculately clean both inside and out.

Once while Mother and we children were staying at the camp, we heard from our father who had gone to the Norbu Lingka summer palace that His Holiness the Thirteenth Dalai Lama was giving a *tsewang* or long life initiation. Immediately our father asked through one of His Holiness' staff, the chief of protocol, if our family could also attend, and obtained permission for us to receive the initiation the next day.

At the time of the ceremony our parents, brothers and sisters, and several servants went together each carrying a ceremonial scarf and a small envelope containing a few silver coins as an offering. The tsewang ceremony was attended by the Dalai Lama's palace staff, their wives and families, and some servants together with some lay and monk officials. Altogether there were about one hundred fifty people. His Holiness gave the initiation of White Tara, a female deity embodying the power of enlightenment and immortality. We believe that during the ceremony His Holiness would manifest himself as White Tara and dispense the blessings of long life to those receiving the initiation.

This was a memorable occasion for all of us since the great Thirteenth Dalai Lama very rarely gave audiences to laymen.

Usually he gave such blessings to the monks in Lhasa during the *Monlam* festival at New Year and on other important occasions. My parents were, of course, very happy to be able to receive the initiation, while to me just to be in His Holiness' reception room seemed like a dream. Even to this day I remember vividly how proud and happy I was. I was eight or nine years old.

Whenever the Dalai Lama passed the quarter of a mile between the summer palace and the Potala, he used to travel on a road near our house. Crowds of people observed the custom of greeting him on the roadside. My mother and all of us children always hurried to take advantage of this opportunity. Although we had seen him in this way at short range many times, the day of the initiation was the only day that His Holiness the Thirteenth Dalai Lama gave us the special blessing of placing his hands on our heads. This ceremony took place in his private audience hall called *Zimchung Nyi-od*, or Sunshine Hall.

There were special assembly halls in both the Norbu Lingka and the Potala where important events of different sorts took place. I used to hear from my monk brother Wangchuk Dorje how all of the monk officials would gather every morning in the assembly hall to participate in the daily ceremonies before starting their official duties. Often appointments by the Dalai Lama were announced through the chief of protocol during this function. All of the tsedrungs (monk officials) and monks were expected to attend, each taking with him his own bowl made out of a rare wood called *dzabyal*, which could be found only in certain places in Tibet. Every day a special tea was made in the kitchen of His Holiness and served in these special bowls. On ceremonial days in addition to the tea there would be some delicious foods. The higher the official, the more elaborate would be the food served to him. Whenever a promotion or demotion was to occur, the official in question would be summoned. When the chief of protocol called his name, the person being addressed would stand before the others with bowed head in an attitude of deep respect. Holding his hat in his hand, he would have to stand in the middle of the hall with all the monk officials surrounding him. Then the chief of protocol read out the order of His Holiness for all to hear. When this was to announce a promotion, it was a very impressive ceremony for all, but when it was a demotion, it would be a deeply humiliating experience.

The reading of the demotion order would be followed by the removal of the badges of the former rank together with the official robe of the demoted person. Besides that, other honorary symbols were taken back by the government. Sometimes when the official did not know beforehand that he was to be demoted, he had to return home wearing only the thin robe usually worn underneath the heavy golden robes made from Chinese brocade. This embarrassment happened to careless officials.

Our father was once demoted. He had teased a woman who happened to be the wife of one of the secretaries of the Dalai Lama. Our father had heard that the woman had rather loose morals, and sent one of his servants to her with a proposal for a rendezvous. It is doubtful whether he was serious since practical joking of that sort is typical among Tibetans. The husband reported the incident to His Holiness through the chief of protocol. When my father was asked about this, he confessed what he had done and could not object to the result of his misdeed. For such an offense it was expected that he would be demoted from his position of commander of the Dalai Lama's bodyguard.

That is how he happened to know beforehand that his demotion would take place, so on the day he received the summons he brought a servant with him who carried a bag of clothing for my father to wear on the way home. He was made to stand before the monk officials and remove his hat, holding it in both hands before his chest while bowing slightly. The hair ornament which indicated his position, a turquoise and gold amulet box customarily worn on the head by a fourth rank official, was removed. We were surprised when he came home without his beautiful ornaments and naturally felt terrible. It was almost like meeting a person who had died, so everyone in the family started to weep. Even the servants wept. All of us were very worried and upset about the demotion, but father himself was never concerned at all because he was a carefree type of person.

It was the custom in Lhasa that whenever an official was demoted or dismissed from his post his relatives and friends would pay him a consolation visit. They came with money wrapped in scarves. My father was well-loved by many, so friends began to visit the family the day following the demotion and continued for five or six days. Even though I was only a child of about eleven years, I was very embarrassed about the entire incident. Since father was still an official, he had to go to government celebrations and functions even though he had no special work assigned to him and no special dress. He had nothing else to do, so he took the opportunity to pray and to read religious books. This period of dismissal lasted for three or four years.

My father's bad luck was not over. The Tibetan New Year was celebrated each year with much pomp and gaiety, which in Lhasa included firecrackers that we bought in the market. On the east side of the Surkhang house was a large crossroad where people, young and old, rich and poor, would gather during *Losar* or New Year from afternoon until dusk. They formed a large circle and sang songs. There was much gaiety, and the people would come and go spontaneously. Some of them used to throw firecrackers into the open area in the middle of the circle for amusement.

During the New Year's festivities in 1924 our father was throwing firecrackers into the center of the circle from the roof of our house. He had put about twenty of these firecrackers into the fleece-lined left sleeve of his heavy outer robe and was throwing them one by one. Someone in the crowd caught one of the firecrackers and tossed it back to him as a joke. Somehow it landed inside his left sleeve. When it exploded all of the other firecrackers ignited at once. He shook his sleeve desperately to try to put out the fire but this only increased his difficulties. His hand and fingers were severely burned, and he remained in intense pain for several days.

Unfortunately there was no good medicine available at that time for burns. However, we had a Moslem friend named Idi, half Tibetan and half Chinese, who took opium. When he heard about what had happened, he came to help our father with the idea of giving him opium as a medication. Idi came every day and gave my father opium to smoke, which enabled him to sleep and get some relief from the unbearable pain. After a couple of weeks his hand began to get better, but it remained scarred for life. Our mother suggested that since Father's hand was better, it would be good for him to stop taking opium. She also said that if he didn't, it would later be the cause of sickness and disease. Although he stopped taking opium at home, he must have smoked it secretly when he went out to other people's houses, because he soon became addicted.

At that time Idi also brought a mahjong set to our house to entertain our father. The game soon became the craze of Lhasa and remained so for the following twenty years. The first mahjong sets that I remember seeing were quite plain and small, made of bamboo with eyes of bone inlay. Before the introduction of mahjong, Tibetans everywhere played *sho* or dice. It is usually played by two persons, although three people can also play at one time. Each player is given about thirty pieces, either black square stones, tiny wooden pieces, sea shells, dried beans, pierced Chinese coins, or copper Tibetan coins. To play the game, two dice are shaken in a cup and thrown onto a small round piece of leather. Depending upon the numbers on the dice, players move ahead or get left behind.

From the time that father's hand began to heal, he went out every day saying that he was going for a stroll. It was about that time that he started having an affair with a young woman named Dawa, who was a neighbor. He might have been taking opium there with Dawa's brother-in-law. Anyway our father and Dawa had been having an affair for almost one year before our mother found out about it. Although my mother warned him that he must not continue, Father paid no heed.

Mother was patient for months hoping he would forget Dawa. Even though our family friends were concerned and put pressure on him, he listened to no one.

As time went on, most of the families in Lhasa knew of the scandal. The Dalai Lama learned about it through the chief of protocol and asked him to investigate the matter. On the Dalai Lama's instruction the chief of protocol said to our parents, "I have heard that you two are not in agreement anymore. It would be better for everyone if you two would make a compromise. What is the matter?"

My mother was always optimistic that her husband would change for the better and asked the chief of protocol to speak to him. When he did this, father answered frankly, "My karma with Dawa has been destined from my past life. It is my fault, but I can't get her out of my mind. Whatever the verdict of His Holiness may be, I am ready to obey."

The chief of protocol reported his findings on the matter to His Holiness and asked for further instructions. His Holiness was very wise and kind, so he gave them more time to settle the problem. His message was, "You two still think it over. If you can agree, then it can be as before. If not, the mother will remain at Surkhang as the head of the house to take care of the estate and all the children. The oldest son Wangchen Gelek together with his mother will assume full responsibility of the Surkhang family. The father must separate from the Surkhang house, but should be provided with furnishings for a new residence. The mother must agree that for the rest of his life, servants, food, and his other needs will be provided from the Surkhang estate of which she will remain the head." Even before the order from His Holiness the Dalai Lama came, Tsarong Sawang had for some time tried to mediate between my parents. Not only was he a person of great influence, but he was also a personal friend of my father. Despite his efforts, nothing could change my father's mind. My mother was willing to reconcile only if my father left Dawa. It was during this period that the separation order from His Holiness the Dalai Lama came.

Twenty days later father made the final decision to leave the Surkhang house for good, and went to stay with some close cousins of ours in Lhasa named Horkhang. There he lived with Dawa and a few servants. The day our father left, we children, now aged from eighteen to eight, were very sad and of course our mother was extremely upset. To her it seemed that the impossible had happened because there was no custom in Tibet for the father to leave his own house. People thought this was very improper, but did not know that it was on the order of the Dalai Lama. We children also felt that mother should remain at the Surkhang house and that we would stay with her.

After father's departure everything turned out well for him. Soon afterwards the Dalai Lama gave him another chance and re-appointed him as depon or fourth rank general. He regained his former rank in the government and could again wear his ornaments when he took his new office. He was assigned as general to the Jadang Regiment in East Tibet (Kham). While there he and Dawa had a son, Nawang Jigme, born in 1929.

When my father left Surkhang in 1928, all of my brothers and sisters as well as my mother agreed to provide anything our father needed. When he established his own quarters with Dawa, we children used to visit him. My parents rarely met and then only at social gatherings, but when they did they were polite to each other. My elder brother was very respectful and loving to our father all through this period, which pleased mother very much. Everyone in the family realized clearly how much she had been upset. Now Father too was remorseful that he had hurt her. He was affectionate to us children and still loved everyone in the Surkhang household even after the divorce.

Although Mother had adjusted nicely to her new life and some admirers had approached her, she was not interested and remained dedicated to taking care of her children. She was then only thirty-six years old, but was turning more and more to religious devotion. Soon after the separation, she took a special Buddhist vow of celibacy, *Tsang Cho Genyen*, combined with a set of precepts formulated for lay devotees, from the great lama Kyabje Khangsar Rinpoche of Drepung Monastery. The commitments or precepts of this type are basically the same as the complete laymen's vows except that the vow not to commit adultery is replaced by one to abstain from sexual relationships. After Father left, Mother lived like a nun for the rest of her life. She devoted herself to daily prayers and meditation, as well as making offerings of butter lamps, incense, and occasionally distributing gifts to monasteries.

In 1917 when they were together, our parents both took the complete laymen's vows from the Most Venerable Budu Dorje Chang of Drepung Monastery. During the ordination ceremony they made these vows after hearing an introductory explanation about the right motivations and methods of maintaining the vows and precepts. Devotees are required to look upon the lama preceptor as an embodiment of Buddha Sakyamuni who is the source of all Buddhist vows and precepts. This was the *Yongdzog Genyen* vow, the basic precepts of which are to abstain from taking life, to abstain from sexual misconduct, not to lie, not to steal, and not to take intoxicants. All laymen, young and old, high and low, could take these vows if they so chose. Our mother had never failed in observing them.

After Father left, our elder brother Wangchen Gelek initially took responsibility for the family. Though he had become an important official, he still attended to the family concerns such as estate accounts, investments, correspondence, and meeting people on business. But nevertheless he discussed everything with Mother. His great love and devotion to her throughout his life set a wonderful example for all of us brothers and sisters, which brought us very close to one another. The love and faithfulness we felt for our mother made our daily life very agreeable. Mother was always as considerate to us as we were to her and to each other.

My older brother, now head of the family, proved to be competent and kind with everyone. He treated all of the servants with fairness, accepting them as family members. He never asked for special treatment for himself. His only diversion was to play games such as dice or mahjong. He loved to relax with just a few close friends, usually no more than three, and play until well after midnight. It didn't matter to him if he won or lost, and it never interfered with his official duties. He became a shapey, or cabinet minister, when he was just thirty-three years old, and held that position for seventeen years. He was always known for his tremendous memory and grasp of details, but most of all for his great clarity of mind in understanding complicated problems. When Tibet was being invaded in 1950 from the east and was not equipped to defend itself against the formidable military power of Red China, he managed to keep things going for quite a few years.

My mother suffered very much at first when my father left, but she gradually adjusted to her fate. Some months after the divorce, she decided to take us on a pilgrimage to the southern province, which included a visit to her mother and sisters living on the estate where she spent her childhood days.

3 Childhood in Lhasa

Although from birth my mother was always there to supervise my care and to give me love, there was also a *mama* who served as a nanny and took charge of my daily needs. Mama literally means "mother" in Tibetan, and according to custom the child of an affluent family was usually in the custody of a mama from its birth until it reached six or seven years of age. If the wealth and status of the family was high enough, there would be one mama for each child.

From the time of my birth, Kyipa was my mama. Her name means "Happiness" and she took care of me until I was six. She had been one of two maidservants given to my mother by her parents as a dowry when she married my father. Kyipa had one daughter a year younger than I, and during the day she took care of us together. At night Kyipa would leave me with my mother while she took her daughter Tsering Choden to her own room on the second floor of our house where she lived with her husband, who was our cook.

In the early morning Kyipa and her daughter would come up to my little room where we would spend most of the day together. Tsering Choden was almost like a sister but she had to eat after I finished my meal, and she would wear old clothes of mine that were given to her. Tsering Choden and I spent many happy hours playing together. When we were tired, Mama told us stories. Although Mama could not read, she was very intelligent and had a wonderfully vivid imagination. When she did not have a story to tell, she used to explain how the birds had their houses in trees and the bird families could talk together in their own language. In this way our days passed pleasantly.

Little Tibetan girls about four or five years of age like to imitate older persons. They try to sing songs even when they do not know the words or tunes. Sometimes little Tsering Choden and I would build tiny little houses out of small pieces of wood, sand and other things and then would laugh when we knocked them down. In those days I was often very naughty so that Mama would scold and sometimes punish me. When we were a little older, we began to play with dolls. Sometimes we made our own dolls with the help of an older person and would proudly show them to others as if we had done all the work ourselves. Then we would keep the dolls in our own rooms.

My brother, who was two years older than I, used to stay with his mama. Since my mother had two other children, my grandmother felt free to take care of my older brother. She became very attached to him and treated him with much love, as if he were her own son. He was literally brought up by her until she passed away.[1]

My mother did not in any way neglect us. She often called us children together just to teach us and enjoy our company. In the winter time when the weather was cold and we could not go outside much, she used to tell us stories. I also remember how she would instill in us the teachings of Buddha through stories that we could understand as children. At first there was only my older brother, but later my younger brother, who was two years younger than I, used to join us. We all used to love fairy stories but were never told ghost stories that might frighten us. Sometimes an elder member of the family or one of the servants would come to recite to us, and we children would gather near the storyteller to listen with rapt attention.

Sometimes my brothers and I would play a game of hide
and seek with other children of the neighborhood. One person would cover his eyes while the others would find a place
nearby to hide. When the seeker found him he would tickle
him. If the seeker took too much time to find those hiding,
they would join together to tickle the seeker.

The girls used to play a game called *teybey*. It was a game
of skill and competition. There was a round disc, about the
size of a big coin, made of lead. In the middle of the disc was
a hole into which some feathers about seven inches long had
been fastened. Each girl by turn tried to kick the disc time
after time into the air without letting it touch the ground. Some
girls could bounce the disc as a many as a hundred times. If
another girl bounced the disc only ninety times, then the girl
who had bounced it a hundred would tap the loser on the fore-
head ten times.

There were other games also. Girls often jumped rope just
like the little girls I have seen in the U.S.A. Sometimes two
girls would hold each end of the rope while the third girl would
jump in the middle. Sometimes the girls would skip alone.
We also liked to play with stones, which we tried to juggle and
throw into the air to see how many we could catch as they fell.
In more quiet times we would be given some cheap beads,
which we would use to make play jewelry. When we were ten
or eleven, we used to enjoy dressing up. We would put inexpensive ornaments in our hair and rub our faces with honey
mixed in water to make them look smooth and shiny. Then
we would stare at ourselves in the mirror.

When the weather was good we went on picnics together
with the family. Or we would go with some of our school
friends or the neighborhood children along with some servants
to a picnic place nearby. The girls used to take branches from
the bushes and trees to make head ornaments while the boys
played together. Both the girls and boys played in the river,
but aside from wading and splashing about there was not much
swimming. We rested in the sand at the riverside. Sometimes
vendors would come selling candy and cookies, which we

would pool our money to buy.

In the winter it was so cold in Lhasa that the rivers, lakes and ponds froze. All children liked to skate on the ice. We didn't have any skates but just went sliding around in our boots. We also used to play a game outdoors by knocking about an oblong piece of bone from a sheep about one and a half inches round called *abchu*. Even though there was plenty of snow in Tibet, there was no custom of skiing.

Sometimes we would accompany our parents when they went on pilgrimage to temples, monasteries and shrines. When we were little, we had seen our elders bow before the images and perform various rituals. When they were not looking, we used to mimic them by doing these things ourselves.

This is what the life of the children in the higher classes was like but the children born into the poorer families also had their fun. They would go on picnics close to their homes. There were many nice places with trees and water in Lhasa and nearby for them to enjoy. The girls in these families were expected to help with the housework. Both boys and girls helped look after their younger brothers and sisters, and could often be seen carrying infants on their backs. Nevertheless, they had their time for fun and play.

Only the children of the higher families and sometimes their servants went to school. The few government schools were intended just for the education and training of boys who would become government officials. However, any boy or girl who joined a monastery would receive an education directly from the monks or nuns.

For the rest of us there were twenty-five or thirty private schools in Lhasa for boys and girls together. Usually children began school at the age of seven or eight, although there was no rule preventing them from starting when they were much older. The only subjects taught were writing, reading, grammar, simple arithmetic, and some prayers. The headmasters of the schools were mostly professional people in some other field of endeavor. Their income from the school was minimal, but in most cases their sole intention of running a school was to educate. It was believed that by doing so, merit would be earned for the next life.

In fact, these schools and the learning process were not at all like the schools in other parts of the world. The students would sit on cushions that they had brought from home. They also were expected to bring all necessary implements needed for writing and reading. Beginners were taught by the more advanced students, who usually were about thirteen years old. All of the students were crowded into one room, whether large or small, for their school work. They would arrive at six o'clock in the morning and then go home for breakfast about eight o'clock and return in an hour. For lunch they went home again for an hour. The school day ended at five o'clock in the afternoon. We used to attend school every day for fourteen days and then take tests. The following day was a holiday. Then we started all over again.

Schools in Tibet were open seven days a week and enrollment was accepted at any time. A new student would be admitted whenever it suited the parents and the teachers. This did not create much problem since teaching was almost done on a one-to-one basis. Senior students and prefects were given the task of teaching the younger ones. Since every day was a school day, my parents were able to decide when my brother and I could start school without any problem.

We were enrolled at Kyiraes school, which was about ten minutes from our home. As was the custom, we informed the teacher through a servant of our desire to join his school about a month before our enrollment. Our servant presented the headmaster with a *kata* (a white scarf) and informed him of our decision. My parents then consulted an astrologer for an auspicious day for us to begin classes. It was around 1919 that my brother and I together with three servant children, two boys and a girl (my playmate Tsering Choden), went to school for the first time. On that day we wore our best clothes. With us was one main servant and seven other servants carrying the gifts for the headmaster and teachers and students. These gifts included refreshments of *droma* (tiny sweet potatoes), rice and tea.

We left for the school that first day at about eight in the morning. On arrival we presented ourselves before the headmaster, after which two of our servants brought forth the gifts. First we presented scarves to the headmaster and his wife who was sitting near him. After we took off our hats and bowed slightly before them, the headmaster told us to sit in front of him. The servants first offered tea and ceremonial rice with droma to the headmaster and his wife.

The servants then left the headmaster's great room, which was on the second floor, to go to the classroom below to offer the ceremonial rice and tea to the students. The students had brought with them that day cups for the tea and pieces of cloth to hold the rice and snacks. If they could not eat all they were given, they took the remainder home. After that the servants presented gifts to the student-monitor who was to be our teacher. These included money wrapped in a piece of paper along with a scarf. He then presented a little of the money to each of the students.

That first day we brought our cushions and boxes of writing implements. The headmaster showed us the alphabet, helping us to write by guiding our hands. He also taught us to say the refuge prayer:

I take refuge in the Lama (Guru),
I take refuge in Sangye (Buddha),
I take refuge in Choe (Dharma),
I take refuge in Gendun (Religious Community).

When the headmaster finished his teaching, our main servant returned to the teacher's room to make the customary request to give all of the students a holiday for the rest of the day. The headmaster agreed and allowed all of the students to leave for their homes. They did not stand up to go all at one time, but one by one each quietly got up to depart.

Before we were dismissed, the headmaster told us individually how to be good students. At that time I was seven and my brother nine; he told us we would have to come to the school every day and while at school must study very hard. But I was so young that I did not understand much of what he said. At last he gave us permission to leave.

Our daily education was a mixture of religious recitations, practical handwriting and later reading and simple arithmetic; but the emphasis was always on reciting our Buddhist prayers. The day began very early in the morning with prayers to the wisdom deity, Manjushri. The student-monitor would lead the chanting of the invocation to gain wisdom and knowledge of religion. After we had repeated the Manjushri mantra one hundred times, we offered special prayers to Green Tara for the prosperity and well-being of the whole universe. These prayers we all recited together in loud voices for about two hours. Then the students who lived nearby went to their homes for breakfast while others took an hour's rest and ate food brought from home. The prayers ended about eight o'clock. The students were expected to be ready for study again by nine.

Besides the prayers the main subjects taught at school were handwriting and reading, grammar and mathematics. The process of writing was very complicated since there were various styles of script to be mastered. Simple arithmetic was taught through the recitation of mathematical problems in addition, subtraction and multiplication. The last half hour in the day was for memorizing. The younger children memorized all the words normally used in a children's vocabulary while the more advanced students memorized all the words from the famous dictionary called *The Lamp of Speech*. They also memorized the sayings of famous bodhisattvas, Sakya Pandit, Nagarjuna's *Sheting* and Shanti Deva's *Chojuk*. The higher subjects, including grammar, were not taught until the students had mastered their written script.

Even though the discipline of the school was mostly under a student-monitor, the school was conducted with great orderliness. Discipline and respect for others was one of the most important lessons for the students to learn. There was much emphasis put on the proper way for the students to leave for the break. We were never allowed to rush in or out of the schoolroom in disorder. We had to form lines with senior students always first and the youngest at the end of the line. We were never allowed to talk loudly in the classroom or laugh or jest with others.

The monitor was allowed to punish the students. If a student was bad, the prefect would order the boy to puff out his cheeks and then switch him on the cheeks twice with a thick strip of bamboo. If the child was very bad, he was swatted on the behind with a whip ten or fifteen times. There was not much punishment, however, for the girls. If it were ever necessary to punish a girl, she was swatted on the outstretched palm of her hand two or three times, or even whipped.

When the students had to go to the toilet, they would approach the prefect with head bowed respectfully to ask permission to leave for going to the bathroom, which was in a small building just outside. He would nod but allowed only one at a time to leave the room. We were allowed to leave the room twice a day, although if we were sick, we were allowed to leave as often as we wished. There was no custom of a recess for play in our schools.

As I have already explained, writing was the main subject. In Tibet two kinds of writings are common but only the *U-Mei*, or longhand, script was studied in school. *U-Chen* is the block printing commonly used for religious texts. To learn U-Mei the students first printed the letters three inches tall and learned the name of each letter. If a new student was young enough, he or she would sit on the headmaster's lap and hold a wooden board (*jengshi*) in his own lap. The student then grasped a pen while the teacher held the child's hand in his to teach him the method of writing. After that some older students would take the place of the teacher to instruct the beginners.

The letters were written by beginners on a wooden board. On this board was sprinkled white chalk powder called *kara*, and three lines were made with a thread. For writing on paper or bamboo, a pen and brown ink made from roasted wheat were used. After filling up the entire board with writing, the student would show it to the monitor. Afterwards he would wash off the board with water before starting again.

After learning to write the large three-inch letters nicely, the middle-sized letters, which were an inch and a half high, were practiced. While writing the large size, only the letters were studied and no spelling of words was begun. Spelling began with letters an inch and a half high. Finally writing itself was practiced with small letters in the U-Mei script. When this was mastered, the students began to write on paper rather than on the wooden board.

No regular tuition fee was given to a school, but on the New Year and other festival days gifts were presented to the head-master. Even if presents were not given, the headmaster would not ask for them as he had other work from which he earned his livelihood. Since the headmaster had to attend another job, he appeared in the school only occasionally during the day. He would leave the eldest and most responsible student in charge as the teacher-monitor, sometimes all day. This monitor stood in place of the headmaster. In addition each student also had an elder classmate who served as a helper, so that the younger students were always tutored by those more advanced.

The fifteenth and thirtieth days of each month were the only school holidays. These coincided with the full and new moons which mark the Buddhist calendar. On every fourteenth and twenty-ninth day the headmaster gave each of the students a grade. On that day he did not go to his work at all, but stayed the whole day in the classroom examining what the students had written. Those who wrote on paper and the younger ones who wrote on wood were separated. First the names of those who wrote on paper were called. They were examined and given a graded number according to their work and then had to sit in that order. When the grading for this group was over, the student who came first would take a piece of bamboo the size of a ruler and snap it on the puffed cheek of the boys and outstretched hands of the girls. Then the second student would take the stick and snap the cheeks and hands of all those beneath him. Thus one by one all the students snapped the cheeks of those whose grades were lower. As the last had no one to hit, he had to snap the bamboo stick three times at an empty yak hide used to hold butter. Then putting the hide in front of him as if it were his teacher, he had to prostrate to it three times. At this most of the students would laugh. The headmaster stood doing nothing during all of this, with a very solemn countenance. Those who wrote on wood would then go through the same grading process. The purpose of the last student's having to hit and to bow down to the hide three times was to create embarrassment for him so he would try harder to learn.

The headmaster then exhorted those who were on the low end of the gradation, telling them that if they wrote well in the future, they would not have to suffer this way. Last of all the headmaster informed the students that the afternoon and the next day were holidays. When these ceremonies were finished, all of the students bade the headmaster goodbye and respectfully left the room with head bent.

A break from this hard work came in summertime when the students went on a picnic together. Pooling their money and food, they invited the headmaster and his family as guests. Such picnics sometimes lasted as long as three to seven days, during which some of the older boys would stay at the picnic grounds overnight in tents. Among the games they played was one in which the students, both boys and girls, stood facing each other calling each other bad names. Other times we played in the water and did many fun things. The students were not required to show much formality in front of the headmaster, who often joined in the games with them.

In my day girls were not so keen to study, so that only about one-fourth of my schoolmates were girls. One of my closest school friends was Rinchen Dolma Tsarong (now Mrs. Rinchen Dolma Taring), who was later the first Tibetan girl ever to go outside Tibet for an education. She left our Tibetan school when she was about twelve years of age to study at Mount Hermon's in Darjeeling, India, an English middle school.[2] Although I was very attentive in my studies, things never came easily to me. I had to spend many hours after school memoriz-

ing the various prayers and multiplication tables. My grades
were low, which meant after a test my hands were always red
from the bamboo sticks.

I went to school until I was twelve years old and then asked
permission from the headmaster Urgyen Norbu to leave. I had
learned all the writing, reading, grammar and mathematic lessons and read some religious books. Very early I had memorized the morning prayers. There was not much to learn in
our schools besides reading and writing so that in about four
or five years a student learned quite well all that was offered.
When a student had finished his studies and was ready to leave
the school, he repeated what he did upon entering by offering ceremonial rice and tea and other presents, according to
the standard of his family. On that day the headmaster made
a holiday for the class in the afternoon. The next day the students would not come to school. I followed this custom when
I completed my studies and my school days came to an end.

Very few young ladies studied after leaving school. They
returned home to help their mothers and learned some crea-
tive work like embroidering or knitting, and supervising house-
keeping. I loved to knit socks for my father and my brothers.
All in all after I left school I was quite free. One of the nicest
things that happened to me was finding a new friend. Her name
was Tsering Lhamo, and I remember her as one of my best
friends from childhood onward. She was one year older than
I, the daughter of a well-known merchant named Gokhrid
Tsongkhang, who was our neighbor. The eastern door of our
main house was just next to his house. Although I had seen
her almost every day for several years, we never had the chance
to talk to each other until I was thirteen.

Our friendship started on the second day of our New Year
when my mother, my brothers and sister were all up on our
roof to perform the incense burning ceremony. Naturally we
were curious to see what the neighbors were doing. At exactly
the same time Tsering Lhamo's family was on their roof following the same custom of offering incense and other items
to the deities. They were also hoisting New Year prayer flags

on their roof.

As we watched all this with interest our mother and her parents talked at length from the roof tops. This little girl, whom I had seen many times before from my roof, had always been too shy to talk to me in front of my brothers and sister. However, that day she overcame her shyness and invited me to come over to her roof.

I went as fast as I could, but by the time I got there, they had finished their ceremony. When I arrived, they were all drinking cups of homemade beer for the New Year good luck. I felt very big when I too was served a cup of it. Then my friend took me down to the second floor to the living rooms. First they served a hearty lunch. Later we two talked and played by skipping as if we had always been friends. I was extremely happy to feel so intimate with her at our very first meeting. In Tibet we always take such sudden friendships to be a sign of some connection from our previous lives. I stayed at her house until evening and from that day on we remained close friends until 1959. I heard later that she had died in Tibet.

Until the age of eighteen when I went to the Treshong family's household, I helped my mother. I did not have much to do. When my mother had visitors but was busy, sometimes I relieved her by entertaining the visitors. Also I would sometimes take charge of the keys of the storerooms. Other days I would go in my mother's place to buy odds and ends or to pay an informal visit for her. I also did some knitting and embroidering.

After I left school, I learned a great deal about running the household by helping my mother to maintain the numerous household accounts and records of transactions that it was our custom to keep. Goods were constantly being received from the various estates and sent on to other locations, or purchased to be kept in storage as provisions for future use. All of these things had to be listed and the inventories kept up to date. Many things were loaned out and had to be separately recorded. Since our family didn't have a steward at the time, these chores naturally fell upon my mother.

During this time my mother often used to help me write my letters. It was a source of great joy to me to see a new horizon open up where I had never ventured before. It also made me feel very mature and important to write my own letters even though they were often filled with errors. I always enjoyed receiving the replies and to this day I have kept up this practice.

4 Losar: Welcoming the New Year

In order to make the Tibetan New Year, called *Losar*, the most splendid and festive celebration of the year, much time and expense was required for all the many preparations. Nearly all of the houses in Lhasa were freshly painted outside. Inside everything was scrupulously cleaned and rearranged, the best furnishings and ornaments were brought out, and many special decorations and foods were made to mark the holiday. Since the Tibetan calendar is based upon lunar cycles, our New Year could occur anytime during the Western months of February or March.

Our family usually began preparing for New Year during the twelfth month. At that time the outside of our house would be whitewashed. First a huge yak skin was stretched and hung from four wooden posts to form a large bowl made of leather called *gumthing*. The whitewash was made from a soft chalk-like powder from north Tibet called *kara*. Forty pounds of kara were placed in the gumthing and water slowly added to make a mixture of two-thirds water and one-third coarse powder. After someone stirred it with a large stick, the mixture was ladled out in a giant spoon into another big wooden or metal tub, leaving behind the pebbles and rough residue in the leather bag.

This mixture, which had the consistency of yogurt, was scooped up in a small pail by special men who literally splashed it onto the walls where it ran down and dried in a day or two. For a tall building two or three stories high, it took a great deal of skill to throw the whitewash upwards far enough to cover everything. If the mixture was very watery, the color would not be white since the dirty wall underneath would still show through a little. But if it was applied very thickly, then the wall became very white and clean looking. Our tenants and lower servants had the work of putting up the gumthing, carrying all the water in containers on their backs from the house well and preparing the whitewash. But the application of the whitewash onto the walls was done by specially hired people. However, for a very small house the owners could do all of this work with the help of a few friends. A few days later the house superintendent with some tenants would paint borders around all of the windows and doors on the outside with black paint mixed with oil and applied with a rag. This was done very neatly so that the shape of the windows stood out providing a dramatic accent to the architecture. If anyone had died in the family during the year, then the whitewash and application of black paint would be omitted as a sign of mourning.

To paint the Surkhang house, it took about six hundred pounds of kara. However, the powder was very inexpensive. All the work would be done in one day by a total of fifteen people. While the work was being performed, tea and soup with meat, flour and cheese were served to the people working, who otherwise were not given pay.

One of our most important customs was to prepare special biscuits called *khabsey*, which were always made for New Year throughout Tibet. Khabsey were made of flour, butter, and a tiny amount of sugar; some were deep fried in oil and others in butter to produce different flavors. Twisted into many different shapes, they could measure from six to eighteen inches in length. In our family, our regular kitchen staff of five worked to help two specially hired cooks. It took the seven of them four or five days to make enough khabsey for the holiday. We used at least six to seven hundred pounds of wheat flour, half of which was white and half whole wheat, two hundred pounds of butter and tremendous amounts of oil for deep fat frying. After being made, they were stacked in piles on cloths and laid down on shelves in a large store room about twelve by twenty-five feet in size. Densely stacked, they reached from the floor at least half way up the walls all the way around the room. In smaller households, just the family would prepare the khabsey. Sometimes families with whom we were friendly asked us to have our special cooks prepare extras for them with flour and oil that they would provide. The large and special khabsey were never made at any other time of year.

At New Year's time we offered khabsey to all of our visiting friends. In addition servants were sent carrying trays of about ten different kinds of khabsey to the houses of Moslem, Chinese and Nepali merchants whom we knew. Whole sides of fresh mutton would also be given to our closest and more important business contacts. The offering tray was attractively arranged and decorated. Later on during the Moslem New Year, our Moslem friends would send us a big covered dish filled with delicious mutton curry and rice. The dish cover was decorated with ribbons. In addition to this they offered us wheat bread rolls similar to scones. On Nepali New Year our Nepali acquaintances offered us a large round tray of special khabsey sprinkled with powdered sugar. On Chinese New Year, which was usually near ours, the few Chinese merchant families living in Lhasa would offer us special imported Chinese dried fruits and fresh Chinese vegetables that they grew for themselves in winter gardens.

In addition to khabsey another decoration everyone needed was a sheep's head, which was displayed for New Year's Day in front of the family altar, placed in a special copper and silver stand. Very few people actually used real sheep's heads like we did. Instead, copies were made from barley flour and butter and covered with colored icing to look real. In addition, the sheep's head was decorated with little colored spots and flowers made from butter. The horns were tied with ribbons.

Just before New Year we always planted wheat in a flower pot so that it would have grown about four or five inches high when New Year's Day arrived. This would be placed next to the sheep's head. On the altar next to these we stacked up like firewood very large and variously shaped khabsey. In front of them different kinds of dried fruit and fresh oranges from Sikkim were placed in separate bowls and dishes. Cups of rice and wheat were also placed on the altar.

Whenever we were having a special function in our house, whether a religious ritual, a marriage celebration, a promotion ceremony or even the New Year celebration, we always made a special decoration on the pathway leading to our house. We would use white powder ground from rock. Starting at the outside gate and leading to the main door, we would draw two long lines, about forty or fifty feet long and about ten feet apart. Then on each side we would draw some auspicious designs appropriate to the occasion, such as the lotus, swastika, vase of nectar, and other Buddhist emblems. This custom was also followed in the monasteries, nunneries and villages.

Hoisting prayer flags on the roof was another important custom. All over Tibet the roofs are flat and have a permanent stand for holding a flag at each of the four corners. Twelve-foot poles cut from a special kind of willow called *gyachang* were put in each stand. It was the custom to leave a few small green branches at the top of the flag poles. Rectangular shaped flags about one and a half feet in length and one foot wide were tied about half way up on these poles. The flags were of special colors: white, yellow, blue, green, and red. Prayers and religious texts were printed on them by means of carved wooden blocks. We believe that when the wind blows on these flags, the wind reads the messages and carries them wherever it travels.

The colors of the flags hoisted at the corners were determined according to the birth year of the main members of the family. According to Tibetan astrology the five elements of earth, iron, water, wood, and fire each ruled in rotation for a period of two years. The color of the earth is yellow; the color of iron, white; water, blue; wood, green; and fire, red. According to the year of birth, each individual would have an element color. Whenever a flag was hoisted in honor of a family member, it would carry his element color. Each flag was one solid color which was always determined according to astrology. At certain special ceremonial times many small flags of different colors would be fixed on a rope that had been tied between two poles. This custom was observed by everyone, and gave the outside of Tibetan houses a very cheerful appearance.

Tashi taring was the custom of hoisting a special kind of multicolored banner on very auspicious occasions. Small strips of silk or cotton in the colors of the five elements were cut and then stitched in certain geometric patterns on a large rectangular shaped banner about eight by five feet, the exact size being determined by the importance of the occasion and the means available for hoisting it in the monasteries, nunneries, or houses. The banner on the roof of the Potala Palace raised when His Holiness was in residence was larger than similar ones elsewhere. This banner used to have some small bells attached to one side so that when the wind blew, they made a very nice sound. Whenever the Dalai Lama was to visit any of the surrounding monasteries or was going on an auspicious mission, the families of all the houses along the route were required to hoist special flags. They were also to draw *karthig* designs on the ground in front of their houses to indicate that a deity, His Holiness, would be present.

The strong flat roofs of the houses and other buildings of Tibet were used for many ceremonial occasions. On every roof of every house there was a special fireplace made of stone and earth used for daily religious purposes. Some of these were as tall as a person while others might be half that size. On religious holidays or auspicious days such as when a lama came to visit, a servant or another member of the household would go to the roof to burn a special offering in the fireplace. This was also done whenever a member of the family was to undertake an important new venture or some good and auspicious work.

To make this special offering, slightly green juniper branches were burned along with two or three spoonfuls of barley mixed with butter, which were added before lighting the fire. When the fire was smoldering, another small juniper branch was dipped into a bowl of clean water and used to sprinkle the flames three times while the mantra, "Om Ah Hum," was repeated each time. This ceremony purified the offering of incense and produced a very pleasant fragrance.

This ritual has been performed since ancient times as a purification and offering to the *lha*, who are the lesser gods belonging to the locality of a particular area. It protects the family from evil forces and brings good fortune to all. Observed by every Tibetan family, fire offerings were made even by the nomads, who used to keep special stoves for this purpose. When there was no stove, they made the offering in an open fire. This kind of fire offering was also made whenever travelers reached the summit of a high mountain, where there often were stoves built for that purpose. Sometimes on special auspicious days the people of Lhasa would go to the nearest high mountains, either Bumpa-ri to the southeast or Gephel-ri to the northwest, to burn incense in the stoves there. They would usually leave for the mountain in the dead of night in order to be able to start the fire at dawn. A huge column of smoke carrying the fragrance would then be visible for a long distance.

In each Tibetan house the largest and most important room was the chapel, which was used only for special occasions such as weddings, Losar celebrations and religious activities. In addition, almost every other room had a few religious statues or paintings displayed on a small altar in a central place in front of which would be placed butter lamps, water bowls, and incense. There was even an altar in the kitchen. This was the case whether a family was rich or poor.

In the Surkhang house the chapel or *tsomchin* was our largest room, measuring about forty-five feet square, and was located on the second floor. Wooden pillars supported the ceiling. On one side there were large windows with glass panes. All of the rafters, doors, window frames, pillars, and altar were colorfully painted with floral designs on a red background. The ceiling itself was painted a lapis blue or green with beams in a contrasting color such as yellow or red and elaborately decorated with intricate designs. On the walls hung religious paintings framed in brocades. At one end of the room was the altar consisting of wooden cabinets with glass doors to protect the images. At Surkhang house there were five life-size statues of the deities Tsepamed (Amitayus), Namgyalma (Ushnish Vijaya), Drolkar (White Tara), Chenrezi (Avalokiteshvara), and Jampeyang (Manjushri), dressed in brocade robes and wearing full sets of our best family jewelry inside the glass cabinets. The statues were made of gilded bronze with painted faces. Their hollow interiors contained holy relics. One hundred and two volumes of the *Kangyur* or Buddhist sutras were wrapped in yellow silk cloth and stored on shelves on either side of the images. In front of the images there was a shelf where offerings and decorations were placed. For Losar sixteen bowls of different kinds of dried fruit from India and China were set out. There were two bowls for each type of fruit as well as large antique Chinese porcelain vases filled with artificial flowers made from paper. Tall piles of khabsey were attractively stacked.

Facing the altar was a row of seats for our family. There were heavy, thick cushions stuffed with deer hair, which was rare and very soft. Cheaper cushions were usually made from straw. Each seat was about thirty inches high from the floor and had a wooden back covered by a brocade slipcover. The seat for our father was higher and had a throne-like appearance. For Losar special colorful brocade covers were put on all the seats. Extra cushions could be put out along the walls all around the room whenever necessary. In front of the seats small carved and painted tables were placed where tea could be served. During Losar beautiful rugs which were usually kept in storage were put on the floors. New katas (long, white silk scarves) were placed on all of the paintings and statues. The altar was decorated with our largest and finest silver and gold butter lamps, as well as many extra ones normally not used which had been brought out from storage and lit to make the holiday very festive and gay. On our roof new prayer flags were strung up and the tashi taring banner hung from the edge of the roof facing the courtyard. Even the doorway areas outside were decorated with auspicious chalk designs. Everything was carefully cleaned so that on walking into the rooms first thing in the morning, one felt surprised at the newness, freshness and beauty of everything.

In the villages New Year celebrations could last from five to seven days, while in Lhasa Losar celebrations lasted for only three days. The first day is the most important. On that day according to custom our family would get up very early, about two A.M. Father wore his best official robes used only on the most special occasions and the rest of us put on new clothes and our best jewelry. Our mother had already gotten up a half hour before anyone else, since she had to supervise the morning's preparations as well as get dressed and put on all of her complicated jewelry.

When we children were six or seven years old, we would be so excited and happy about Losar that we could not sleep the night before. We rarely got to wear new clothes, so we really enjoyed putting them on for New Year's celebration. After finishing the family ceremonies, which ended just before dawn, we would be allowed to play with sparklers and small firecrackers bought from India. This was a very special treat only for New Year's Day.

Early in the morning of New Year's Day, after taking a cup of tea in our rooms, we greeted each other happily saying "*Tashi Deleg!*" meaning "Good Luck!" Our family gathered in the chapel where Father would place a very long kata about ten feet long on the altar. Then everyone sat down in order of precedence, with Father sitting first in the highest seat, then next to him our mother, and finally the children from the oldest to the youngest. Tea was then served in our best cups which were of antique Chinese porcelain with carved Tibetan silver lids and saucers decorated with gold inlay and semi-precious stones. A servant then brought into the room the *droso che mar,* the symbol of the New Year.

The droso chemar was a painted wooden offering box about twelve by eighteen inches in size. One of its two compartments held tsampa (barley flour) mixed with butter and the other was filled with wheat kernels. Each offering was piled into a small mound and decorated with colorful butter sculptures of the eight auspicious symbols (traditional designs called *tashi tagye).* For the decorations, colored butter similar to cake icing was applied to a very thin wooden board about five inches tall and two inches wide (called *ashang pangleb*—ashang means uncle, pangleb means board). This was stuck into the top of the offering. The droso chemar was placed on the cabinet or cupboard near the entrance to the main room. Next to this was set a beautiful large pitcher filled with beer, and a cup reserved only for special times such as this. Ours was made of silver, but other people might use a wooden one with silver decorations. The droso chemar was first presented to our father, who took a pinch both of tsampa and wheat and threw it into the air as an offering to the deities. Then the servant offered it to Mother, who followed Father's example, and one by one each member of the family had his turn to make the offering.

Afterwards a woman servant entered and presented a large pitcher of beer to everyone starting with Father, who dipped the tip of the third finger of his right hand and then flicked a drop of beer into the air as an offering. Then, two small bowls, one of cooked rice with butter and the other of droma and butter (droma are tiny dark brown sweet potatoes the size of beans) were served to each person, and placed on a small table before him. In their bowls, the rice and droma were each molded into the shape of a mountain, on top of which a little bit of sugar was sprinkled like snow. The offerings of rice and droma were left on the table, and we would take a small pinch, first tossing it into the air and then lightly tasting it. Tea was served and drunk and the cups immediately refilled several times in quick succession.

The *changtzod,* who was the head servant or treasurer, then offered Father three katas by placing them on the small table in front of him. After placing the first two, another servant standing by would reach over just as the third scarf was being presented, and courteously accept it on behalf of the head of the family. Then he placed it around the neck of the servant making the presentation. The head servant offered *chambul* or salutation of respect by removing his hat with one hand and bowing slightly. Women would join their hands together, palm to palm in front of their faces and move them up and down briefly. Afterwards each of the twenty-five servants in turn presented Father with three katas, and then of offered chambul to each member of the family one by one. Altogether this took half an hour. When this was finished, there would be a huge pile of katas heaped in front of Father, which made everything seem very festive.

Immediately following this ceremony, hot wheat porridge with butter and dried cheese was served to each person at his seat. Then a special hot drink called *chang-go* made of beer, butter, tsampa (barley flour), natural sugar and dried cheese was poured. When these had been eaten, a few minutes later another servant brought a large decorated teapot into the room and signalled with a slight circular motion of the pot that the morning's ceremony had been completed. This was known as *drol-cha* or end tea.

At about this time, although it could be a little earlier or later, a beggar would arrive dressed in a white costume and white mask. He was known as the *dregar,* meaning white rice, and would sing about himself as being the bearer of good omens for the New Year. There were always five or six men from among the beggars of Lhasa who had good voices and had memorized the dregar's auspicious songs, which had been handed down for centuries. When he came to our house, he would be received in the courtyard and would be given some khabsey and a kata which was accepted by the assistant who accompanied him. This practice was observed all over Tibet during New Year. The dregar's stories were chanted in a strange high-pitched sing-song voice.

Our father then set out with a few servants for the Potala Palace along with all the other government officials in Lhasa to offer New Year's greetings to the Dalai Lama at about three A.M. Those who were not government officials would get up at five or six A.M. All of the customs and observances were followed more or less the same way by everybody, varying only by their station in life.

On all three days our family stayed in the house to receive visits from just a few of our closest friends who would stop by informally to wish us a happy New Year and offer a kata. They might stay for a little while to play dice or perhaps join us for dinner. Upon their departure we gave them khabsey. During the holidays, everyone wore their best clothes, ate special foods, and enjoyed the festive atmosphere in order to start out the New Year in a happy frame of mind.

After dinner on the evening of the last day, the family gathered again in the chapel at seven o'clock, where all of our men servants and a few of our women servants awaited us. When we were children, my parents always presided at this celebration. But after my older brother was ten years old, our parents stayed only briefly until finally they just sent us to represent them. Although they were probably bored, we children were thrilled and felt terribly grown up to be a part of an adult party.

After the family was seated and tea was served, a woman servant went over to the altar where a large silver beer pitcher was placed along with a large silver bowl that could hold the equivalent of three regular bowls. She filled the bowl and carried it over to my father, pouring some beer from it into his bowl from which he took a few sips. After a few moments she went over to the altar again to refill the silver bowl. Once again she refilled Father's and then placed it before him. As soon as she stood to one side holding the pitcher, Father picked up the silver bowl and gestured to the head servant to come forward. Father then filled the head servant's bowl from the large silver one. When he took a few sips, Father refilled his bowl, and then he very politely withdrew doing chambul to my father and removing his hat. This was repeated one by one by each male servant, of whom six or seven sat opposite the family on cushions while the rest stood.

When everyone had been served, four or five of the men stood up and began to sing traditional songs accompanied by dances called *shalchin*. After ten or fifteen minutes, the head servant gave katas to the singers and dancers on behalf of the family to thank them for their entertainment. Everyone then sat down and was served tea. A little later, a man servant entered carrying the large teapot for drol-cha (end tea) to signify that the ceremony was over. On the fourth day after New Year's about fifteen khabsey were given to each of our servants. The changtzod (head servant), *nyerpa* (storekeeper), and *trungnyig* (secretary) each received double this amount. This was how the Surkhang family celebrated Losar. Officials' families celebrated just as we did, while others only varied their observances according to their financial means. Losar was the most important celebration of the year for all Tibetans whether laymen or monks, rich or poor, townspeople or villagers.

5 The Pilgrim's Life

All Tibetans, high or low, rich or poor, were extremely fond of going on pilgrimage. I know from first-hand experience that even children liked it. Besides enjoying the beauty of the places of pilgrimage, which were often in very remote areas, pilgrims also got the opportunity to see how other people lived in different parts of the country. While there were many well-known pilgrimage spots all over Tibet, the most holy were Lhasa, the capital of Tibet; Samye, an ancient temple established by King Trisong Detsen in the eighth century, sixty miles southeast of Lhasa; Tsari, an area of holy places associated with the deity Demchog, also in the southeast approximately 140 miles from Lhasa; and Gang Rinpoche, the sacred mountain of Kailash, near the border with western Nepal. Besides these there were countless sacred places known only to the people of particular local areas. Of course since Lhasa was the seat of His Holiness the Dalai Lama and many other high lamas and was the location of the three largest monasteries in Tibet, to visit Lhasa was the first priority for all pilgrims. Among the holy images in Lhasa the most important was the image of Lord Buddha in the Tsuk Lhakhang or Central Temple. This image was believed to have been made by a deity and blessed by Buddha himself.

The purpose of going on pilgrimage was to achieve two essential aims: to increase the pilgrim's store of merit and to purify his negative tendencies. The hardships of the journey did
not lessen the inspiration the pilgrims experienced. As soon
as any pilgrim reached his destination, he would be in his best
spirits since an important goal had been achieved. This also
kindled an unshakable faith in the power of the deity who
helped him fulfill his vow.

Entering the temple, the pilgrim first made prostrations in
front of the altar, presented a kata, and then made offerings
of butter lamps and incense. Butter lamp offerings were the
most usual and most popular form of worship. It was somewhat like the flowers Hindus give to their deities or the can-
dles Catholics burn in their churches. Worship was made to
the images of deities and also to the sacred texts and the other
symbols of wisdom kept in these holy places. Pilgrims usually
circumambulated the temples as many times as they could.
Giving gifts of cash and food to monasteries, nunneries and
the poor was also considered a pious act. In their concluding
prayers pilgrims do not pray for themselves alone, but always
say "wish prayers" for others. In this way the pilgrim shares
his own merit with all beings, and multiplies this merit into
limitless power, the source of the Buddhahood that we hope
to achieve. Even though there is obviously little merit to be
gained by selfish deeds, people cannot help praying for their
own personal gains. Nevertheless, pilgrims are supposed to try
to imagine that their deeds will help other beings.

In my days in Tibet there were no means of transport except by beasts of burden, nor any hotels or restaurants along
the way. A short pilgrimage might take one day only, leaving
in the morning and returning at night. But for longer pilgrimages, which might take weeks, months or even years, many
elaborate preparations were required. These preparations varied
a great deal according to the financial status of the family.
Sometimes food and other necessities including tents and cooking equipment were to be carried along for the whole journey. Tsampa, butter, tea, salt, brown sugar, dried meat, rice,

and wheat flour were some of the foodstuffs carried on the backs of horses, ponies, and mules. Both cooking utensils and wooden bowls for eating had to be included. Of course some foods could be purchased along the way according to what might be available in a particular district, but pilgrims could not depend on this. Tents for the night's lodging would be necessary whenever there were no villages or monasteries in which to stay. When, for example, the family members and servants would number about ten, it would necessitate as many as twenty-two to twenty-five horses and mules for riding and carrying supplies. These animals were cared for by two or three muleteers. Naturally all families going on pilgrimage could not afford such elaborate preparations. Sometimes part or all of the food supplies had to be carried by the pilgrims themselves. Those coming from far away places like Kham and Amdo in eastern Tibet were usually less affluent and had fewer animals and less money. They had to travel on foot and beg for food and lodging along the way.

There were many beggars in Tibet—as many as a thousand living in the Lhasa area alone. They came from different parts of Tibet, wandering all over the country to make a living. Many of them had been beggars for generations and had deliberately chosen this way of life. There were also many religious mendicants—those who had given up the material world, devoted their time to prayers and depended on alms for survival.

The beggars in Lhasa lived in tents around the Lingkhor area, the path of circumambulation around the city. They began their day early in the morning, going from door to door seeking alms. As the great majority of Tibetans were Buddhists, we willingly gave the beggars something, either foodstuffs or money. In so doing, we believed that we gained good karma. The small Moslem population of Lhasa was also very generous in their charity to the beggars.

At festival times and other auspicious occasions, it was the custom for the government to give the beggars roasted barley and other food. The richer families would do the same, and the beggars would wait in lines along the path of the Lingk-hor. On such occasions I too went to circumambulate, along with a servant carrying a cloth bag full of coins that we would distribute. When we went on pilgrimage it was considered especially important to give generously to the beggars.

One summer in June my parents took us children and four servants to a place outside of Lhasa called Phorong Kha in order to go on retreat. There were about twelve monks and twenty hermits in this mountainous spot. The monastery had been founded in the seventh century by Srongtsen Gampo and contained a temple with many statues inside. Although our family took four horses, a mule to carry water, and three other horses borrowed for the servants, on the day we visited most of the pilgrims there had walked. At that time I was seven years old and my younger brother Lhawang Topgyal was five, and we each rode double in front of a servant. We did not make trips like this very often, and we really enjoyed ourselves. Because our mother had told us the story of Phorong Kha we sensed the holiness of the temple, statues and the surrounding area. After we visited the temple the monks gave us tea at the monastery guest house. We had also brought a picnic lunch.

Phorong Kha was famous for its celestial burial grounds, regarded as very sacred because they had been blessed by Srongtsen Gampo. The celestial burial grounds were in a deep valley. On large flat stones human corpses were spread out. I was very frightened to see the corpses and cried for a long time. All of us were deeply affected by the experience, and we quickly returned to the monastery. I thought that since I was crying so much my father would scold and punish me as he would normally do, but on that day he did not. We believe that if someone pretends to be a corpse and lies down on the stone slab, he can overcome the bad karma in his life. We had planned to do this but didn't. Instead we went home. It had been a day that I both feared and enjoyed at the same time.

Motivated by the desire for religious merit, my mother took

us for a long pilgrimage when I was seventeen years old. My elder brother had to stay behind for his official duties so our pilgrimage party consisted of my mother, two brothers, one sister, and myself with eight servants and three muleteers. Leaving Lhasa we traveled in a southeasterly direction towards Drak, my birthplace. It took two and a half days to reach Drak, after which we rested at our house Kunsang Choeling for a few days. Then our pilgrimage really began.

In the Drak area there was a very famous place of pilgrimage known as Drak Yang-Dzong, high up on the mountainside. Guru Padma Sambhava, who had come from India in the eighth century to give Tibetans the teachings of the Buddha, had one day happened upon a huge rock cave concealed high on this mountain. Inside he found many natural forms of the Buddha and other deities in the face of the rock walls. From that time onward pilgrims counted it a great blessing to visit this cave. In order to get into it, pilgrims had to climb a thin bamboo ladder with twenty-one steep rungs. Because the ladder shook so badly, nervous people often could not climb up. It was considered a special blessing if the pilgrim could conquer his fear and enter the cave.

Years before when I was only a little girl, I had gone with my mother to Drak Yang-Dzong. I thought I was brave, but when I began to climb up the ladder it started to shake, and I became so giddy that I was afraid to continue. Many years had passed and again I returned. But this time after five or six cautious steps, I overcame my fear. I took it as a very good omen and climbed the rest of the way up safely. When I reached the cave, I found it was breathtakingly enchanting. My eyes feasted on the many Buddhas and the other deities that were natural formations of the rock walls. These were not hand-carved but appeared to have formed when the rock was in a molten state. We Tibetans believe that they were supernaturally created. At one place there was a natural opening leading down a three-hundred-foot pathway into another deep cave containing a tiny lake at the bottom. It was very dark, but the caretaker had brought a torch to light the way, and he described in detail all the auspicious sights. The caretaker told us how occasionally when pilgrims were standing at the edge of the lake they would hear the unexpected sound of an ox, which was a bad omen for one of those present. This bad omen seemed to signal disaster for the unlucky person in the form of accidental death, loss of wealth or sickness. That is why there was always an element of anxiety creeping into the thoughts of people when they stood beside the lake. They could not help wondering who would be the next to hear this strange portent.

Since the weather was not too severe in this area, endless streams of pilgrims came to visit throughout the year from all over the country. It was the duty of the caretaker there to provide shelter and to act as the guide for the pilgrims. There were always four monks in the cave doing daily pujas. I heard that they came from a big monastery of the Nyingma sect called Dorje Drak which was about sixty miles distant across the river Yarlung.

The formations of the stone deities in the cave at Drak Yang-Dzong were surely not made by any human hand. The sight of them was so startling that it held us spellbound. Even now my heart rejoices when the images in this cave come into my memory. There is no doubt in my mind that this place had once been blessed by the great Guru Padma Sambhava, whose name means the Lotus-Born One who sees past, present, and future events clearly.

Since Drak is a very beautiful place, we stayed about ten days enjoying the scenery before beginning our journey to Samye, our next destination on this pilgrimage. On the way we halted one night at Pangchung where we also owned an estate. Between Drak and Samye there were other sacred places associated either with Guru Rinpoche (another name for Padma Sambhava) or some other great Buddhist teacher. Not far from Drak was an enchanting small lake called Tsogyal Lhamtso. This was the sacred lake of Yeshe Tsogyal, considered to be an incarnation of the female Buddha of Wisdom, who was born there in the eighth century. The lake was said to have appeared suddenly at the instant of her birth. Later she became the disciple and consort of Guru Padma Sambhava and herself was known as a great dakini, or goddess having special powers. Local people say that all the girls born in the Drak valley have good personalities because it was the birthplace of Yeshe Tsogyal. This seemed true to me, as I found that the girls living there had very calm and sweet natures.

Samye, one of the most sacred places in Tibet, was for many centuries a great Buddhist center of learning and it was there that the volumes of the Buddha's teachings were first translated from Sanskrit to Tibetan. Samye was fashioned after Udantapuri[1] in northern India. The first Buddhist monastery of Samye was established and developed during the reign of the thirty-seventh king, Trisong Detsen, in the eighth century. It was during his reign that the great Indian Tantric saint Guru Padma Sambhava was invited to Tibet to teach Buddhism.

Among the many temples of interest in Samye, the most famous and magnificant of all was the enormous temple known as Migyur Lhungyi Drubpai Tsuk Lhakhang. This four-storied temple was built in the midst of a huge desert in the style of a mandala with fourteen smaller temples clustered around the main one, called Samye Chok. The main temple contained numerous small rooms housing many images and volumes of scriptures of both Tibetan and Sanskrit origin. On the advice of Padma Sambhava this temple was built in the same style as the great temple of Udantapuri in India. Instead of the Tibetan style flat roofs, the roofs of these temples were constructed in a pagoda fashion and covered with gold. Not only did the architecture of these temples have a special beauty but also the statues of the deities were considered to be very powerful. Among all the images, that of Guru Padma Sambhava found on the ground floor was the most life-like. When it was first finished the image had been heard to say, "I am exactly like him." After that it was said to have spoken many words of wisdom.

This town of temples was surrounded by high walls built

in a square. Atop these walls one hundred and eight small stupas had been constructed at regular intervals. There were four great gates, one in each of the four sides of the wall. Besides the temple inside the great wall there was a monastery called Rabjung Dratsang. About two hundred fifty monks stayed there as caretakers of the temples. At one side of the wall was a two-storied house with about twenty rooms. Butter offerings for the temples were prepared there, and part of the house was reserved for pilgrims who wanted to stay a few days. We took advantage of this and rented some rooms.

The Rabjung Dratsang and Samye Chok Temple owned some estates that had been granted by the government for their maintenance. Besides the profit gained from these estates, the monastery was supported by the Samye Dzong district, situated on one side of the town, where about sixty families lived.

There were three other big temples nearby built by the three queens of King Trisong Detsen.[2] These were located in different areas at a short distance from the town. From their appearance and architecture we could guess that they were once residences of the queens that had later been converted into temples.

For a few days we were very busy visiting these magnificent and absorbing temples in and near Samye. On the fifth day we went to visit another holy place called Chimphu. A monastery had been built at a bend in the trail high up on a mountain about fifteen miles from Samye. We rode up to the half way spot, left the horses in a village, and walked the rest of the way. It took us several hours because the trail was very steep and we often had to stop to rest. We were naturally very tired when we reached the top.

This mountain was different from others in that it looked like a huge blooming lotus flower. It was a strange sight to see so many kinds of bushes and trees covering this sacred mountain in striking contrast to the surrounding barren peaks. All around us beautiful birds sang in the woods. Colorful wildflowers bloomed here and there. Many giant blue pheasants roamed about in the bushes making long shrill sounds. The atmosphere was so pleasant and peaceful that I wanted to remain forever.

On this mountain were many holy caves where Guru Padma Sambhava had remained for years in meditation. It was here that he gave the esoteric teachings of Tibetan Buddhism to his famous twenty-five disciples who at that time attained enlightenment. In addition to the many caves consecrated by their meditations and teachings, there were huge magic footprints of Padma Sambhava in the rocks along with the tiny footprints of some goddesses. Many other sacred locations in Tibet besides Chimphu were also first discovered by Padma Sambhava who blessed them for us by using them for spiritual practices.

At the time we were in Chimphu about twenty hermits were living on the mountain in scattered caves and hermitages. We gave donations of dried tea and alms to each of them. Staying all night in the monastery at Chimphu enabled us to absorb deeply the holy atmosphere. The next morning we returned to Samye and stayed long enough to make the rounds of the temples again. When the time came for us to take leave of the monks, we gave them a donation and thanked them for their hospitality.

Early in the morning we started our journey to the Gerpa ferry. Progress was very slow because we had to cross a vast desert-like plain where the trails were covered with sand. Not until the afternoon did we reach our destination. To my brothers, my sister, and myself the light blue river Yarlung looked extremely wide. We could hardly see the other side. We knew we had to cross and, any way we looked at it, the crossing seemed very dangerous. We watched the preparations with mixed feelings.

Only one boat was apparent, a large wooden barge tied at the riverbank. It was long and box-like in shape with one narrow side that opened for boarding. On the bow of the boat was a big carved wooden horse's head. We wondered if we were going to have to cross the river in this curious vessel. Then a boatman approached my mother and suggested that she might prefer to hire a small hide coracle instead of waiting for the barge. We were greatly relieved since it was clear that the big boat would have taken a long time to reach the other side, and the heavy load and strong current would have made it very difficult for the boatman to manage a safe crossing. Indeed we thought it would be very lucky if the big boat did not sink from its weight somewhere in the middle of the river. Mother decided that the small hide boat was a good idea. However, only seven of us could fit into it. There was no other choice but for the rest of the servants, animals, and our supplies to risk crossing in the barge.

Even today I can remember how our boatman looked. He was a young man dressed in a white wool cloak with a bright geometric pattern on the collar. As it was in summer, the river had fully risen and the current was very strong. We children shuddered just at the sight of it, and we grew even more afraid the moment we got in the boat and felt it slide into the water.

Our fright was not unfounded. We had hardly left the shore when the motion of the waves and whirlpools began to shake the boat so violently that they nearly turned us upside-down into the turbulent water. Never in my life had I been so scared. We have a Tibetan saying which translates as: "I was so frightened that my heart nearly came out of my mouth." Well, this exactly describes how we were all feeling.

We were thankful that our boatman was young and strong and could row hard. He struggled vigorously trying to get us out of the danger. Miraculously after a little over half an hour he was able to bring the boat under control. When we could see that he was master of the boat, a little ease came to our minds and we began to smile slightly at each other. Still fear hovered in our minds, so we all continued to mumble prayers intently until we safely reached the other side.

Crossing this river was always a dangerous undertaking. Since it was so wide, there were no bridges. Nor was it possible to ferry donkeys or horses in the small hide boats. These animals cannot stand still, so when they stamp about they can easily cause the boat to turn over. Besides, their hoofs might tear a hole in the bottom and cause the boat to sink. Difficulties always increased whenever there was a strong wind. Even though it was summer, there was so much wind in that place that one could only cross the river early in the day. It was quite impossible for anyone to cross in the evening when the winds were the strongest.

We all rejoiced when we reached the other side and realized we were safe. We had been told that every year there was at least one tragedy in which a hide boat sank here. Although we seven had crossed safely, we now had to wait anxiously on the bank for another hour for the ferry to arrive. We tried to eat but could not relish the tea and tsampa because we were so worried about the rest of our party and our supplies. But at last the barge arrived. Gladly we paid the fees and continued on our way as soon as we could get organized, but it was not until evening that we were able to leave the riverbank.

We traveled only a few miles to reach the Gerpa estate, which belonged to the Nechung Monastery in Lhasa. We were all exhausted by the time we met the manager who was living in a large house in the midst of a grove of willow trees. He knew our family well and received us warmly. After halting there for the night, we traveled all the next day until we came to a small village called Jangthang. Now we were nearing the most important part of the journey. That night we all were so excited we could hardly sleep. The next day we would meet our grandmother at the Ludhing estate near a town called Rong Lukhang.

On the following day when we were still quite far from the house, we met Grandmother's servants. They had come to welcome and accompany us to the gate where Grandmother Lhagyari and her three daughters were waiting to greet us. We dismounted, and as we approached, our mother took out a long white silk scarf from her pocket and presented it to her mother. Then according to Tibetan custom they touched foreheads. Grandmother kissed and patted us and asked whether we had found our journey hard. We all rejoiced at this meeting because we had not seen one another for eight long years. Our grandmother was eager to show us her two-storied house with a small park in the front which she had just finished building.

As is our custom, as soon as it was convenient my mother presented Grandmother with a load of brick tea and Chinese silk. Grandmother must have been sixty-nine years old at that time but her mind and senses were very clear. Her weight was about two hundred and fifty pounds. She was so huge she could hardly move. My grandfather had died more than twenty years earlier, but even as a widow all of her needs were taken care of nicely. Most of her daily necessities came directly from the Lukhang estate nearby. Other items not available there were brought from Lhagyari which was the largest estate of the family. She did not have to take any responsibility at all for the Lhagyari family. Neither did she have to bother with her own household for she had a nun assistant named Kunsang Wangmo who stayed permanently at the estate to manage the household affairs. There were eight servants living in the Ludhing house including the cattlemen, cook, water carrier, and so on. In addition there were also ten women who did spinning and weaving to make woolen cloth and carpets. These products were sent to Lhasa from time to time to be sold.

Grandmother's elder daughter Urgyen Chozom was a nun. She had devoted her entire life to religious practices and stayed at a hermitage called Tshawa Ritod, which was in the upper regions of the mountains nearby. It was a steep climb of about seven miles from Ludhing, but she often used to visit her mother. At the time we made our visit, she was forty-nine years of age. Another daughter, Yeshe Wangmo, was also a nun. She stayed most of the time at Lhagyari,[3] which was one and a half days' journey from Ludhing. It was she who had charge of the welfare of the family. She moved between Lhagyari and Ludhing every few months. My grandmother's other daughter Kunsang Dekyi usually stayed in Lhagyari.

We were lucky that during our visit all three daughters were with our grandmother in Rong Ludhing. Grandmother was obviously very happy to have us there and entertained us in a most hospitable way. Not only did other family members staying nearby come often to visit but also Rong Lukhang itself had much charm in both beauty and activities. That is why my grandmother loved to stay at this estate.

Sometimes we visited temples and monasteries, sometimes we went on picnics, and sometimes we just enjoyed visiting together. After staying about a month in Ludhing, we traveled for a day and a half to reach the Eh Lhagyari palace. The Lhagyari family was expecting us and had prepared a welcoming party. A large tent had been pitched in an open grass meadow where a delicious supper was served. Later we went to the main house which was so huge it looked to us like a large monastery. It had four stories with archaic designs and decorations on both the inside and outside. The Lhagyaris had occupied this palace since before the seventeenth century. During the reign of the Fifth Dalai Lama, the head of the Lhagyari household was bestowed the title "Trichen," which was equivalent to the rank of a cabinet minister.[4] The palace was ancient even then and had attached to it a large monastery called Rego Chosde.

Two rooms had been arranged for us on the third floor close to the rooms used by my aunt and my cousin, Trichen Kalsang Nyendak, and his wife Rigzen Choden. Trichen Kalsang was the heir to the house. The rest of the servants stayed on the ground floor in guest rooms. As in Ludhing, we were lavishly entertained by the Lhagyari family.

The twenty day stay in the Eh Lhagyari palace was a time of joy and fun. There was a stream and pool beside the *trokhang* or pleasure house set in a huge park, where on sunny days we could take baths and the servants could wash our clothes. Within the park there were several houses in one of which our aunt Kunsang Dekyi lived with her husband Pema Gyalpo and several of their children. Sometimes we played a Tibetan dice game or else another game similar to checkers with white and black pebbles that were moved on cross lines. On other days we went to see small monasteries and nunneries in the area.

My mother had spent her childhood days in Lhagyari. One of her intimate friends still lived near the palace. One day this friend invited us and four of Mother's other friends from nearby villages for a luncheon party. Although our hostess's husband was a servant of the Lhagyari family, this did not stand in the way of their social friendship. My mother's friend was not rich but their rooms and inexpensive furniture were kept very neat and clean. Their meeting was a revival of their past. Mother gave each of them presents of red silk material for blouses.

Many days before our departure from Lhagyari our aunt Yeshe Wangmo was making the preparations for our long pilgrimage to Tsari. She herself was going along to keep company with our mother. This made our caravan much larger than it had been. My aunt had arranged for nine more servants and fifteen mules to carry extra rations and three more tents. Our party now totaled six family members including our aunt and twenty servants all mounted on horses, plus four muleteers watching after at least twenty pack animals.

When the day came for departure, we started out in a southeasterly direction. Towards the evening of the first day we reached a village called Eh Chundo Gyang. It was a windy place, but since it was late in the day we had no choice but to stay there. Luckily for us the Lhagyari family had previously arranged a rest house for us for the night, so we did not have to pitch our tents and brave the cold. As our Tibetan custom required, the next morning we gave thanks to our hosts for their services and paid for the fodder we had used.

After we left that place, the landscape gradually began to change. Soon we reached the Lha Gong Thang steppes and traveled three days through this beautiful expanse of vast grasslands with low small hills here and there. All over the hills there were small bushes called *pangma*. They had soft needles of a light green color like that of the juniper. As these needles dropped, they made interestingly shaped patches on the ground. The branches of these trees provided the only firewood we could find in this area.

It took three long days to cross this Lha Gong Thang steppe, the land of nomads. At the foot of the low hills, nestled between the slopes and all over the steppes, groups of two to five black nomad tents were huddled together. Sometimes our trail took us quite close to them. We all were frightened when their huge dogs barked at us. The dogs were chained; otherwise I am sure we would have been bitten.

Seen from a distance the nomads' tents made little black dots in the green pastures. It was summertime and the steppe was like a large enchanting natural park where many wild animals roamed. Often we saw tiny tunnels dug by little grey creatures with cute faces, called *chiphi*. These little animals were something like the prairie dogs found in the western part of the United States. Sometimes our trail took us near lovely blue streams where we could see herds of antelopes and wild blue sheep. Deer and wild ass also were roaming the steppe freely. Even dangerous animals like wolves were said to be there, but fortunately we saw them only in the distance.

Of course in the grasslands there were many herds of yak and dri and flocks of sheep all along the way. The nomad herdsmen and shepherds were always walking lazily behind these animals. They carried small sticks made out of yak hair for tending the flocks. Besides this they also carried daggers and slingshots decorated with beautiful patterns used as a sort of game. Our aunt told us that water and grass in the Lha Gong Thang areas were very nourishing for the animals. We noticed that the butter and cheese made by the nomads here were tastier than that made in other places.

Before our departure from Eh Lhagyari, Aunt Kunsang Dekyi had prepared elaborate and delicious lunch packs for our long journey through Lha Gong Thang. She knew that firewood would be scarce which would make cooking difficult. She had prepared several pounds of cake made of tsampa, butter, dried cheese, and brown sugar. Along with this she had packed a lot of dried yak and sheep meat. All of these foods she had wrapped in separate lunch packs, so we enjoyed delicious meals all the days we were passing through the steppe.

Whenever we were hungry and tired, our guides looked around for a favorable site. We would then all dismount and spread our saddle carpets over the ground. We had only to wait for the water to boil for tea. Then we each would open our lunch packs and eat sitting on the open ground. During this break the horses and mules were given water and grain. We usually rested for two hours at a lunch break. The cooks and some of the servants who carried the tents would go on ahead to find a suitable camping site for the night.

During one of these sojourns, my aunt chose a camp site not too far from some nomads' black tents. She sent two of the servants to buy some yogurt from them. It was dusk and the nomads thought two dangerous intruders were coming, so they let their fierce-looking dogs loose to run at the strangers. The servants bravely fought their way to the door of the tents and explained quickly that they were only travelers who had come to buy yogurt. The nomads then became very hospitable and gave them plenty of it free of charge. They also sold them one fourth of a mutton so that in the evening we had an especially delicious feast.

During the journey across the steppe we had to get up very early every morning. Before sunrise we had always finished our morning tea and tsampa with dry cheese, in order to be ready to leave the camp by dawn. Although we were straining all the time, it was not until the third day toward evening that our travel across the wild steppe came to an end. Finally we came to the mouth of a narrow valley called Dakpo Drolung, where a river rushes down a steep gorge making a thunderous noise. At the head of this valley was a small village with only six householders. The only place large enough to pitch our tents was near one of the houses. Our tents were so close to their sheep shed that all night long we had to endure unpleasant smells. Also the camp site was full of rubbish probably left by previous camping pilgrims. All in all we had a very uncomfortable time there. Although we bought hay for our animals, it was unusual that these villagers did not offer us any of the customary Tibetan hospitality.

We left that place as early as we could the next morning. All that day we traveled in the Dakpo Drolung Valley and only by nightfall did we reach the end. As we watched the servants pitch our tents, we were thinking how we had at last reached the place of pilgrimage. Now that we had finally come to the Tsari district, we were all eager to start visiting the holy places.

This region was a very remote area isolated from the adjoining districts. It started from a place called Bumdha Serbum. There was no regular seat of the government in all of Tsari, which belonged to the district of Dakpo Kunam Dzong. The people of Tsari did not have to pay taxes. Instead they were assigned to help the pilgrims by keeping rest houses ready and aiding them in other ways. The pilgrims were not required to pay anything to the keepers of these rest houses, but those who could afford it always gave something in return for their hospitality. It was our custom to give all the keepers along the pilgrimage route presents of brick tea and inexpensive cotton materials to show our appreciation for their services.

Tsari was very well known all over Tibet as a sacred place. There were three different pilgrimages for those going to Tsari. The small circle was the easiest since it took only a few days. The middle circle was the route we followed. The third was a very special pilgrimage called the large circle, which was by far the hardest, the longest, and the most holy of all.

Many years later my cousin Tsering Yudon Drumpa told us all about the large circle pilgrimage, which is open only every twelfth year. In 1944 she made this pilgrimage following a route that included most of the places we visited in the middle circle and in addition a place called Tsari Rongkor, meaning "circling of the mountain base." The powerful deities blessing this place were the Chakra Samvara (Demchog) and the Vajra Yogini deities who had their abode on the peak of a snow covered mountain in that area called the Pure Crystal Mountain. The sacred nature of this place was first discovered by one of the disciples of Milarepa named Tsangpa Gyari who had meditated in the mountains of Tsari for a long time. Later one of Tsangpa Gyari's disciples, Kyibu Yeshe Dorje, performed many religious practices there. When people learned of his experiences, it became a very important place for pilgrims.

One of the reasons this area was not open to pilgrims every year was because of the extreme difficulties faced by travelers. Even so, some years the number of pilgrims had exceeded twenty thousand. All were expected to be ready to sacrifice everything, even their lives if necessary, when they chose to follow the large circle going to Rongkor. That is why my cousin's decision to go in 1944 was not taken lightly. We had all waited anxiously for her return to hear her tell about it.

Tibetans believe that if they can earn enough merit during their lifetime, they will be reborn in a human form; but if they accumulate negative karma by committing evil deeds towards other sentient beings, they will be reborn in an animal body. If, however, they could make the pilgrimage to Tsari Rongkor with an earnest desire to correct their faults, they believe that after death they would certainly be born again as a human being.

My cousin told us that going to Rongkor on pilgrimage was not at all easy because of the many obstacles. It was not like going to other holy places in Tibet. The area around the holy mountain was inhabited by a primitive race of people called the Lobas. Though they officially were subjects of the Tibetan government and were nominally Buddhists, they would not submit to government authority. In many ways they were uncivilized and undisciplined. They did not wear any clothes except a small piece of cloth just large enough to cover their sex organs. The Loba men always carried knives as well as bows and poisoned arrows. They were said to eat insects. Their presence always posed great difficulties and dangers for the pilgrims. In the past the Lobas had killed some pilgrims with their poisoned arrows and taken away their belongings. Our cousin Tsering Yudon had heard many stories like this from the guides who were helping her group of pilgrims.

The Tibetan government made special arrangements for those who wanted to go on the Rongkor pilgrimage tour. Two senior officers, one monk, and one layman would be appointed to arrange the details for the tour itself, and the government would send along one hundred soldiers to protect the pilgrims from the Lobas. In addition the Tibetan government sent many presents to the Lobas to try to pacify them. The presents included hand-bells, cymbals made of brass, cotton clothes, some costume jewelry, some woolen cloth, and about twenty bags of salt and sugar. All these added up to about one hundred loads.

On reaching Mikyim Dun at the edge of the Loba territory, the pilgrims would rest while two government officials sent three or four natives of Tsari who understood the Loba language to call them for negotiation. Usually about thirty Loba men and women would respond. The negotiation took place in a village called Seven Households. The two groups would sit facing each other. Through an interpreter the officers would lay out the presents the government had sent and request the Lobas to guarantee that the pilgrims could pass through their area without harm. They were also asked to help them if the need arose. If the Lobas were satisfied with the gifts, they happily accepted the presents and assured the officers that they would allow the pilgrims to go on their way peacefully. But even then they could not be trusted entirely.

When an agreement was made, the Lobas would be asked to confirm in a peculiar way their promise to give the pilgrims safe passage. Of course it should be understood that these people were even amongst themselves so undisciplined that a sworn promise was not a complete assurance that there would not be trouble. Even so, the officers tried their best to make all the Lobas feel the responsibility of keeping the agreement.

When the officers thought that they had come to the best possible agreement with the Lobas, they would arrange the necessary things for a Loba swearing ceremony. A wooden gate, which some of the pilgrims were expected to help build, was erected out of bamboo for the special ceremony. When the gate was ready, the meat of freshly killed yaks was tied to the posts on each side. Then the Lobas were expected to show their good faith by passing under the gate. In passing each would cut a small piece of raw meat from the yak's carcass and eat it. Although the pilgrims were expected to build the gate itself, the government officers arranged to pay for the animals that were to be slaughtered for the ceremony.

Sometimes the Lobas would not negotiate because they were unsatisfied with the number of presents that had been sent by the Tibetan government. In such cases the only recourse the officials had was to bargain and sometimes offer more presents that they had held in reserve. These officers had to be ready for almost any contingency when they faced the Lobas.

Seven Households was a large village situated in a strategic place for pilgrims and was a good resting place. Here pilgrims from all over Tibet gathered in preparation for the long journey ahead. Special arrangements for them had to be made by the government. Since food had to be provided for the rest of the journey, the government estates in the district of Dakpo sent fifteen hundred to two thousand sacks of tsampa. When the pilgrims were assembled there, the government officer made the distributions. Usually each person received three pounds of tsampa which he had to carry himself unless he could hire others to help him.

After the Lobas had confirmed their promise and the food had been distributed, the officer divided the pilgrims into groups of one hundred, with leaders appointed for each group. The first group was different in that all hundred pilgrims were either volunteer soldiers or natives of Tsari. They were sent ahead to clear the way for the other groups, which would follow them one by one.

The road was rough and hazardous. Sometimes there were steep cliffs to climb. Everyone had to keep pace with the others. Pilgrims were warned not to leave much gap between the groups while moving. Sometimes before they could reach a convenient place for spending the night, it became dark and they could not go further.

My cousin Tsering Yudon Drumpa and the other pilgrims faced all these difficulties for the fifteen days it took to circle the mountain. All along the way they said their prayers and were expected not to talk unnecessarily. They read religious texts whenever they stopped to rest and also at night by candlelight. In this way the blessings of the deities Demchok and Vajra Yogini were expected to influence them for the rest of their lives as well as in the next life.

The larger circle taken by my cousin was much more difficult than the middle route I took with my family. We had completed the long journey across the steppe through the narrow Dakpo Drolung valley and had arrived safely at Bumdha Serbum. Although there was a rest house there, we chose to pitch our tents once more so that we could be near the temple. We were all eager to begin our visits to the holy places.

The next day we came to a place called Drup Chu Kha. We made the usual offerings to the deity in that temple and prayed for the betterment of all sentient beings. On the second day we left for a big village called Choezam which consisted of about sixty households. We rested there for two full days so that both we and the animals could recover from the hardships of the journey. The pilgrimage ahead would be very difficult. We decided to leave behind all the riding horses except two for my youngest brother and sister. Because we needed only eight mules to carry our rations, bedding and other necessary items, the remaining horses and mules were sent away to a pasture area that was owned by one of the Lhagyaris' friends.

A drizzling rain fell most of the time, making the paths wet and slippery so that it was necessary for us to use walking sticks. Our servants cut nice bamboo sticks for each of us from the woods nearby. When we left Choezam on foot, we all carried these bamboo sticks. In addition each of us had to carry a cotton bag slung across our shoulders containing lunch packs, refreshments, and tea cups.

Since it was our first day of walking and we were not used to trekking along unfamiliar trails, we easily tired and had to rest after almost every mile. Even with all the delays we probably covered a distance of eight miles before we halted for the night at a sacred place called Do Tsen.

Do Tsen translated literally means sex organs of the male

and female, and in that place there were natural forms of the male and female organs in the rocks. Since these forms were not manmade, they bestowed special powers of procreation, enabling any childless couple who prayed to them to be blessed with children. It was interesting for us to note that neither the temple nor the rest house in this area had any particular name.

As we were getting settled in the rest house for the night, we were surprised to see a person coming straight toward us from a distance. He told us that he had been sent by a high lama whose name was Drukchen Rinpoche. This lama had a strong connection with the Lhagyari family, so when he received word that we were at this place, he sent one of his servants named Dhenod to be our special guide for the rest of our pilgrimage. As most of the people in Tsari were the devotees of Drukchen Rinpoche, the guide was a great help to us.

The next day Dhenod took us on foot to a sacred place called Lugyal Wangdak. Here we saw a huge boulder that looked a little like a two-storied house. It was almost square in shape and had bushes growing all over it. According to the Tsari legend, whoever made the round of this rock with devotion and faith would never suffer from leprosy. Furthermore, anyone already suffering from leprosy who was able to make the rounds with enough devotion and faith would be cured. That day we saw some lepers walking around the rock doing prostrations. I felt such compassion for them. I prayed that their faith would be strong and that neither I nor any of my family would ever suffer from such a dreadful disease.

We kept right on going until we reached a nice camping site. Since by this time it was raining heavily, we pitched only three of our tents. Everything inside was alright except that a fine drizzle kept leaking through the canvas in various places. Nevertheless we managed to stay dry. The next day we moved on to a holy place called Chikchar, which was a small village of about fifteen families. In the center of the village was a nice rest house where we stayed for the night. This was near a small monastery that housed about ten monks. Inside was a famous life-sized statue of the deity Vajra Yogini. As usual, we made offerings and prayers to the deities and gave donations to the monks. The rest house was very comfortable and the area very beautiful. We lingered for eight days in Chikchar before leaving for Seven Households, the same large village where the people who were going on the Rongkor pilgrimage always gathered. Long ago this village began with only seven families, but when we were there it had grown to more than one hundred.

The pilgrims who visited Seven Households begged food from the inhabitants following a long-standing custom. It was said that a living deity dwelt in the locality who was always ready to give a physical or spiritual boon depending on the prayer of the pilgrim. There was only one hitch: no one knew where she stayed and no one could recognize her. It was said that she gave the blessings through food begged from the inhabitants living there, but even the families in this village did not know when and how the deity blessed the food. In the hope that the food they gave to the beggars had been blessed by the deity and that they also would receive a blessing, the villagers gave generously to the begging pilgrims.

Inspired by this tradition, the pilgrims did not want to miss the opportunity to get this immense spiritual and worldly blessing. So with their begging bowls they went to as many of the houses in the village as they could. They had firm faith that somehow at one of the houses they would receive some food that had been blessed by the deity. It is strange that although the villagers never knew from which house, theirs or another, the blessed food had come, still they too believed in the legend and always gave food to the begging pilgrims.

In our case, we sent the servants with bowls to beg from every single household and warned them not to skip even one. The village was divided into sections each of which was taken by a different servant. It wasn't until late in the evening that all the servants returned to show what they had collected. They had brought a variety of foods: tsampa, meat, potatoes, green vegetables, dried peaches, some walnuts, and grains. All this was cooked together and was distributed equally between the family members, servants and even the animals. We never did know just who the deity was. We did not know which food had been blessed, but neither family members nor servants ever forgot the wonderful feast that was made from the alms. This was our last full meal in Seven Households.

The trail which we had to follow the next day was very rough. We had to cross through three different passes known respectively as the forest pass, the grass pass, and the boulder pass before we could find a suitable camping site. The forest pass was very high and to reach it we had to climb a steep winding path through a thick forest. With great effort we reached the top and were relieved to see ahead of us a straight and gently sloping trail. Soon that trail again started to rise, and so we climbed the grass pass, which was not much higher than the forest pass. Then we found ourselves at the most taxing part of all. We had come to the beginning of the much steeper and higher boulder pass. After a great struggle by both beast and man, we reached the summit exhausted and discouraged. The sun was already setting but before we could stop for the night we had to climb down into the deep canyon below on a very rough and dangerous trail.

Dusk fell as soon as we came to the place where the trail started downwards. We could not even see the path. It was too dangerous to move since there were piles of boulders of various sizes in the way and the trail went first one way and then another. We all were worried about our safety. Even by the time we had reached the pass, some of our servants had already become so tired that they had lagged behind. Our aunt was worried too, but she was not one to succumb to fear. Taking our guide Dhenod and some of the servants, she went on ahead. All we could do was wait and see what would happen next.

Mother said we could not move in the dark. Meanwhile she told us all to say a prayer to Tara. We all chanted the prayer loudly in unison. We had been praying and sitting there for about an hour when suddenly we saw flames moving toward us from the bottom of the canyon. At first this frightened us more than ever. What could these be? Had some friendly deity come to help us? Or had we offended a hostile deity?

The flames kept moving in our direction very slowly. As the light came closer and closer we nearly fainted with fear. Then we heard some calls by our guide Dhenod who had a high-pitched voice. In great relief we called back to give our location. We soon saw that our guide together with an innkeeper from Tsokar (White Lake) had come carrying torches to rescue us. They had been sent by our aunt. We were very much relieved and thought that Tara had heard and responded to our prayer.

Now that we did not have to spend the night on the trail in misery and fright we quickly forgot our fatigue, which had been greatly increased by the feeling of fear. Together with the servants, including those who had lagged behind, we went down the steep canyon trail as fast as we could. Even so, it was midnight before we reached Tsokar. Thanks to our wonderful, brave aunt, tea and food were ready for us when we arrived there. But we were so exhausted that we could not do justice to the hearty meal before we fell into bed.

I thought that Tsokar was the most beautiful place in the whole of Tsari region. It was situated in a closure of low rocky mountains. Small green bushes made little patches among the rocks. There was a breathtakingly lovely sky-blue lake in the center of the valley, which we were told was the holy lake of Goddess Tara. Around the edge of the lake were green swampy pastures. On one side herdsmen who tended dairy animals had pitched their black tents. There was a rest house and a temple nearby amidst scattered groves of trees. Our guide told us that whoever visited the lake and offered prayers to Tara would have her blessings of religious knowledge and a long life.

We enjoyed five peaceful, restful days at Tsokar. The weather was perfect, and each day we took the two hour walk around the lake. The innkeeper's daughter, a charming girl, often came along with us to point out the special places. She carried a long stick to point to the natural formations of the many deities which could be seen on the face of the rocky mountains nearby.

We had to return to Seven Households through the same three passes, but this time we were familiar with the hazards. We decided that it was too much for us to make the trip in one day so we found a nice safe spot between the grass pass and the forest pass to pitch our tents for the night. The next day we reached Seven Households easily. From Seven Households to Yulmey it took us three days. We slept in tents since the houses along the way were small.

From Yulmey we wanted to go to Gonpo Rong, a journey of about eight hours. As we walked along, we were thinking about the many mysterious attractions in the Tsari district. For instance there is a sacred plant called Tsa Ludud Dorje and a holy spring known as Chu Drowa Drenpa, both found only in Tsari. Neither the plant nor the spring can be recognized by everyone. Only those who have been blessed by the deity are lucky enough to find them. Those who had seen the water said that rays of rainbow colors radiated from it like an aura. It was said that persons who drank this water or ate the plant were purified of all negativities and would gain spiritual power.

As we walked along the path to Gonpo Rong, I was thinking about the mysterious stories I had been hearing in Tsari when a very odd thing happened to one of our own party. Along one part of the trail the going was so difficult that we separated into several groups according to who wanted to walk slowly and who wished to walk faster. A middle-aged couple, our grandmother's servants, had accompanied us. The wife was called Azom and her husband was named Samten. That day Azom and her husband were walking on ahead with two of the other servants, while Mother, my brothers and sister, our aunt, and I followed more slowly. Suddenly Samten and the other two became aware that Azom was no longer with them. They had no idea when or how she had disappeared. Of course they were alarmed and searched frantically in every direction without finding any sign of her. They called out her name at the top of their voices. Still no reply came.

Not knowing what else to do, they sat down to wait for the rest of us. When we caught up with them, they explained that Azom had vanished without any trace. My mother told them that we would have to go on as there was nothing to do until we reached the village and could find someone who was familiar with the area to organize a search party to find her. We continued on, marching as fast as we could.

When we reached Gonpo Rong we first went to the temple, made offerings and prayed that Azom would be found. Then we hired a guide to go along with one of our servants and Azom's frantic husband. The three of them went back towards Yulmey but fortunately did not have to go very far. After only one hour's journey they saw Azom at a distance coming towards them. After she joined them, it took two hours for them all to reach the rest house where we were anxiously waiting for news. Azom looked happy but she was a little breathless. We could see that she was glad and relieved to be back with us.

She sat with us and explained her strange adventure. She said that while she was walking along with her husband and the servants, a tall, good-looking monk wearing rich robes appeared out of nowhere on the right side of the path. He looked straight at her and told her to follow him. Suddenly she realized that she could not see her companions any more, but without hesitation blindly followed him. She walked for some time with the monk when all of a sudden he was nowhere to be seen. By this time she was in the middle of a thick forest where even the path had vanished. She realized that she was lost. She was frightened and in near panic. She sat down for a while and prayed; after a while she felt as if she had awakened from a dream. There was no forest anymore. Not only was the path there but the monk was again in full view and walking on ahead. Not knowing what else she could do, she started to follow him.

Before long they came to a beautiful spring with rainbows hovering about, and a little pond into which it poured. As soon as she saw the spring, she realized that she was very thirsty. She was about to drink the water when with horror she noticed something frightening about the monk who was now standing near the spring. His benign appearance had suddenly and mysteriously changed. She had been carrying some food in a small bundle on her back, and suddenly the monk was demanding to know what she was carrying. She told him that this was a bundle of pears for her mistresses. He ordered her to put the bundle on the ground. He then opened it and scattered the contents all around. By this time Azom had already drunk some of the spring water which she was sure was holy because it was reflecting the colors of a rainbow. The monk told her to do a prostration of thanks and respect to the spring. This she did three times.

Whereas before she had felt protection from the monk, now she was frightened because she couldn't understand all these things. The strange look on the monk's face and his stern attitude had frightened her so much that she could hardly breathe. Even so she collected the things that had been spilled all over the ground and packed them back properly in the bundle. Then she put the bundle back over her shoulder. Again the monk told her to follow him. What else could she do? She followed him for what seemed to be a long distance when he suddenly disappeared again. This time she was standing on a path, but she was not sure whether this was the same trail she had been on before or an imaginary one. All she could do was hope for the best and assuming that she was going in the right direction she started her march alone. She had not gone far when to her great relief she saw that her husband and two others were coming towards her at a distance. This ordeal had lasted for about six hours.

We all were shaken by this strange experience, but relieved that Azom was safe. About six years ago this couple had come from Bathang in Kham to live as servants at the Ludhing estate with my grandmother. Azom was a good-natured person who had the reputation of never telling lies. We had no reason not to believe that whatever she had told had truly happened to her. In fact she was lucky that she had been led by a protector monk. The local men told us later that many such mysterious things had happened in that area. They told us how in the past some wicked men who displeased the protector deity were lost and never found. In winter when all the leaves fell down from the trees, they had sometimes found the skeletons of these unfortunate persons in the thick forest. It seems that this protector deity appreciated the simplicity of Azom. It is clear from the story that only Azom among our group of pilgrims had found and drunk the holy water.

When we left Gonpo Rong for Yultod, you can believe that we did not have to be urged to stay close together! In Yultod there was a rest house as well as several homes. It was to be our last day on foot. We would soon reach our riding horses and the mules, which were now waiting for us in the same small village where we had stopped to rest many days before.

Early in the morning two days later the servants prepared our horses and we started to ride again. We all were relieved to be riding after such a long and hard journey on foot. Never before had I appreciated riding on a horse so much. The path was steep and riding difficult as we ascended to the summit of the high pass called Takar La, but I remembered how difficult it was to climb such trails on foot. This mountain pass, half forest and half rock, marked the boundary of Tsari.

We had to descend through the Takar La pass all the way to the foot of the mountain before we could find a good place to pitch our tents. This was the beginning of a region known as Jar, which was famous for its big monastery called Druk Sangak Choeling. As I have already mentioned, the head lama Drukchen Rinpoche had a strong connection with the Lhagyari family, so he invited us to stay there for several days. This provided a much-needed break in our journey.

All during our pilgrimage in Tsari we had been accustomed to a simple diet with practically no variation from day to day. Now this austerity was over. Drukchen Rinpoche served us so many rich dishes that we had difficulty digesting them. We were grateful for the luxurious accommodations of this monastery after the many hard nights we had spent in rest houses and tents. We had not, however, stopped at the monastery only to enjoy these comforts. We were on pilgrimage and did not break our reverent mood. We continued to observe the customs of visiting the temples many times, offering butter lamps and giving donations of money. Once we arranged to serve tea and refreshments to the three hundred monks of the monastery.

Now that we were in the Sangak Choeling monastery, our guide Dhenod spent most of his time with Drukchen Rinpoche. He had been very helpful all during our journey. Dhenod had, among many other useful qualities, a wonderful sense of humor, and he had often lightened the feeling of hardship we experienced along the way. Since he was not going further with us we began to realize how much we would miss him. For the many kindnesses he had shown us all through our journey together, my mother and aunt presented him with gifts.

After we left this monastery, we traveled along until we reached one of the Lhagyari estates at a place called Jar Gegye. We stayed there for two nights. Then we started a four day journey through a strip of nomad land that was far less interesting than Lha Gong Thang. There were only a few black tents near the road and almost no wildlife in this part of the country. We missed our guide Dhenod who somehow had always managed to lighten our spirits in all kinds of trying circumstances.

Leaving the steppe behind, we had to halt one night at Eh Chundo Gyang before we finally reached the Lhagyari palace. This time we stayed only three days, and my mother was busy every minute. There were streams and streams of visitors who wanted to see her one last time since they knew that it would be many years before they would meet again. Of course we went to the protector's shrine to do puja and made farewell visits to Aunt Kunsang as well as the rest of the Lhagyari family.

We were all very happy that our next destination would be Ludhing. Our grandmother and aunt Urgyen would be waiting eagerly to receive us. At first sight my grandmother could easily see that my mother and all of us were very tired. With the kindest words and most tender concern, she comforted all of us including our mother, as if we were small children. This time we rested for a whole week. There was not much opportunity for gaiety and activity because it was almost winter. Instead we found it pleasant to rest inside the house and avoid the cold.

When we felt refreshed enough to proceed, we left Ludhing once again to face the crossing of the Yarlung River by the Gerpa ferry. This time we knew what to expect; however, the crowds had now thinned. When we were safe on the other side, retracing our steps once again we visited the great temples of Samye. On the fourth day we finally came to Drak Kunsang Choeling where we stayed to rest for five days. Only my younger brother and I could find the energy to go to the old estate house nearby so that I could do a special puja to my birth deity and the other local gods.

All along on the return journey the weather kept getting colder and colder. Whenever we came to a high pass we traveled as fast as we could. By hurrying it took us only two days this time to go from Drak back to Lhasa. Our eldest brother Wangchen Gelek had come to the Lhasa riverside with tea and refreshments to welcome us. We were meeting after a long absence and happily sat together drinking the tea and exchanging our news. Then we all mounted our horses and went riding in a procession to our home in Lhasa.

We had been away on pilgrimage for six months, but every month our brother had managed to send one messenger to us with a letter telling in detail all the home news. Besides this he had sent many provisions to replenish our supplies. In return Mother had always managed to send back letters and some presents of various village crafts such as colorful Bhutanese bamboo baskets or wooden tea cups and bowls. Sometimes she had sent dried fruits and once included some pairs of socks I had knitted for him.

For all of us Tibetans, pilgrimages held a special significance and were considered very important in our religious life. The teachings of the Buddha are very profound and the goal of Buddhahood can be achieved only after many lifetimes of rigorous practice, including meditation and chanting. We had been gone a long time and it was good to be back home. We took up our household duties as before, but now, inspired by the spiritual renewal gained on our pilgrimage, all our work seemed lighter and our lives happier.

6 Mistress of Treshong, the Lucky Valley

In the district of Nyemo, one hundred twenty miles north-west of Lhasa, there was a big village called Shu, meaning "Bow." In Shu there was a large estate called Treshong, owned by a family bearing the same name. The Treshong family were of the gerpa class of the nobility in the service of the government and for a few years it looked as if this estate was destined to be my second home. The name Treshong means "Lucky Valley."

The relation between the Surkhang family and the Treshongs was established in the early 1800's when a son of the Surkhangs went to Treshong as a makpa or bridegroom in order to continue the lineage of their family. There was one son from this marriage whose name was Tsewang Topgyal. Tsewang Topgyal married and had one child who died very young. His wife died when he was sixty. Having no other descendants or relatives he requested the Surkhang family to give one of their children as the heir of his estate to continue the lineage after his death. According to government rules if no will was made establishing a definite heir, then ownership of the estate, which originally had been granted to the family as a compensation for government service, would return to the government.

Whenever there were no heirs to a family lineage, it was the custom in families of all classes to adopt a boy or girl as the head of a household. However, this probably happened in only two cases out of one hundred. It was considered desirable to have a prior connection between the household of those who were adopting and those supplying the new family head. Such was the case with the Surkhangs and Treshongs, who had enjoyed a long-standing relationship of mutual trust and blood ties.

For a few years no definite decision was made by my family as to which child would be sent to inherit the estate of Treshong, so the matter was pursued no further. Then at the age of sixty-five the lone survivor Tsewang Topgyal was stricken during a flu epidemic and succumbed at his estate. With no relatives at his side and knowing that his last moment was approaching, he instructed his trusted servants that it was his wish to pass on his estate to one of the Surkhang children. Expressing this intention in his last will and testament, he died.

Treshong had six main servants headed by Karma Tsering and Dorje Samdup, both of whom looked to be about forty to fifty years old. They were known as *nyerpa* or storekeepers. After the death of their master, they made all the traditional offerings to the monasteries. In 1923, these two servants came to my parents to ask them to allow our eldest brother Wangchen Gelek to be the head of the Treshong household. Our parents agreed, with the provision that Wangchen Gelek should stay in Lhasa serving in the Treshong family's hereditary government position but still remain a Surkhang. Thus, although he would oversee the management of the estate, he would not be adopted. By this arrangement Treshong would have to belong to or become a branch of the Surkhang house. Karma Tsering and Dorje Samdup discussed this and agreed that this was the best arrangement for the time being. Afterwards our eldest brother Wangchen Gelek became a government official in the treasury office as a representative of the Treshong estate, and went to that office every day to study accounting and government procedures.

In 1927 since my parents were not getting along and were planning to separate, the Dalai Lama ordered that our father should establish a separate house of his own and that his son Wangchen Gelek should act as the head of the original Surkhang house. He was to discharge the obligations of the Surkhang family by serving the government as an official, so therefore he had to give up the position he was filling for the Treshong family. His Holiness then ordered that another child should be given the place of Wangchen Gelek to represent Treshong.

The Dalai Lama had settled the Surkhang family affairs; however, our mother had no wish for any of her sons to be adopted by another family and thereby give up the Surkhang name. Therefore she had another discussion with the two managers of Treshong and decided that my younger brother Lhawang Topgyal would discharge the obligation of the Treshong estate to the government in the treasury office, while I would be given to Treshong to become its actual head and owner. Later when I married, my husband would be expected to forsake his surname and take the name of Treshong. At that time my younger brother Lhawang Topgyal would hand over his position to my new husband, and would then return to Surkhang.

Thus it came to pass that in 1929, at the age of eighteen, I was sent to Treshong as head of the estate. The Treshong servants had come to Lhasa to arrange for my journey as well as to attend to other business. Before leaving they set a date some months ahead when they would return to accompany me back to Treshong. During this period of waiting for their return my mother was busy making preparations for my clothes and jewelry as if a bride were being sent for marriage. A few months later, Karma Tsering came from Treshong to be my personal escort. Accompanying him were some other servants including a cook and a groom to take charge of the horses. There was one horse for me and one for each of the servants. In addition there were ten pack mules with two muleteers.

The day after their arrival at the Surkhang household, according to custom they paid their respects and presented gifts to my mother and brothers. Among the gifts were one hundred twenty pounds of butter in bags made from untanned yak skin that still had hair on it, two crates of dried yak meat, and five hundred eggs carried in a wooden box. It was customary for people from the villages to bring these kinds of gifts when visiting Lhasa. On the other hand, when city dwellers visited the country they would take some commodities or finished goods that the villagers could not get in the countryside.

When it was time for me to leave, all the members of my family gathered in the grand reception room of the Surkhang mansion in a ceremony to bid me farewell. My mother put a special kata around my neck. The servants of the household, excluding the ones who would accompany me, also offered scarves. One by one each placed a scarf on the table in front of me. The Treshong servants were each presented a scarf around the neck by a senior servant of our Surkhang family.

Before I left for Treshong my relatives and friends had given me many presents such as silk material for dresses and cosmetics from India. Even though I was not in fact a bride going to my husband's house, my mother gave me a dowry and a maidservant just as if I were. This dowry consisted of four or five boxes of clothing and jewelry.

My departure from the Surkhang household for Treshong was quite a grand event, in the style displayed by nobility when traveling to distant places. I was dressed in a silk brocade dress with elaborate jewelry and headdress. Under ordinary circumstances the servants accompanying me would not have worn their best clothes, but on this day they wore their finest black wool robes, black leather boots, and Stetsons or Italian Fedora hats to match. All of this was a sign of the high social standing of the Treshong family. Sometimes on such important journeys even the servants of the highest ranking Tibetan families wore clothes made out of heavy silk brocade. Such servants were loved and trusted, and their position in the social structure was higher and more dignified than servants of most other cultures.

The time had come to say goodbye. The servants all removed their hats as a gesture of respect and made a bowing motion called *chambul*. Since I had an ornamental headdress called a *patruk* on my head, I could not bow. Instead I joined my hands at chest level, then raised and lowered them in a quick motion. This is the custom of showing special respect when one is hatless or when it is not practical to take off the headdress. When these ceremonies had finished we went to the courtyard to mount the horses and mules that were all saddled and ready. In this fashion, with the scarf given to me by Mother around my neck, and with all the servants wearing their scarves presented by the Surkhang household, we left Lhasa. My father at this time was posted in faraway Kham as a general or depon, so was not present to see me off.

This departure was an extremely sad experience for me since it was the first time I had ever been parted from my family. Though Treshong is only one hundred twenty miles from Lhasa, I felt that I was being sent to the other side of the world. This was due mainly to the difficult and tedious travel conditions within our country. There were no proper roads, and horses, mules, or yaks were the only modes of transportation. Some of the servants carried silver relic boxes and some carried guns for protection along the way.

The one hundred twenty miles from Lhasa to Treshong usually took four days, but since I broke my journey at Yargag for one day, five days passed before I arrived at Treshong. As I have already mentioned, Tseten Dolma was my personal maid who was sent along by the Surkhang family to be my constant companion and servant. She was a few years older than I. Her mother and several generations of her ancestors had been in the Surkhang family. Tseten Dolma herself had been born in our household. She carried my personal prayer books tied in cloth in a pack on her back. The pack animals carried boxes of clothes, bedding, provisions for the journey, and presents for the villagers who would give us hospitality along the way. The bedrolls of the servants were under the saddles on their own horses and their personal belongings were carried in saddle bags. A few of the male servants were armed with German Luger pistols that they strapped to their waists.

The first day of our journey took us through a level valley, the width of which varied from one to two miles. Both sides were bordered by very high mountains. Since it was midsummer, the whole valley was lush and green as if covered by a carpet. There were wildflowers everywhere, and higher up we could see some coniferous shrubs that sparsely dotted the mountainsides. Farms lay all along the route. Their crops of barley, wheat, and peas stood tall, since harvest time was only a month away. The farm houses were separated from each other by one or two miles, but we also passed some villages of as many as thirty or forty houses. Most of the houses were one-storied but there were also a few two-storied ones. Some of the larger villages had a common park where trees had been planted. Often the houses displayed a garden in front, which would include a tree or two, shrubbery, some wildflowers, and occasionally vegetables.

Our route for most of the day followed the large river called the Thulung Phuchu which flows south, joining the Tsangpo River at some distance below Lhasa. I noticed how the many rivulets and streams flowing into it were utilized by the villagers to irrigate their fields. They had also built water-powered mills to grind barley into tsampa, the roasted barley flour that is the staple food of Tibetans. In some places they were grinding wheat. Most of the villages had no shops since almost all necessities were produced locally. Things that were not available, especially tea, cotton cloth, and implements for farming and other necessities, as well as luxury goods, were purchased in Lhasa when the villagers went to sell the produce from their farmlands.

Towards the evening, we had to cross the river on an ancient bridge known as Thulung Lumpa. It had been built more than two hundred years earlier. Made of wooden logs tied together by yak rawhide ropes and railings, the bridge was suspended from foundations made of stone and mortar. One dared not ride a horse across it. Only two or three persons at a time could walk across in single file, each holding on to the railing and going carefully step by step. I felt very glad to reach the other side safely.

A quarter of a mile further on was a village called Para with twenty households where we planned to stay the night. The muleteers and the cook had gone on ahead and had everything prepared at a house called Sharlampa, which the Treshongs had patronized for many years when traveling to and from Lhasa. We stayed at places like this at all of our stopovers until we reached our destination.

There were many private houses where travelers were welcomed as guests in the towns and villages, especially along the well-traveled routes. These houses would have an extra room or two for accommodating guests. Most travelers would bring their own provisions, purchasing only such things as eggs, fresh meat, or vegetables when available. A small fee would be paid for the use of the rooms and kitchen facilities and for the purchase of fodder to feed the horses. If the travelers were well-known to the hosts, no money would change hands except for the price of the fodder. Instead a present would be given which would actually be of more value than the fees. The hosts themselves usually would give a present in return. If the relationship between the host family and the traveler was close, the hosts would entertain the guests lavishly and the gifts exchanged would be more elaborate.

Since this was the first time I had traveled in this way, I had no personal knowledge as to how such payments were to be made to the hosts. That did not matter though because the Treshong head servant Karma Tsering dealt with all such matters. I assume that they must have given presents brought from Lhasa since they were closely acquainted with each household and had been accustomed to staying with them over many years.

Although we left early the next morning, the cook together with the muleteers and pack mules left even earlier, as was the custom. This was so that they could reach the next destination ahead of us to make the necessary preparations. As we continued that day the scenery gradually began to change. The going was more difficult because the road sloped gently upward, and the surrounding mountains were much nearer. Again we came to a valley, where there were fewer farms and houses. At midday we came to a small village called Tulung Nangar where we stopped to eat lunch. As soon as we were able, we had to continue on so that we could reach a town called Tsurphu. This town of about one hundred households was located near the walls of the famous monastery of the Gyalwa Karmapa, the highest lama of the Kargyupa sect of Tibetan Buddhism. Since we could stay there only one night, I did not have the privilege of paying homage to the monastery, much as I wished to do so. We spent the night at a guest house.

The next day we continued through the valley, and at first the terrain was no different from the day before. Before long we had to start a gradual eight-mile climb that started at about 13,000 feet and finally reached a plateau at an altitude of approximately 14,000 feet. The plateau was a huge pasture land from which we could see high mountains at a great distance on all sides. There was no cultivation of any kind on this plateau. The only inhabitants were the sparsely scattered nomads. These nomads lived in big tents made of yak hair, although a few of them had small one-room houses built of sod next to their tents. These were used primarily as storerooms. Most of these people raised yaks; some raised sheep as well. The majority were lessees of the government. The government had originally given each of the families about fifty male yaks and one hundred female yaks (dri) with the right to the use of the pastures. In return, each year the nomads paid the government about fourteen pounds of butter for each original dri. Nothing was levied on the male yaks, which the dairymen used for breeding purposes and transportation. Some of the nomads kept sheep that had also been provided by the government. The sheepherders paid their taxes in wool.

This system had been established many years ago in most parts of Tibet. But during the reign of the Thirteenth Dalai

Lama it had been improved when the government gave the peasants more yaks and dris. The successful ones now had more than one thousand head of male and female yaks. Others were not so fortunate, and found it difficult to meet their commitments to the government. However, there were only a few rare cases in which families had to surrender their leases because of their inability to make a success of their work. In such cases, the government would appoint a new, more efficient lessee to replace the one who had failed.

The third night we rested at a place called Karkhang. This was a community of three separate households, each having two round yak hair tents. The tents were enormous in size, up to forty feet in diameter, with no partition whatsoever inside. The stove for cooking and heating was in the middle of the tent and surprisingly the place was very well furnished. Being only a black tent from the outside, it was not at all a beautiful sight.

Inside the tent and on one side were stacked many sacks of barley that were probably bartered from the farmers of the lowlands. The other side served as the living quarters and was decorated with a few *thangkas* (religious paintings mounted in brocade) and a small altar. Since there was no privacy and we were not accustomed to live in this way, it was embarrassing for us to sleep together in the huge tent. I had never imagined such an experience. It was surprising that, though it was quite cold outside even in summer, it was very warm inside the tent. Even in deep winter it was far warmer in this kind of tent than in a house. Each tent was set in a secluded place far from the next neighbor so the people used to keep watchdogs for protection.

Our fourth night's halt was at Shupho with the Yargag family. It was from this place that I got my first distant view of the huge dark Treshong house. The Treshong estate consisted of about fifteen families. I could see it across the green sparse fields dotted with occasional houses towards the southern horizon. We could have continued our journey to Treshong on that day, but since the Yargag family was a very good friend of Treshong, we made a halt here.

The Yargags were once tenants of the Treshongs, but during the time of the Thirteenth Dalai Lama the family had become freeholders. This had come about in the following way: It was customary for the Private Office of the Dalai Lama to select secretaries and scribes from among the intelligent and attractive young boys from the districts of Eh and Nyemo. One of the Yargag sons named Thupten Kunphel had been selected as a secretary owing to his hard work and intelligence. Later when he became the Dalai Lama's favorite he took the vows of a monk, and although he served as a personal representative within the government for His Holiness in many important affairs, especially between the different bureaus or departments, the Dalai Lama did not give him any special appointment. When the Treshong family had no natural heir, he could have easily taken the Treshong estate for himself. But out of respect for the Treshong family for whom he had once worked, he did not do that. He was a very honorable person.

The mother of the Yargag family had died some time ago, but their father Tashi and his daughters made me very comfortable that night. One of the daughters who was about my age, Dechen Choden, later became a very close friend. She was a nun living at Kharag Gonchung nunnery, which was hidden behind a hill on the north side of Yargag village. The nunnery was two miles from the village, and housed about a dozen nuns. On special religious days they would gather together in the main hall to say their prayers. Otherwise there were not many activities. Some nuns used to go home every day to pray.

Dechen Choden was given some land by her family to help support herself. She would supervise the farming by herself and sometimes took some nuns to assist her. The heavy work such as ploughing the fields was done by her family. She also had two cows. From the surplus milk she made dairy products which she sent home. Her family would call her to assist them whenever there was a need, so that she usually visited them twice or three times a month. Her family had arranged a small room near the kitchen for her that was usually kept locked, and whenever she visited them she would stay in that room. Whenever she needed money or provisions, she would be given them by her family. During my stay at Treshong she often visited me, and we would talk about our spiritual aspirations.

When we left the Yargag estate the next morning, we went only half way to Treshong, to a village called Barlek. A reception had been arranged for us there by the servants of the Treshong family together with the villagers. There were about twenty families in the village who worked on the Treshong estate. Counting the servants from the estate and the villagers living in Barlek, there were about eighty in all waiting to greet us. A large tent had been pitched inside of which seats and tables had been arranged. The place of honor where I sat was higher than the other seats. It was at the head of the row; everyone sat in order according to their rank and seniority. The servants accompanying us sat in their respective places. Among those who had come from the Treshong estate were two senior servants and two headmen who represented the villagers. These four were given seats near me. As soon as everyone was seated, tea and many tasty foods were served after Karma Tsering welcomed me by placing a scarf on the table before me.

Immediately after this brief ceremony we left for the manor of the Treshong estate. Here and there along the route people came to stand by the wayside to watch us pass. In this part of the world it was seldom anything happened to interrupt the routine, and for these village folk this was a big occasion. The group of friendly onlookers got larger and larger, which delighted me, but in spite of all this I was still feeling anxious about my future life in such a faraway place among strangers.

When the Treshong manor finally came into view, my first impression was not at all good. I saw only a huge, dark, ancient building and wondered why it had not fallen apart. My heart sank when I thought that this was where I would have to live. The house was situated on a hill, and as we drew nearer its details gradually came into focus. I soon realized that I had seen the house at its worst angle and now it did not look quite so bad; although I still felt that the huge castle-like structure had a gloomy appearance. The Treshong house was about three hundred years old and was made mostly of natural stone. It was built during the childhood of the Fifth Dalai Lama when a Treshong wife was appointed as his nursemaid. Later during the eighteenth century the interior of the house had been redecorated very nicely but its appearance had not been altered since, either on the inside or outside. The walls, both interior and exterior, were from three to five feet thick. The beds were placed in niches carved into the walls.

In order to approach the main gate of the manor we had to ride up a slight incline. To one side of the big gate a terrifying Tibetan mastiff was chained. Beside him stood a dog house constructed of stone and mortar with a flat roof. Almost the size of a donkey, the dog had a very deep and thunderous bark and kept pulling at the chain. This mastiff was kept as a sentry, and he was very good at warning the household of approaching strangers, especially at night. As we entered the big courtyard I saw on the right side and in front a covered area used as a stable that housed about thirty horses and mules. We dismounted there and then entered the main building through the inner gate. The storehouse was in the main building flanked by the central courtyard on the left side. We turned to the right through this building and into the main house.

As soon as we entered, I was led upstairs to the chapel. In all of the big houses in Tibet the chapel was used for ceremonial occasions, and my welcoming ceremony was to be held here. The seats were arranged in an L shape, with the main row opposite the main altar. At the head of this row was the highest seat, the place of honor where I was made to sit. The servants of both the Treshong and the Surkhang families who had accompanied me from Lhasa took their respective places. Then tea and ceremonial sweet rice, which is customary for such occasions, was served to all. Assembled to welcome me were about thirty household staff members headed by a nyerpa or storekeeper. He presented the scarves on a table in front of me as a sign of respect for the new mistress of the household.

Next I was taken to the protective deity of the house. All Tibetan houses have a guardian deity and Treshong also had one. It is the custom in Tibet that one should always pay homage before this deity whenever one arrives or departs. Prayers and offerings were made daily by a monk designated specially for this purpose.

When the ceremonies were over, I was shown to my own rooms. Although the outward appearance of the house had disappointed me, the rooms were surprisingly nice and comfortable. Even so they did not compare to what I had been used to in Lhasa and much was left to be desired. While I was thinking about all this a sumptuous dinner was served in my private chamber before I retired for the night. My maid servant Tseten Dolma also slept with me in the same room. Both this and the day before had been so eventful and full of new experiences that we were extremely tired. Although I had brought my own bedding I did not take the trouble to use it. The Treshong household had prepared new bedding for me consisting of a thick yarn rug (*tsuk dru*) and quilts of excellent quality. Thus passed my first night.

In honor of my coming the Treshong servants had brought all the way from Lhasa one special cook who was very skilled in the preparation of the ceremonial meals. He stayed at Treshong for two weeks. Every afternoon there was a general party where the Surkhang attendants and the Treshong servants enjoyed themselves drinking beer and gambling with dice and the Tibetan game *bakchen* in their quarters, and shooting at targets with bows and arrows outdoors. Some of the Surkhang and Treshong servants used to entertain me every other day by playing bakchen for several hours to help me pass the time. While the Surkhang staff remained I did not miss my home in Lhasa very much, but after they returned to Lhasa, I began to feel very homesick for my family. I thought Tseten Dolma would be as homesick as I, but she made friends with the Treshong servants quickly. She and I were together until 1959 when I had to flee to India. At that time much to my sorrow she had gone on a visit to a farm belonging to the Surkhangs called Nangkhor near Gyantse where her husband was the estate manager. That is how it happened that she was unable to escape with us.

Since there were no postal services in such far away places, whenever letters were exchanged it was necessary for someone to personally carry them back and forth. For the first month at Treshong there was no mail from my family in Lhasa. It seemed to me like years since I had received any news from home. I could only hope every day that someone would come from Lhasa. Tseten Dolma and I would go together to the roof to stare in the direction of Lhasa for half an hour or so to see if anyone was coming. Then at last one of the Surkhang servants, an excellent horseman, was sent from our home in Lhasa. When he arrived at Treshong, he was first met by all the servants and then he came as soon as he could to my quarters.

I had been constantly wondering what was happening at home and wanted to ask about everything at once. When first I asked about everyone in the family, it made my heart happy when he told me that they were all very well. He had brought a long letter. Then he explained that since he had come alone on horseback, he had not been able to carry many gifts. Even so he had brought English tea, sugar, and dried fruit sent by my mother. He went on to speak a lot about everyone in my family until I was very happy and content. Within a week he left for Lhasa. I never told him how much I missed my family since I knew that this would upset my mother greatly. Instead I sent her several pairs of embroidered boots (*thil*) made by the peasants in Shu. Even with this exchange of news I was still very homesick.

Gradually, however, I began to adjust to my life in Treshong, and it became more pleasant. At that time I had two maids and eight general domestic servants. As head of the Treshong estate my duty at first was to try to heed the advice of the two estate managers when every two or three days they presented their work plans to me. Two months after my arrival the two estate managers told me that they would carry out the duties of the estate as usual, but they asked me to take charge of the money matters and the keys for the different storehouses. They said that when Tsewang Topgyal, the last heir of Treshong, was alive, this was how he did things and how he preferred them to carry out his instructions.

I had a feeling that while Tsewang Topgyal had been the rightful heir when he replaced his parents, mine was a different case. It would be improper for me to take charge of so much so soon. Not only was I inexperienced, but the servants might not like to hand over these duties so quickly to a newcomer. After all, they had worked for more than nine years without a master, and had done so honestly and faithfully. Therefore, in the beginning although I talked to the servants about their work, most of the time I just said, "Please decide for yourselves." As time went on I developed much confidence and respect for most of the servants. I also grew to love them very much so that I was really sad when I later had to leave these people and the estate for good.

But I had to accept some duties. I kept the numerous keys to the storerooms and trunks, and a money chest in my room. Whenever there were any transactions, the manager-servants would make a notation of them, which I also used to do. Since there were no banks, we kept a record of our money in this way. I also supervised the servants who worked in the house and the cook who prepared the special dishes that were brought to me in my room. I never liked to eat much when I was alone so the servants noticing this took turns to stand in my presence and talk pleasantly with me until I was finished.

Usually in the morning I would get up at seven o'clock. Every day after rising I prayed and did two hundred prostrations, which took at least two hours. During the day I sometimes read holy books or else I chanted and prayed. Sometimes some friends came to call.

The amenities back home in Lhasa and those of Treshong were very different. While I tried my best to adjust to the shortcomings of my new home, I also tried to make some improvements. For example, in our house in Lhasa we had a big copper bathtub. Flat copper was imported from India and made into bathtubs by Tibetan craftsmen. The tub was then placed in a little room near the kitchen where towels and so forth were kept. The servants would carry in hot water for our bath and depart after closing the door. I missed this convenience very much. Later I brought an aluminum bathtub from Lhasa and had it installed in the Treshong house. In both summer and winter we always bathed four times a month in the house but in the summer time we also liked to bathe in pools on the edge of the Tsangpo River.

About a year after my arrival at Treshong a new project was started. Four or five people were hired to spin wool into thread. At the same time we hired some weavers who were expert in making rugs and *nambu*, a heavy, tightly woven woolen cloth. Tibet is famous for this woolen cloth, which is almost waterproof. My maid Tseten Dolma had the responsibility of overseeing this work, giving instructions, and checking on the spinners and weavers every now and then. The rugs and nambu cloth they made were partly for use on the estate and partly for giving to friends as gifts.

In the summer the servants often went to the fields to inspect and check on the farms and discuss how things were going with the farmers and their crops. Sometimes they used to take me with them, and we would ride on horseback up and down our little district of Shu. "These are the Treshong farms over here...those are some more Treshong farms over there...," they would say to me. Our land was not all in one place but scattered over a wide area. There was a certain farm in Shu where we went sometimes at midday to rest and the family living there would prepare a special meal for us. When we visited that place we unsaddled the horses and gave them grass and grain. After taking something to eat ourselves, we rested for a while peacefully. The whole atmosphere with the village tenants was very cordial.

There is a tradition among all the farmers in Tibet called *wongkhor* (circling the field) which takes place sometime in autumn. Every year while I was at Treshong I would look forward to this occasion. At this festival all the farmers would get together from our estates Dzong-Shul and Dho-Shung, about seventy people in all, and they would invite eight monks from a nearby monastery. The monks would come with their bells, cymbals, and drums and would also be accompanied by eight lay people who would carry religious texts. Together they would chant special prayers for a good harvest and make the rounds of all the farms on the estate. They would be followed by all the other farmers single file, dressed in their very best clothing. The procession would last for about one and a half hours. During these occasions I would observe the festivities from the rooftop of my house. After they did the rounds they would go home. But all the farmers would return with food, fuel, and *chang* (barley beer) and gather at an open space just behind our house around seven P.M. to light a huge bonfire. For our part, we would supply the farmers with enough broth for a hundred people. Since the weather was so predictable in Tibet, this festival was always arranged to fall on a clear autumn night. The dancing would start around eight P.M. and would not stop until well after midnight. People from various households would take turns dancing around the fire and much barley beer and food would be consumed. Many would be happily drunk, and everyone would make the best of this happy day.

I wanted to get acquainted with the people of the locality and always met informally with everyone regardless of social status. On seeing us, farmers would often come out smiling and laughing to offer little gifts of fresh tea, beer, meat, and eggs. There was a strong family-like love between the owners of the estates, the managing servants, and the tenant villagers. Going around the farm like this gave me an intimate contact with the villagers. Inspecting the fields took almost the whole day. Such days have left many pleasant memories.

There were about fifty-three families on the Treshong estate. They were situated in four different areas: Sho-Phu, Barlek, Dzong-Shul, and Dho-Shung. Any problems regarding family quarrels and land disputes by these families would be brought to the attention of the steward who resided in the main Treshong house. There was also a person called *ge-o* appointed in each of the four areas to supervise the running of these estates. Adjacent to Treshong were five small families called *mo hrang* whose main task was to provide us with water, which they hauled in wooden buckets. They would carry out this chore twice or sometimes three times a day. Although there was a slight incline, the distance to the spring from which we got our water was only about two hundred yards.

Sometimes I rode a few miles to a small bathing pond at a hot spring, along with my nun friend Dechen Choden and two or three servants. Around the hot sulphur springs were lush grasses and about thirty shade trees. Encircling the area was a ring of hills covered in some places with thick grass while in other places there were only boulders. Nearby there was a tiny cottage belonging to the Treshong estate. The door was never locked and whoever wanted to use it could stay there. Inside there were stones arranged to serve as a simple stove for cooking. Whenever we bathed in the springs, we would put down our saddle rugs and linger for about three hours drinking tea and chang and eating the foods we had brought along. Tibetans would mostly go to these hot springs for a cure or to prevent illness. Although I had no illness at all, I loved to go there with my friend simply for relaxation and enjoyment.

In the upper, lower, and middle area of Shu there were three nunneries, each located at the base of a mountain. One nunnery was called Chubzang, meaning "Good Water," where about fifty nuns resided. I was introduced to this nunnery through Dechen Choden, who was herself a nun in this order. I stayed there with her several times, each time for four or five days. One day would be spent talking about religion, and the next day we would fast and remain silent when not reciting the special prayers. The first time I attempted to fast one day by neither eating nor drinking was at this nunnery. I must admit that I felt terribly thirsty and found it difficult to keep chanting the prayers, but it was possible for me to succeed in this peaceful atmosphere. This experience was to provide a milestone in my spiritual practice.

Each nunnery usually had an incarnate lama in charge, but in Chubzang there was none. The older nuns taught the younger ones to read the religious texts. Most of these nuns had come from nomad areas in the north to practice religion. The formal head of their nunnery was the Gyalwa Karmapa, and the lamas from Tsurphu monastery often came to give special religious teachings to the nuns.

Nunneries have always played an important role in Tibetan culture. Probably two women out of a hundred became nuns. Some of these lived in nunneries while others remained in laymen's households living as nuns. A few chose to live alone in caves to practice in solitude. Many girls entered nunneries at the age of nine or ten with their parents' consent. Older women who became disappointed with secular life, or who realized the impermanence of things and wished to abandon worldly attractions, took vows to enter the life of a nun. Since nuns were much respected, most families felt they had been honored when one of their daughters chose to become a nun.

If all the nunneries existing in Tibet before the Chinese invasion were counted, they probably would number more than a thousand. Although there were a few exceptions, nunneries were not usually located in cities. Even in the vicinity of Lhasa there were only three: one in the center of Lhasa called Tsam Kung, founded by Srongtsen Gampo, and the others in the foothills just outside the city. Most nunneries were located in some remote place at the foot or at the top of a mountain and were usually surrounded with beautiful trees and flowers that had not been planted there. Ancient nunneries still existed that had been founded by Padma Sambhava in the eighth century, Milarepa in the thirteenth or Tsong Khapa in the fifteenth century. The more recent ones were established by great lamas. The atmosphere of these nunneries was surprisingly enchanting and peaceful. In the smaller nunneries there might have been as few as ten nuns living together, but in the larger ones there were as many as two hundred.

Most of the nunneries owned some land and depended on

its cultivation for their subsistence. Sometimes they kept cattle and dri to make butter and cheese from the milk. The nuns
themselves did some of the work in the fields but the heavy
work of ploughing was done by the village farmers. Not all
nunneries allowed their nuns to indulge in such worldly activities but would depend instead on gifts from donors or contributions from wealthy families. The poorer nuns would go
out during the harvest season to beg from the farmers, who
always gave generously. The nomads contributed butter, milk
and cheese. Nuns as a class were so much respected that they
had no trouble obtaining enough food to eat and clothes to wear.

Usually a monastery would oversee the activities and instruction at a nunnery but this was not always so. There might be
three or four elder nuns in charge of the general affairs, positions that rotated every three years. Likewise the work in the
kitchen, the cleaning and so forth, were assigned for a period
of three years. Each nunnery had a hall where the nuns could
pray and meditate several times during the day for an hour
or two. This also served as a hall for general assembly and special celebrations that lasted the whole day. If the celebration
was a short one, tea and sweets would be offered but when
it was for the whole day, food would be served in the hall during
the ceremony.

When a woman took ordination as a nun her head was shaved
and thereafter her hair was not to grow longer than the breadth
of one finger. Nuns wore robes and shoes of a reddish or yel-
lowish color and were not allowed to wear even a single piece
of jewelry. They were not allowed to use any facial make-up,
but were permitted to put butter or liniment on their faces
when it was windy or very hot. There was an emphasis on
cleanliness. Life as a nun began with the taking of vows. The
first vows were against killing sentient beings, stealing, sexual intercourse and the boasting of divine qualities. The vows
were taken from a lama, either male or female, who had already taken such vows himself or herself. In between each vow,
the novice was asked, "Are you able to uphold such a vow?"
and the answer was given, "I promise to do so." The first vows

were compulsory but after that further vows were taken according to wish.

For those who broke the vows there were specific rules of discipline. In the case of lower vows the nun could confess to herself, to a lama, or to an image. However she would have to forsake the order if she broke the vows against killing, adultery, or becoming a disbeliever. Usually she would have to donate food and money to the nunnery as a means of repentance.

The internal practice for all nuns was to receive teachings and to meditate. The nuns received their training from lamas, either monks or nuns, and received exhortation from the elder members of the nunnery who instructed the young ones about both religious and worldly affairs. The younger nuns were also expected to nurse the elder ones when they were ill, and to perform simple duties such as bringing water and tending the fires. The most important external activities for a nun were reciting prayers and doing services for others. The more dedicated nuns sometimes spent their whole lives in retreat. They stayed in retreat for three years, three months or only three days. Nuns who reached a high level in their religious practice had no difficulty in staying alone over a long period of time. During the time they were in retreat they avoided all worldly activities, even writing or receiving letters, and only in case of illness would the nun in retreat consult a doctor or meet with any of her family members.

About half a mile from our house there was a farmhouse belonging to the Tsurphu monastery. The estate manager Ngedon Chokyi Dolma was the daughter of the late fourteenth incarnation of the Gyalwa Karmapa. She lived there with her husband. Shortly after my arrival at Treshong she and I became close friends and often took turns visiting each other. Ngedon told me some very interesting stories about religion and about her family. Since I did not have much work to do, time went by very slowly in Treshong, so that having a friend like this was very important to me. I still missed my family and companions, but whenever she and I talked together the time passed very pleasantly.

I used to stay at Treshong through the spring, summer, and fall seasons, about eight months altogether. For the other four months of the year I used to return to Lhasa. Shu was too cold in winter, being at a much higher altitude than Lhasa. During winter the tenants could not do any work outdoors, nor could I do anything outside, so there seemed very little reason for me to remain. Besides I was homesick for my family and Lhasa, and would not want to miss being with them during New Year when there were many festivities and parties.

The four day journey to Lhasa always required much planning. I always took Tseten Dolma with me. Also accompanying me were two or three servants, a cook, someone to take care of the horses and another person for the mules. This made altogether about seven or eight attendants. In case of unexpected trouble, just as on my first trip to Treshong, several of the servants were armed with guns. Sometimes while traveling all day we would not meet a single person and especially at such times I feared we might meet a band of robbers. Such trouble in Tibet was very rare but it felt good to be prepared.

Once in a while we would meet other groups traveling along the lonely mountain roads. Usually the rich farmers from Nyemo and Shu sent barley, wheat and peas to sell in Lhasa. The farmers and other villagers also would send special paper made in the village, yeast for barley beer and embroidered boots to sell in the villages just outside of Lhasa. Most of our villagers were not poor, but they enjoyed making these things and also liked to get the extra income from this work.

Whenever we went from Treshong back to Lhasa, we took meat, butter, tsampa, and flour loaded onto about ten mules as a present for my family. All of these foods were stored in one of the Surkhang storerooms. The Treshong servants would stay on in Lhasa for a few days, visiting the holy places and buying whatever they needed for themselves and for the Treshong house. Then they would return to the estate while my maidservant Tseten Dolma and I would stay with my mother in Surkhang for the next few months.

While I was in Lhasa I heard many wonderful stories about

Kyabje Khangsar Rinpoche of the Drepung Gomang monastery from my cousin Dekyong Wangmo (the daughter of Changlochen). She and her husband Nyendak were his disciples, and they often spoke of his exalted spiritual activities. Hearing these wonderful stories, I was very keen to see him. During one of my stays in Lhasa I asked my cousin Dekyong Wangmo to make an appointment for me to visit Kyabje Khangsar Rinpoche. In June 1930, about the time I was to return to Treshong, my request was granted. While on the way back to Treshong I went to visit him in the Drepung monastery, taking two servants with me. The rest of my provisional needs, servants, and mules were sent ahead to the place where I would spend the night. Just from first glimpsing this Rinpoche I felt great joy, faith, and happiness. Being able to spend a little time in his presence caused these feelings of mine to increase tremendously. Kyabje Khangsar Rinpoche offered me lunch, but due to fear and shyness I could not eat much. Afterwards I had the opportunity to receive many teachings on the Sutras and Tantras from him. Rinpoche's presence was like bright sunshine suddenly dispelling my mental darkness. I felt that it was a great blessing to see him and to receive these teachings that so deeply impressed my mind.

Kyabje Khangsar Rinpoche was born in Lhasa in 1888 in an average middle class family and in our day was recognized as one of the greatest incarnate lamas in Drepung Monastery. In addition to being a great scholar and saint, he was a Drepung Tsokchen Tulku, a title given only to the highest category of lamas. He was recognized as the reincarnation of Lobsang Namgyal, who was an abbot of Drepung Monastery, by Gomang Khenpo Khenrup Tenpa Chobi. He came to be called Khangsar Rinpoche after he dwelt in one of the houses in Drepung called Ashu Khangsar Metsen. He became a monk at the age of five and was regarded as a child prodigy since he was able to both read and write even before he became a monk.

Although he preached the holy teachings to many monks and lay people in all of the provinces of Tibet, he always preferred to live very simply. He and his disciples had kept only four to five rooms for their own use in the Ashu Mitsen of Gomang Dratsang in the Drepung monastery. Only his nephew, one servant, and one cook lived with him there. About ten miles from the Drepung monastery was a farm called Yebda. At this small farm Kyabje Khangsar Rinpoche had some plots of land that he rented from other people for his provisions. One monk from among Rinpoche's disciples managed the affairs of this farm so that his own personal needs and the needs of his disciples were provided for.

Whenever Kyabje Khangsar Rinpoche came to Lhasa he used to stay in the homes of his disciples. If someone asked him for religious teachings, Rinpoche would answer in great detail, but if someone asked him about worldly things his answers were very brief. Later we invited him to our house to give the Tara and other initiations, and my husband became one of his disciples. At such times Rinpoche would stay for a few days or sometimes longer. We always tried our best to see that both he and his attendants were very comfortable. We gave each person in his party his own separate room and as much attention as we could. Although Rinpoche received many offerings of material things, he never kept them. He always gave these gifts away either for religious purposes or to poor people. Kyabje Khangsar Rinpoche was loved very much for his pure nature. When he was at the height of his fame he became ill and in 1941 at the age of fifty-five this great Rinpoche passed away. We were all very sad to have lost such a great teacher.

Around the time of my first arrival at Treshong, I was seriously contemplating becoming a nun. If I had done so, I would have wished to live at Drak, my birthplace, in our house Kunzang Choeling, just as my great aunt had done when I was a child. Despite my calling to join the order, I was never able to fulfill this desire because of circumstances and also because of my fear that I would fail. Whenever I went to see my mother in Lhasa, as well as encouraging me in my spiritual life she would talk to me about marriage. Several times she even proposed some names and urged me to give an opinion, but none of the persons she proposed pleased me. In fact I told her that I had no intention of getting married for the time being. I explained that whenever I found a man of my liking I would tell her. She was very understanding and did not further press me to marry.

At that time my family used to be the customer of a Nepali merchant in Lhasa. One day while I was spending the winter with my family, this merchant handed me a short love note from Yuthok Tashi Dhondup, saying that he had been requested to present it to me on his behalf. I had seen Mr. Yuthok once or twice but had never spoken one word with him and was very surprised to get his letter. Mr. Yuthok was twenty-nine years old at that time and very handsome. He was a general in the army and in a very short time, only through these letters, I began to realize that I was falling in love with him. We exchanged several letters through his servant and about two months before I was to leave for Treshong we fixed a date to meet.

When the meeting time came, I suddenly felt very shy. I thought I could not dare to even speak to him. "What am I going to say?" I wondered. I had asked my brothers to stay at home with me in the room where I would meet him but they just laughed and refused. Then I asked Tseten Dolma and a few servants to stay just outside the room at the appointed time. Mr. Yuthok, as expected, came on horseback with two servants at nine o'clock in the evening. I did not see him when he first arrived with his attendants since he followed the usual custom of going immediately to a small reception room where he was served tea and refreshments.

When he finally came into the room where I was waiting I was surprised to find that my shyness had almost vanished. In our house we had electricity but that night the electricity had failed and there was only a dim oil lamp burning in the room. This lamp was placed far away from where we were sitting so that we could not even see each other's faces clearly. After we seated ourselves and the servants had brought tea and left, he immediately drew closer to me. While drinking tea he made light conversation. I was too shy to talk but responded the best I could and offered him something to eat, but he replied that he had just come from a party and had already eaten. Suddenly he took my hand in his and on this very first meeting kissed me, but I did not dare respond. This was the first time I had ever been kissed. I was twenty-three years old and a virgin. I had not had any experience with men and I had come to know Mr. Yuthok only through our correspondence. I was very shy and practically unable to speak. Although we did not say much that night, from that time on we continued to fall more and more in love.

The next day I felt somewhat self-conscious when I met my family but no one said a word about the meeting nor did anyone tease me. After that Mr. Yuthok came very often, whenever he had a chance. Sometimes he spoke with my brothers and then I remained in my room, but most of the time he came to see me alone. During the period when he was visiting me regularly, the marriage of my two brothers to Dekyi Lhaze, the daughter of Rimshi (my suitor Yuthok's older brother) began to be discussed. My mother sent a representative to the Yuthok house to request that Dekyi Lhaze be given as a bride to the two brothers in the Surkhang family. Both families agreed to the proposal so the proper arrangements were made for the engagement ceremony and the marriage. As I began to be attracted to Mr. Yuthok, my two brothers, although they said nothing, were clearly pleased with his visits to me since this would make another bond between our families, and would make their engagement more secure. These events were all happening about the time I was expected to return to Treshong. I had received a letter from the Treshong servants saying that whenever I wanted to return, they would send the escort. Part of me wanted to return to my quiet life there, but another part of me wanted to stay longer in Lhasa.

According to Tibetan custom it would not be proper for Mr. Yuthok to talk to me directly about getting married. Since I was a very serious and straightforward girl, I was thinking that all the attention he was giving to me surely showed his intention to marry. Thus, I was not surprised when I heard that Rimshi Yuthok had sent a representative to my mother asking that I be sent to the Yuthok house as a bride. My mother gave her consent but told him that it was expected that my husband was to go to Treshong as a makpa (bridegroom) and thus take the Treshong name. About that matter Rimshi Yuthok made the firm decision that because of his family situation, I would have to go to my husband's house as a bride rather than Mr. Yuthok going to Treshong as a makpa. My mother agreed to this. Rimshi Yuthok was fifty-four years old and not in the best of health. His younger brother, my suitor, was already the father of two sons from Rimshi's deceased second wife[1] and had taken much of the responsibility for Rimshi's three daughters.

Not only was I very disappointed when I knew that I could not return to Treshong, but the servants from there were also very sad. They expressed their feelings to the Surkhang family, saying "The one who is making all of this trouble is the man with the long legs." What they were referring to was this: At that time Mr. Yuthok was a depon or general, and wore a British-style officer's riding breeches and coat. To our servants, who did not usually see this style of dress, it seemed as if my future husband's legs were absurdly long. Our servants said this to me and my mother, but I was still determined to become the bride of Mr. Yuthok.

Since I was not to return to Treshong, my mother and elder brother then decided that my younger sister Lhawang Dolma would replace me as the rightful heir to that estate. The servants of Treshong also agreed. When this was all arranged I would be free to go to the Yuthok's house as a bride. When it was decided that I was not to be the heir of Treshong, I felt strongly that it would not be good to remove even one small thing from there, so I tried to be very careful to keep only the things I had brought with me from my home in Lhasa. However, later when I arrived at the Yuthok house as a bride, I discovered that I had not been completely successful. I found

one of the beautiful Treshong lacquer jewel boxes unsuspect-
ingly still in my possession, but decided that it would be permissible to keep it as a remembrance of my happy days there.
Even the jewelry, clothes, and other things I had made or purchased while at Treshong were passed on to my sister Lhawang
Dolma. When I arrived at the Yuthok house, I took with me
only my own jewelry made from stones that were a part of my
original dowry. At the time of my marriage to Mr. Yuthok my
bridal trousseau was presented to me by my mother.

About that time it was decided that a makpa should be found
for my sister Lhawang Dolma in order that the Treshong lineage be reestablished. One noble family named Shekarlingpa
had a son Sonam Topgyal who needed a bride. A tsedrung
(monk official) named Gyatso Choephel who was a mutual
friend of both the Surkhangs and Shekarlingpas had the idea
that a marriage merging the two families would be very good
for both sides.

The Shekarlingpas had no other children apart from this
son. In the course of negotiations between the Surkhangs,
Shekarlingpas, and Karma Tsering and Dorje Samdup of the
Treshongs it was mutually agreed that all would benefit if the
union took place. My sister and the son of the Shekarlingpas
were consulted, and when both consented, they were married.
Shortly after the marriage, the son of the Shekarlingpas entered the government service in the name of Treshong since
the Shekarlingpa estate was already represented in the government by his father. Later a son named Thondup Phuntsok
and a daughter named Chunden Dolkar were born of this marriage, thus providing the Treshong family again with an heir.

At the time of their marriage they were both very young and
attractive. The husband was twenty-one and my sister Lhawang
Dolma was twenty-two years old. At the beginning they were
happy together but in the later years each suspected that the
other was having a lover. Furthermore, the Treshong servants
and the Shekarlingpa servants did not get along at all well together because the Shekarlingpas tried to take power away from
the old trusted servants. This trouble with the new servants

aggravated the dispute between my sister and her husband.

My sister and her servants sent a letter about the situation to the regent Reting Rinpoche. At the same time a letter was sent by the Shekarlingpas telling their story in an entirely different way. Without carrying out an investigation or making any inquiry into the real facts, the government committee dealing with such matters suddenly issued an edict that all of the Treshong property except for lands and buildings had to be divided between the husband and wife. The Treshong houses, servants, land, and peasants would be taken over by the government. This was in 1938. Both sides had no choice but to agree. They had to follow the unexpected decision. Our view is that such a hasty decision must have been caused by karma from another life.

The father and his son then moved back to the Shekarlingpa house. My sister and her daughter returned to live with my mother at the Surkhang house in Lhasa. Although such disputes were by custom and law settled by a government committee, it was extremely unusual for the government to take such drastic action without a thorough investigation. It was unthinkable that the government would confiscate the estate merely because of the incompatibility of the husband and wife and their respective retainers. Such harsh judgement was usually reserved for a serious crime such as treason. My sister and her supporters were of course disappointed that the problem between her and her husband had been settled in this way. After this decision the government committee dealing with these matters treated the Treshong house and land as public property and gave the Treshong estate to Regent Reting Rinpoche in recognition of his part in finding the incarnation of the Thirteenth Dalai Lama. Perhaps all along some of the government officials had wanted this estate for this purpose.

In Tibet when after an unsuccessful marriage a bride returns to her family home, it is customary that she be reinstated as a rightful member of her family together with any daughters remaining with her. In this way my sister Lhawang Dolma and her daughter Chunden Dolkar lived as family members in the Surkhang house. The story does not end there. In Lhasa there was one noble family named Rongtrak who had only one daughter and no son; Rimshi Yuthok's son Tsering Dorje (by his first wife of the Sholkhang family) was sent to Rongtrak's home as a bridegroom thereby taking the name of Rongtrak. They had a few children and after a while the wife died. The husband was about the same age as my husband. A few years after my younger sister Lhawang Dolma separated from her husband she went again as a bride to Tsering Dorje now of the Rongtrak family. In other words, she married my husband's nephew. Lhawang Dolma and her second husband had five children. This marriage was very happy. Chunden Dolkar, the daughter from the first marriage, stayed on at Surkhang. Her brother stayed with his father's family, the Shekarlingpas.

7 Marriage

Before the nineteenth century, most marriages in Tibet were arranged by the parents of young men and women. Girls usually had no say in the matter but boys could occasionally choose their brides. At the time of my marriage, there were few who married because they were in love, but this custom gradually changed.

In some instances, the couple had never seen each other before the day they were to be married, as might be the case if the bride lived at some distant place or the immediate family members had never met. However, among noble or middle class families, this happened only rarely.

When a young man decided to marry, a representative of his parents would visit and talk with the parents of several suitable young women, but if the families were well known to each other, the family members might discuss the matter between themselves. A relative, friend, or even a trusted head servant of the boy's household would take the initiative, and go to the head of the girl's family to present a ceremonial scarf. If the girl's family was willing to consider the marriage, they would give a copy of her horoscope to the boy's family. This was then taken to an astrologer to be compared with the boy's own stars and signs.

In all families, rich or poor, the astrologer played a very important part in selecting the bride. There were many astrologers throughout the country who could handle these matters. If the astrologer found that the requisite signs were slightly unfavorable but the groom's family still wanted the marriage, he would recommend that special rites be performed by the two parties. These rituals were expected to remove the obstacles. When several girls were being considered, the boy would help the family choose the bride after the astrologers had made their report. If the astrologer found that out of five horoscopes given to him for analysis three were acceptable, then further help might be obtained by consulting a lama who would perform a divination ritual to select the one most suitable. Only after the boy's family had considered all this would the final decision be made.

The young man's family always took the initiative in marriage proposals. In finding a suitable bride there was no hesitation to consider a girl from a family of lower status. Strong priority was placed on the horoscope and the nature and capabilities of the girl. The girl's family, on the other hand, did not want to see their daughter marry into a family of lesser status. If for some reason the girl's family did not want to consider the proposal, they would give many polite excuses. For example, her family might say that this matter had to be discussed among all the family members and relatives. Then the boy's family would know that this was only a polite way of declining the offer so they would drop the matter.

After the astrologers had given their reports and the word of the lama was known, the boy would be called in to discuss the matter with the family. The family of the girl who had been selected would again be approached by the boy's representative. If they agreed to the marriage, preparations would be started. Only at this stage would the plans come to the attention of the girl and no one would try to conceal it from her any longer. Still the young couple did not meet.

Even in my day most girls never knew beforehand when proposals for them were being made. For example, when I was sixteen years old, one of the sons of the Ramoche Changrag family wanted to get married. His family consulted mine and my name and stars were included along with several others for possible selection. In this case they took the horoscope to His Holiness the Thirteenth Dalai Lama for the final decision. Since the requisites of one of the girls suited the boy, the Dalai Lama recommended her for marriage. I knew nothing of this until six years later when my mother told me all about it. Until then she had kept it a top secret. I would have felt sad and worried if I had known that my mother had given my name and signs. This boy had been a schoolmate and was well known to me. I never thought he was good looking and was not at all attracted to him. That I was not destined to this marriage helped me feel that we are protected against an inappropriate destiny even in marriage. Nowadays when I compare the custom in Tibet of choosing a mate with the system of love marriages in the West, I am satisfied with our Tibetan traditions.

The marriage was always preceded by a *longchang* or engagement ceremony in the bride's house on an auspicious day set by an astrologer. On this day a written marriage contract would be drawn up in duplicate and signed by representatives of the two families. Although elaborate preparations had been made, the only participants at the longchang would be the specially chosen friend or relative acting as a representative for each family, the family members of the bride, as well as some servants from both households. The ceremony was never attended by the groom or his family.

The contract set out the basic provisions for the marriage, including wishes and prayers for a happily married life expressed in beautiful poetry. Added to these was a description of the duties and behavior of the groom and bride to each other so that they could expect an honorable life together. As a last item the document would often mention how the property was to be divided if unfortunate circumstances caused a divorce.

After two copies had been properly signed by both sides, one would be retained by the groom's family and one by the bride's. With this finished, the time had come for presentations to be made by the groom's representatives to the family of the bride. The traditional gifts expected at this time included a sum of money known as *nurin*, which literally means the price for the breast feeding given by the mother to the infant. Besides the nurin there were many foodstuffs and another sum for covering the cost of the longchang party. In addition an individual gift would be given to each member of the bride's family. After her family had accepted all the gifts, the party would begin. The representatives from the boy's side were always treated very warmly on that day. When all their official duties had been completed, they would be escorted into the main room of the house and seated formally. Tibetan beer, tea, and refreshments of sweet rice and droma were served and the guests would make merry by singing, dancing, and playing different games together. Last of all there would be an elaborate dinner served to all the guests. Some days later the date for the wedding would be set by the groom's family.

These same customs in general were followed by Tibetans of all classes. The people in the villages were mostly illiterate so they simplified the written agreement. The presentations of money and the other gifts were offered according to their means. They followed the same custom of longchang being at the girl's house and the serving of barley beer with tea and rice followed by dancing and playing dice, but all this was done in a simpler fashion.

On the day of the marriage, the bride would be taken to the house of the groom early in the morning. If the distance was long, she would travel with some servants as well as a few of her own family members if possible. After a long journey the bride's group never went directly to the house of the groom, but stayed with relatives or friends for a few days awaiting the day of the marriage.

The villagers also followed the same general custom for taking the bride to the groom's house on the marriage day. When I was in Treshong, I used to see marriages take place among the villagers. The attendants would hold the bride on each side while she walked along with her head bowed. It always looked to me as if the escorts were trying to hurry the bride along while she dragged her feet.

My own mother came to Lhasa as a bride from Eh Lhagyari along with her mother, sister, and about ten servants. In Lhasa they stayed with relatives of the family by the name of Drumpa. About a week later the Surkhangs formalized the engagement with the Lhagyaris. All of this took place without the knowledge of my mother, who was purposely sent to one of the Drumpa estates outside of Lhasa with some of her cousins. On her return to Lhasa she found out about her pending marriage and was greatly saddened to think that she would have to part from her family.

I have already mentioned that the marriage between my husband and myself was a love marriage. Even so, there were certain routine procedures to be followed. My husband's elder brother sent one of his friends, Gajang Tenpa, to my mother's home to talk with her about my going to the Yuthok family. My mother knew that there was already love between us, so she agreed to the proposal. Since the marriage was settled this way, we did not call in an astrologer for matching our stars. However, my family did have to consult the astrologer to find a suitable day for the longchang. He decided that the nineteenth day of December, 1933, would be auspicious.

Almost a month before the day of our engagement ceremony, His Holiness the Thirteenth Dalai Lama died unexpectedly. All Tibet was in mourning. In the hope that soon afterwards he would be reborn, the high lamas began looking for signs of his new incarnation. Nevertheless, mourning and sadness were present in everyone's heart. The families agreed not to postpone the engagement ceremony since the date had already been fixed. Of course we downplayed the occasion. I put on my best dress but I did not wear much jewelry. Otherwise the longchang ceremony was observed as usual. A government official named Gyalkhar Nangpa was our family representative. He came to our house early in the morning. After that Gajang Tenpa, the representative of the Yuthok family, arrived with their senior servant leading another fifteen or sixteen servants to carry the presentations. The servants were all accomodated in a separate room while the family representatives were seated in our main hall with my brothers.

After the marriage document had been read by the two representatives, they and the servants of the Yuthok family all assembled in the main hall with my family. As soon as everyone was seated, rice with droma and butter tea were offered by the servants to the image of Buddha. Then cups filled with more of the same were set before each person. After that Tashi Tsering, the senior servant of the Yuthok family, offered scarves to the deities on the altar. When this was finished, he and the other servants placed the presents they had brought at the feet of my mother and brothers. The gifts consisted of boxes of brick tea, several loads of butter wrapped in skin, and as a special delicacy, many different kinds of fruits which had come all the way from India. Also among the gifts were some pieces of imported brocade silk of many different colors for making dresses. In addition there were about twenty packages of money each containing twenty dotse wrapped in clean white cotton cloths in order to make them beautiful. After these gifts had been presented to my mother and brothers, the Yuthoks' senior servant offered scarves to the representatives and family members who had come to attend the engagement ceremony. A sum of ten dotse was then given to be distributed to each of the servants, who, of course, liked to be included in this part of the festive occasion.

This presentation of gifts was followed by the ceremony of signing the marriage agreement. First our representative Gyalkar Nangpa stood and read the document in a loud voice so all could hear. When the reading was over, the contract was signed and sealed in duplicate and a copy of the signed agreement handed over to the senior servant of each of the families.

I was not present to witness any of these happenings because it was not the custom for the bride to attend the long-chang function. On this day, although I had put on my best dress, I stayed in my own room with my sister Lhawang

Dolma. The Surkhang servants brought to my room whatever was served to the others in the main hall. At one time the main servant Tashi Tsering along with a couple of other Yuthok servants came to my room and laid a scarf on the table in front of me and then went away. I did not know what to say so I just smiled. The servants who had carried the gifts to our house returned to the Yuthok house after they had taken lunch, but Tashi Tsering and a few other servants remained until the function ended.

When it was time to depart, a servant of the Surkhang family came to the main hall with a silver kettle. This ceremony was called *drol-cha*, which literally means "finishing tea." He stood in the center of the hall and slowly moved the kettle in circular motions, took one step back and went away. This meant the engagement function was over and it was time for all to leave. While departing, the guests removed their ceremonial scarves from their necks as they left by the main gate. This was in deference to the mourning period for His Holiness the Dalai Lama.

After the longchang ceremony very few people ever broke the engagement. In fact this ceremony signified that the marriage had been concluded. However, if there was a very special reason for either party to back out, then the marriage agreement could be broken. In such cases the representatives of the two families concerned would meet together again to decide the matter. If the girl's family did not like the boy and it was their side that wanted to break the contract, then they had to return all the money and presents given at the time of the engagement ceremony. Such cases were not taken to the court for decision, since the rule was so clear that everyone had to follow it.

Such a problem had arisen in our family many years earlier. It happened in 1905 when my mother, her two sisters and her grandmother had gone to Nepal on pilgrimage. During that time my uncle Lhagyari Trichen Rinpoche had gone to Lhasa. It was through this uncle that the Tsogo family had asked for my mother in marriage for their son. Without consulting any of the family members, he accepted the proposal on the family's behalf and celebrated the engagement ceremony. When my mother and grandmother returned from Nepal, they discovered what he had done. My grandmother protested strongly that it was not correct to decide such an important thing while she was away, and she refused to give her consent. The case was brought to the attention of the Tsogo family representatives. After that they had to determine the details for breaking the marriage proposal and returning the money and presents given to the Tsogo family at the engagement ceremony.

This did not happen in my case, and the Yuthok family decided to celebrate the marriage ceremony during the Tibetan New Year. This was in part an economic measure since there were always many elaborate activities organized at that time. By taking advantage of this neither of the two families would have to make special arrangements for decorations for the marriage ceremony. Thus it was planned that both the marriage and the New Year could be celebrated at the same time.

On the first day of the Wood-Hog year, the Yuthok family sent their senior servant Tashi Tsering together with four other servants and an astrologer dressed in white to our house to escort me. They had brought with them dresses, jewelry, and a mare for me to ride the next day to the Yuthok house. It was the custom in Tibet that the bride's mare should be carrying a foal yet to be born as a sign that the new bride should be able to bear many children afterwards, but the mare on which I was riding was not bearing a foal simply because they could not find one in this condition.

All the servants were dressed elegantly in dark yellow clothes made of flowered Chinese silk brocade. According to custom they were to spend all night at the Surkhang house as there were many arrangements to make for the following day. On that same evening some of my relatives and Tsering Lhamo, my best childhood friend from next door, came to our house, and we all played *sho* (dice) while my mother and brothers busied themselves with preparations for the next day.

Early the next morning, at about half past two, I went to

my mother's room as her unmarried daughter for the last time. My sister and brothers joined us for morning tea. After tea we each went back to our rooms to get dressed. Tashi Tsering and one of the servants had brought some dresses and jewelry for me from the Yuthok family, from which I was to choose what to wear that day. They handed these things to my mother's favorite attendant Kyipa, who helped me select the most suitable attire for the occasion and then helped me to dress. When I was almost ready my mother came to my room to make finishing touches.

Both the dresses and ornaments given to me from the Yuthok family were extraordinary and costly. They signified the wealth of the family and were passed from generation to generation. However, I was not happy when I wore the Yuthok heirlooms that day. In the first place, I was not particularly fond of jewelry. But weighing more heavily on my mind was an awareness of the previous generations who had worn and preserved these things but were no more. Now it was my turn to wear and preserve them and pass them on to the next generation. I could feel the impermanence of life and the profound truth of the Buddha's teachings.

I do not know why these things should have come to me on a day that should have been only a happy one. Of course, just wearing the ornaments was most uncomfortable. They were so heavy that I could not lift my head at all. I felt somewhat like a doll with whom everyone seemed to do whatever they pleased. When finally they finished dressing me to their satisfaction, the servants of the household came and led me to the main hall where my mother, brothers and sister had already taken their seats. I was made to sit facing them. While the ceremonial tea and rice were being served, the Yuthok changtzod Tashi Tsering came to fix the turquoise on the top of my head and tied the *dadar* (a small decorated lance) to my collar. Then he started to recite a verse in praise of the turquoise and the dadar. This was the sign that I now belonged to the Yuthok family. Although inwardly I was not sad or nervous like most other brides because I already knew my husband and his family very well, when I saw my mother crying I could not help crying myself.

Accompanying me from the Surkhang family were five escorts and one maid servant. In addition there were two extra servants to steady me on the horse. The five male servants wore light brown robes of silk and the maidservant also wore a silk dress. The extra servants wore their best robes, but they were not of silk like the others. When we were ready to leave, one of the main servants of the Surkhang family offered all of the escorts from both the Surkhang and the Yuthok households the traditional katas or ceremonial scarves, which they wore around their necks for the whole trip.

When the departure time came, our main servant began to sing a sad song of departure. At least ten of the other servants started humming along with him. Hearing this song, I suddenly became very sad. While I was still crying, about ten of the escorts approached me on all sides, helped me to stand up, and started to carry me to the mounting stone, a platform with several steps used by everyone for mounting horses. Holding me from all sides, they carried me down two flights of steep stairs out to the mounting stone, some holding my arms, some my legs, some my waist. While this was going on according to the custom all of my family had to remain seated inside the chapel.

When we had somehow reached the mounting stone, the servants lifted me up on the horse and placed a cushion on the horse's neck. All the jewelry was very heavy and my head was aching from crying. I was feeling so sad that I put my head down on the cushion. The two extra servants came to hold me steady on the horse and, as a last gesture, the escort put a huge, heavy white woolen shawl over me.

There is a legend concerning this custom of draping a white shawl over a bride. It is told that in ancient times in Damshung in northern Tibet, a certain young bride was put on a horse early one morning to be taken to her new husband's house. The escort thought it would not make any difference if they did not cover her with the white shawl. Rather than weary her with its weight, they decided not to follow the usual custom. Having mounted their own horses, they all left together and arrived sometime later that morning at the groom's house. Along the way the attendants felt her presence on the horse and took it for granted that she was there. But when they went to help her dismount, the bride was no longer on the horse! Those who came to assist could still feel her presence, but no one could actually see her. They all thought she must be there even if they could not see her.

Sometime later when a few persons in that area saw her in a strange kind of body, she told them that the god Nyenchen Thangla had put a magical manifestation in her place and taken her away as his queen. She had no wish to return among them, but wanted to stay in the subtle world as Nyenchen Thangla's queen. Since that time all brides have worn the white shawl to prevent some god from seeing them and taking them away.

First in my procession to the Yuthok house was the astrologer. He wore a white robe and carried a banner on a pole to bring good luck and to ward off the ill effects of any inauspicious planets and stars. Behind him were five of the Yuthok servants mounted on horses, with me under the white shawl following on my mare. Two of the Yuthok servants led my horse on foot and two of the Surkhang servants steadied me on the horse. The maidservant and the rest of the Surkhang servants followed behind riding horses. We proceeded with the escorts singing all the way to the Yuthok household. The entire time I was crying. Because they were singing so loudly, no one heard me, and thus no one offered me any water or comfort along the way. By the time we reached our destination, my throat was very dry. The ride from the Surkhang house to the Yuthok residence seemed to me to take hours. Actually the distance was only about a quarter of a mile so the journey really could not have taken very long. Upon arriving at the Yuthok household two women servants wearing beautiful dresses with elaborate jewelry and holding silver cups of beer were waiting for me at the mounting stone. One man servant, also dressed very handsomely, was holding a wooden bowl filled with a mixture of wheat and barley powder, sugar and butter. They brought the offerings to me so I could sprinkle a tiny portion as an offering to the gods, but with my head bent down on the horse's neck I did not even see them. My maidservant Tseten Dolma, who told me about them later, did the sprinkling for me.

All the servants gathered at the mounting stone to lift me off the horse. As soon as they took the large white shawl off I became much more comfortable. Then the servants carried me up the steep stairs into the Yuthok chapel. According to custom I kept my head bowed and covered it with another, smaller, silk shawl called *rinchen nenga*. It is brightly colored with wide stripes in five colors, much like a Tibetan apron.

My husband and the sons and daughters of the Yuthok household were waiting for me in the chapel, which had been decorated in a most beautiful fashion. My husband's elder brother was an invalid and could not be present, but on first glance I saw that there was an empty seat waiting for me next to my husband. After the servants seated me there, my maidservant took her place standing behind me. I began to feel a little better. The Yuthok servants offered scarves first to my husband and then to me. After that all the other servants one by one offered scarves to us. Finally the main servant presented the customary offerings of rice, droma, and butter tea to the Buddha on the altar and then set some on the table in front of us.

This marked the end of that part of the ceremony of welcoming me into the Yuthok household. The time had come for us all to leave the chapel. Two servants came to help me get up, and then with all of the Yuthok and Surkhang escorts and all family members, we went to the roof. The reason for going there was to perform a special ritual to be observed on the first day of marriage. My family had given the Yuthoks a special flag that they were to raise on the roof that day. This flag indicated that the Surkhangs had sent a bride to the Yuthok family of which she now had become a member. When they had fixed the flag they said a prayer of victory to the gods while

tossing some tsampa into the air. The color of my flag was
blue because the element of my birth year is water.

After the flag had been raised, the Yuthok servants led me
to my husband's room while the Surkhang servants were taken
to the servants' visiting room. I remained in my husband's
room while relatives and friends came to the house to offer
him scarves and gifts. On the first two days about twelve visitors came each day; on following days there were fewer. They
did not come to my husband's room nor did I have to go to
meet them. My husband went out each time a guest was announced, and personally received their scarves sitting on a high
seat in the chapel. In a room nearby two or three servants were
stationed to receive and list the many presents that arrived.
Families higher than my husband's would not come personally
to offer presents, but instead would send their gifts with servants. The families equal to or beneath his status came personally to pay their respects.

According to custom those who came on the day of marriage would not talk much but merely would say that they had
come to offer a gift and to wish us good fortune. Those who
were very close might stay for five minutes to make polite conversation on some impersonal topic such as the weather. The
visitors carried the scarves while the servants carried the
presents. When there were no visitors, my husband would return to our room. We passed pleasantries back and forth and
ate there together. And thus night finally arrived and it was
time to sleep. When the time came to go to bed, several of
the Yuthok servants entered the room. Under our bed they
drew a swastika with wheat. The reason for drawing this was
to discover whether the young lady and man are agreeable to
each other: if they are agreeable, the grains of wheat will scat-
ter by morning. This is our ancient custom.

Our ages were late for marriage in Tibet; I was twenty-three
and my husband was twenty-nine. Even so I thought that, according to custom, the servants would stand at the head of
the bed to offer beer after we had settled in bed—not to drink
but just to be sprinkled about as a good omen. I thought also

they would stay to sing and perform a special dance done when the time comes for the bride to be alone that first night with the groom. But when we were in bed all the servants left quickly without further ado and closed the door. They did not do any of these things probably because it was commonly known that we had been living together prior to our marriage.

Many young Tibetan girls are unprepared and shy when they are alone with their husbands for the first time. They may even become afraid and call out. Sometimes they have been known to flee from the room. If that happened, a maid servant would try to console the girl and would accompany her back to the room, sometimes remaining with her through the night. Usually by the next day the situation would begin to appear more agreeable and the girl would feel more friendly with her husband and would sleep with him alone. I myself have known young women who have reacted in this fashion at the beginning of married life.

The marriage festivities, including merry-making and feasting, lasted five days. On the first day, only my husband's family participated. On the second day my family came, and according to custom brought all of the dowry. For this formality the two families were gathered in the Yuthoks' big chapel where my husband and I sat side by side on two high seats. Two of the main Surkhang servants stood in front of us and then opened one at a time the six large boxes that had been brought for us. These boxes contained my dowry. As they removed the gifts a few Yuthok servants standing nearby took them, and put them back into the box after an account was made. At the end some gifts were presented to each member of the groom's family. All through the ceremony everyone was curious about my gifts but would not say anything. They were following the custom of not showing any outer opinion or feeling and sat quietly with head bowed only smiling a little. I also sat with my head bowed throughout the presentation.

In Tibet there was no custom of offering a huge dowry even in rich families. Tibetan wealth mainly consisted of the ownership of large estates with their many animals, including yaks, sheep, cows, mules, and horses. It was very seldom that any of these were given to the daughter as a dowry. My dowry was an image of Buddha, a volume of scriptures, a shrine, and some pearls. There were also some very precious stones set in twelve types of jewelry in the form of head ornaments, rings, bracelets, and necklaces. There were thirty dresses, about ten of which were made of black Tibetan handwoven woolen cloth, both long-sleeved and sleeveless, as well as blouses and aprons. Three of the dresses were of silk lined with sheepskin. The rest were an assortment of silk and imported woolen dresses in various colors, and for all occasions. These things along with one complete set of bedding were all put back into the six large wooden boxes and were to be kept for the time being near my husband's room.

After the presentation of the dowry was over, everyone stayed in the chapel only five minutes longer while tea was being offered. Then all of my family were escorted by the servants to the rooms where they would be staying during the next four days. The Surkhang family had to bear all the expense of the party for the second day. It was customary for the family of the bride to stay at the groom's house throughout the marriage celebrations.

Five days later all of the festivities were over. When the Surkhang family and servants had returned to their home, my life as a wife in charge of the household duties began to take shape. My husband's parents had died many years before. At the time I came to the Yuthok house only my husband's elder brother and the children lived there. The eldest child was sixteen years old and the youngest was five.

Even when the bride and groom's families lived near each other, there was a custom for the bride not to visit her family right away. It was some days after my marriage that the Yuthok family established an auspicious date for me to go to the Surkhang house for the first time as a married daughter. This first visit was not a simple affair. Beforehand the Surkhang family was to be informed, and they were expected to prepare the festivities.

An auspicious day was found. After a month and fourteen days I went back to the Surkhang house. On that occasion the Yuthoks again were to present gifts to the Surkhang family. There were so many presents this time that it took twenty-two servants accompanied by two main servants of the Yuthok household to do the job. They had to leave at eight in the morning to make all things ready for our arrival. Their first task was to lay out all of the gifts in the big room next to the chapel.

My husband, the children, and I left at ten o'clock in the morning and took twenty minutes to reach the Surkhang house. All of my family were waiting in the chapel when we joined them. As soon as everyone was ready, the Yuthoks' main servant offered the presents to the family and then gave fifteen dotse to the Surkhang servants as a group. This party lasted for seven days, somewhat longer than usual. The reason for this was that my elder brother had just finished a successful term of office in Kham, where he was an assistant to our father who was the governor there. He was expected to give a party in celebration. This party was added to the festivities held in honor of our marriage. Many visitors came and returned to their homes each day but the entire Yuthok family stayed all week in the Surkhang household. When we all returned to the Yuthok residence, I had to settle down as a married woman and assume the responsibilities of the head of the house.

Thus one can see how custom and order in marriage among Tibetans was quite clearly set out. However, love marriages occurred frequently, especially among the peasants. Love marriages happened in the village in a natural way because the boys and girls often met and came to know each other, for example, when they worked in the fields together. Sometimes when it was not convenient to hold the longchang and marriage ceremonies, the boy and girl would start their life together without them and several children might be born. But when it was possible, they would arrange for the traditional ceremonies. When there was no marriage celebration, the couple lived together in a marriage relationship without offending the social standards of the village. Both the villagers who were married officially in ceremonies after their married life had begun and those who had not performed any marriage ceremonies at all were free to stay. However, they lived either in the house of the young man's family or in a separate house built for themselves.

There were also allowances made for girls of noble families who chose to live with their love partners without marriage. These cases were very rare and happened mainly when the girl belonged to a much higher social class than the boy. Such an occurrence took place in my family when our aunt Kunsang Dekyi fell in love with Pema Gyalpo, a servant to Guru Rinpoche from Tawang monastery. They were not allowed to marry because of the difference in their social status, but they lived together and had children just like any other married couple. They stayed in a guest house in Eh at the Lhagyari estate and their children were accepted into the family in a normal way. They remained together for the rest of their lives, but my aunt always had a little inferiority complex and seldom joined the family in festivities.

All of these social customs accompanying family life served to produce stability in the community, but human frailty sometimes showed its face when young ladies conceived when marriage was not intended. This did not happen very often, but when it did, it always presented a very embarrassing situation. When the pregnancy came to the second or third month, it could no longer be ignored so the girl would have to tell her mother. Some mothers would take their daughters to a distant place and try to find a young married woman whom they could trust. They would offer her some money to pretend that she had given birth to the child. When the baby was born, the actual mother tried to make it look like she had not given birth to any child and the adopted mother would keep the child as if it were her own. Of course in most cases there would be some suspicion that something had happened, and talk would start that so and so had given birth to a child in this way. But no one was unkind enough to say these things in front of the girl. Since the government under the inspiration and guidance of the Dalai Lama always recognized that there are frailties in human nature, there were no laws governing these circumstances and the people concerned were left free to make the best they could out of a difficult and embarrassing situation.

The practice of polyandry served a special purpose in the social structure of Tibetan life. Polyandry was useful sometimes when there were many sons in a family. To try to maintain one wife for each boy complicated the management of the family property whether it was in the form of an estate, a more modest farm property or the activities of a merchant. On the other hand, when there were only daughters left to carry on the family, sometimes it worked out better to bring only one husband for the girls. Polygamous marriages thus could serve the social structure of the family and were not a result of lust.

Although these practices may seem very strange and even barbaric to people of other cultures, for the Tibetans they had many advantages. Our country is very big and the holdings of land were often large. There was much demand for manpower to take care of the land. In the case of peasants and poorer families there was always a need for the family to remain together as a unit. For all classes these problems were somewhat solved by the practices of polygamy and polyandry.

A polygamous marriage took place in my family when my brothers both married Dekyi, a daughter of the Yuthok family, a few months before my marriage.[1] Both my brothers were in their early twenties and from that time onward both in Tibet and as refugees living in the United States all three lived a happy and contented life together. Since both brothers were in government service, it was very convenient for one to remain in Lhasa with Dekyi while the other brother had gone away to some far off place on government business.

In ancient Tibet there was almost no incidence of divorce. Even as late as the days of my grandparents, there were no divorces in the Surkhang or the Yuthok families. I have already told the story of the divorce between my father and mother and later I shall tell the story of my own. Starting from about 1900 and continuing up to 1959, divorces gradually became more common. The circumstances leading to the divorce between my parents and to my own were quite similar, but the cause leading to my sister's as described in the Treshong story was quite different.

8   Yuthok: House of the Turquoise Roof

The Yuthoks had been nobility in the service of the Tibetan government for many centuries. Their house was built near an ancient small bridge on the outskirts of Lhasa that enabled people to pass over the dank marshes on the way to the Potala. This bridge had a roof covered with turquoise tiles, hence *Yu* (meaning turquoise), *thok* (meaning roof). From this they took their name.

During the reign of the Fifth Dalai Lama in the seventeenth century, Yuthok Losang Thargye was made a depon or general, and fought in the war with Bhutan. Later, in the early eighteenth century, during the reign of the Eighth Dalai Lama, Yuthok Tashi Dhondup became a *sawang* or cabinet minister. Then in the 1800's the Yuthok family had no heir. This problem was solved in a very special way.

It is well known that when a Dalai Lama dies he is expected to take a new birth within a short time. The discovery of when and where the child is to be born and the identification of the new incarnation are determined very carefully and according to specially prescribed rules. Thus according to Tibetan custom whenever a newly incarnated Dalai Lama was first recognized, he would be brought to Lhasa along with his parents, brothers and sisters from his birthplace. The parents would be given a permanent residence in Lhasa and were also given an estate. This honor was signified by the name "Yabshi," indicating descent from the father and mother of a Dalai Lama. The descendants were made nobility in the government service. Sometimes the relatives of the new Dalai Lama would be assimilated into the family of an existing noble house without an heir, ideally another yabshi family or else one of the midrak rank. This saved the government from having to allot the family of the new Dalai Lama a separate estate. At the same time the service to the government rendered by a family without an heir could be continued without interruption.

This is what happened in the Yuthok family about 1820 when His Holiness the Tenth Dalai Lama Tsultrim Gyatso was brought to Lhasa as a small child from the Lithang village of Dron-Dok in Kham. At that time the Yuthok family had no heir to the estate in their name nor anyone to carry out the obligatory government service. The government merged the new Dalai Lama's family into the ancient Yuthok house, and the family of the little Dalai Lama consequently changed their name to Yabshi Yuthok. The few elderly Yuthoks who remained from the original family lived together with the new Dalai Lama's relatives who had become their heirs. This was a traditional arrangement and everyone lived together happily. According to this custom the family of the Dalai Lama then became the legal holders of the estate that long before had been given to the original Yuthok family in exchange for government duties assumed by its members. From that time onward the family of the Dalai Lama took the name of Yuthok and did the government service assigned to them. That is how it happened that the present Yuthok family members are the blood descendants of the Tenth Dalai Lama's mother and father and their other son, Kalsang Phuntsok.

The Yuthok family like all nobility were expected to furnish a government officer. The head of the family would attend to this and to all other family affairs. If there were only one son then he was obligated to become a government servant; otherwise the estate would be forfeited. If there were more

than one son, the other sons were free to do government service or could become monks. When there were only daughters, at least one of them would be expected to marry a man
who would take her name and work as a government official
under that name.

When I joined the Yuthok family, my husband's elder
brother Tsering Wangdu was a high government servant with
the title of Rimshi. He was one of the two officials who were
in charge of the government treasury in the Potala Palace. This
position was called *tsechak*: *tse* means Potala and *chak* means
changtzod or treasurer. The other official was a monk, with
the title *tsedrung* (monk official). Their main function was to
distribute the government income for the expenses of the
Norbu Lingka Palace, Potala, and the various monasteries.
They did most of the important office work concerning this
and also sent traders to India and China to procure tea, silk,
and foodstuffs. They had about twenty laymen working under them. Ten of these were from the lower ranks of the government, and were concerned mainly with the clerical and secretar-
ial tasks. The other ten employees were responsible for the
general maintence of the office—sweeping, cleaning, and taking messages.

Rimshi Tsering Wangdu held this post for ten years. He was
so respected that even when he had to resign his post because
of the kidney trouble he had developed, he was given the special privilege of retaining his title. He was always calm and
capable in dealing with any official or family duty and his advice was always sound.

When Rimshi took ill, he decided that it would be best if
his younger brother Tashi Dhondup, who later became my husband, married Rimshi's second wife, Chime Yudon. In order
to help the family life continue in an uninterrupted way, they
therefore all stayed together, and the younger brother assumed
the responsibilities of the husband. Chime Yudon, who was
the niece of the Thirteenth Dalai Lama and whose family was
called Yabshi Langdun, had had six daughters by Rimshi before he became ill. Thereafter she had two sons by Tashi

Dhondup.

I came into the Yuthok family long after the death of Chime Yudon. By the time I joined the family two of the daughters of Rimshi and Chime Yudon had already been given to other families in marriage and the third daughter Dekyi Lhaze had been married to my two brothers. The three younger daughters who were fathered by Rimshi (Tseten Dolkar, Tsering Paldon, and Mingyur Dolma) and the two sons fathered by my husband (Ringzin Tseten and Jigme Dorje) were still living at home.[1] Except for the youngest son, all the sons and daughters of the Yuthok family were attending a private school called the Tarkhang School. Tarkhang means telegraph house: the school was so named because it was near the telegraph station. The youngest son, Jigme Dorje, was not of school age yet, so he stayed at home with a governess named Penpa who looked after him.

When I first joined the Yuthok family, my aunt Yeshe Wangmo and my other two aunts became worried that I would have a difficult time adjusting to so many children. Although my mother feared the same, she decided not to say anything. Since I was in love with my husband, it would not have been helpful.

The children used to call me Achak Dorje Yudon. Achak means elder sister and when added to a given name it is a very polite form of address. On my side I used to call the children by adding Kushab to their name; e.g., Kushab Tseten Dolkar, etc. This word of respect can be added to the names of both boys and girls within the family. In this way we showed the intimacy of family relationship but with a flavor of respect as expressed in the honorific language used by the nobility in Lhasa. The children and I maintained a very good relationship. As far as I can remember none of us showed an angry face to another, nor did we ever quarrel. This was due to the atmosphere in which we were brought up. Every one of us in the family was well-mannered. Even now it gives me great pleasure when I think back on the enjoyable relationships between all of us. I was very happy, although when I thought of the peaceful times at Treshong I missed them very much.

The staff at that time consisted of at least nineteen retainers and servants who were permanently a part of our household. Many of them were really like members of the family. Tashi Tsering was the changtzod or treasurer; his father had also been a servant of the Yuthoks, so you might say Tashi was born and brought up in the family. Unlike many of the servants he had received an education. As changtzod his duties were to oversee the management of all our estates. Since managers of various estates were rotated every three or four years, it was his duty to oversee the whole operation so that they could continue to be managed in an efficient way. He went back and forth between the farms and Lhasa overseeing everything, which included shipping the products from the farms and arranging for the necessary supplies to be sent back. However, his powers were limited. He had to do everything according to the plan and orders of the head of the family.

Thinlay Namgyal was our nyerpa or steward. He looked after the storerooms and turned over the daily rations to the cooks. The other servants who were charged with special duties included the *trungnyig* or secretary, two men servants for Rimshi, two men servants for my husband, one maid for myself, two maids for the Yuthoks' daughters, two men servants for Mr. Yuthok's two sons, two cooks, one sweeper, one groom, one man to care for the cows, one gardener, and one manager for our rental properties. This total of nineteen did not include their husbands, wives, children, or retired parents who might be living with them in their various quarters. In addition to the servants who had their own special duties there were many others whose work was to serve our meals and accompany us whenever we went out. Some washed our clothes by taking them to the nearby river. Extra servants would be added whenever there was a need by having the changtzod request an estate manager to send one.

The household servants would come early each morning bringing warm water for us to wash our faces and tea to start the day. Their morning duties would also involve sweeping each room. The elder ones usually spent the time reading their prayer books while the younger ones just talked. They brought their own food and tea to partake of whenever they had the opportunity. Actually the duties were never very long and most of the time they were idle. Today I realize that they might have suffered from boredom when they had nothing to do but wait. As they had no freedom to come and go, they just had to sit and wait and wait. Perhaps this thought comes to my mind because I am now in America where people enjoy so much freedom and like to be very active. However, they were accustomed to the prevailing conditions and thus probably did not mind much.

This group of about twenty servants attended to all our various household responsibilities and jobs. Some were sons and daughters of elderly servants who, after serving us for a long time, had retired although they still occupied the same quarters in our household that they had had before. All the house servants lived in a one-storied building behind the main house. Each person or couple had his own small room.

In the main house, there were one large and two small sitting rooms for the servants. One of the smaller ones was adjacent to the suite of rooms my husband and I occupied on the third floor. This suite at the front of the house included our bedroom and large sitting room where we had breakfast. Near our rooms were those of our children. The daughters shared a bedroom and sitting room, behind which was a smaller waiting room for their attendants. Further on, the large servants' hall adjoined the suite for my husband's two sons. These servants' halls were quite comfortable and had enough seating along the walls for all of the indoor staff. They could stay there in between regular chores or when not needed by a member of the household. There they would talk or rest. It was also our custom that the servants would wait for the family to finish its meals and then eat what was left over in their sitting rooms.

Our food was served on large trays with many small bowls containing special dishes and condiments. On the table were also large heated serving dishes containing rice, noodles, *momos* (steamed dumplings), and curry, from which we helped ourselves. Dishes were always made fresh for each meal since we had no refrigeration. Therefore, when we had finished, the leftovers were eaten by the house servants. In this way they did not have to use all of their ration of grain, which was their salary, and thus could gradually accumulate enough to sell outside at the market.

Whenever the family was in need of an extra servant a note would be sent by the changtzod to the estate manager of one of the family estates. The manager would select a suitable person from among his workers and send him to our house. Since it was considered a great honor to be selected, his family would feel pride. The young men and women who had been chosen to become servants in rich families, especially the families of government officials, were also much pleased because they would have a chance to get educated and to acquire good manners. The servants always expected that they would learn from their new surroundings in the city.

Although the facilities enjoyed by most servants in Tibet were fairly standard, our head servants, the changtzod, the secretary, and the steward of the family, always enjoyed higher status than the others. Each lived in a small one-storey cottage that we provided rent-free. These were located on the east side of our house in a cluster of about fifteen one-storied buildings that were rented out to tenants. The treasurer's cottage had four or five rooms while the other head servants had cottages containing three or four rooms each. Each cottage had its own kitchen so they never ate with the rest of the house servants.

The outdoor servants such as the gardeners, stable keeper, sweepers, and so forth, each had their own quarters attached to their working places. They brought their own food and tea to the main kitchen in the big house to prepare it whenever they wished and took it back with them to their own quarters to eat.

Our maids used to do the family washing at a nearby river.

Men servants never did the washing. Although sometimes one of the men servants might be living with one of the women servants, usually their partners were not from our household staff. If a man servant had a woman in town, she stayed there with their children and he would visit her at night. Men from town might also visit a woman servant in her room in our house; the children always stayed with the mother.

The ordinary servants were given two dozen *khels* of grain in a year and an extra four khels as a clothing allowance. Other supplies like tea and butter were given to them every month. I myself remember distributing the tea, butter, and meat from time to time to the servants. We used to give them new clothes regularly as well as provide them with medicines. They were never poor. Actually we regarded them as family members, as most of them had been living with our family for several generations.

When the maid servants had children they could not do their work as efficiently and regularly as before; however, we never complained. Nor were the names of the servants who were too old to work struck off the pay list. They were always given the same amount of rations that they had received before and were looked after by the family with much care as long as they lived. The relation between master and servants was in general very good with the servants remaining faithful to their masters. They were much more like relatives than employees. It was unheard of to dismiss or replace a servant. Although what was given to them in exchange for their services was more than enough, I sometimes look back with regret that I did not give them more. But it is useless to regret now because it is too late. Furthermore I could not foresee the terrible circumstances that would come into their lives as well as into my own in the very near future.

In Tibet there was no modern plumbing. We had four toilets in the main house, two on the second floor and two on the third. Of these, two were considered mainly for the family and two for the others. However, there was no strict rule as to where one could or could not go. Outside, there was one more for the outside staff. The toilets basically consisted of a wooden seat or chair in a small closet. The waste dropped into a metal container on the floor below. Our household sweeper kept the toilets and receptacles clean, and daily added cold ashes and dried yak dung to the containers to eliminate odor. Once a month villagers from our estate near Lhasa arrived to carry away the containers. The waste was needed for fertilizer on the farms. There was little smell because of the cold climate and use of ashes. It would be carried in big baskets by donkeys.

As can be seen, we had a large household with many people coming and going freely in a very relaxed way. We usually left the doors of our rooms wide open. Only when actually sleeping would we close the door to our bedroom. People walked in and out very freely all over the house. At dawn, the huge main door of the house would be opened by a servant and not closed until evening, after eight or nine o'clock, or later if my husband was out.

From olden days the Yuthok family invited high lamas and monks from nearby monasteries to perform special rites and prayers for the family. When I came to the Yuthok family, the monks in our house included four geshes (highly qualified scholar-monks) from the Gyuto monastery in Lhasa and eight monks from the Beser monastery situated in the lap of a small hill a distance of fifteen miles from Lhasa. The Yuthok family had an ancient tie with those monasteries. Prior to 1912 the family used to invite eight geshes and sixteen monks from those two monasteries to stay continually in the house. They had their own small kitchen in their wing of the house. The original house of the Yuthok family had been destroyed by the Chinese during the 1912 war between Tibet and China. After that the family could not accommodate more than eight Beser monks and four geshes at a time because the new house was somewhat smaller and it was difficult to arrange accommodation for sixteen.

None of the other noble families in Lhasa permanently kept such a large number of monks at home. The monks who stayed with us received generous rations, and besides this we gave them a little money every month. For this they performed many religious duties for us. I think the monks were glad to come and stay with us because it was a good place for them to pursue their own religious practices. They used to perform rituals in our chapel every morning and evening; after that they devoted most of their time to their own religious activities. Their life was quite free. They had their own kitchen and living quarters and were undisturbed most of the time. These monks were also invited by other families in Lhasa to perform rituals and prayers and would receive money and goods from them in return. Every six months the geshes returned to their monastery and new ones would come to take their place. The eight monks of Beser Monastery stayed on for longer periods of time.

It was our custom in Tibet among high as well as low families that the husband should be the head of the household. The man always preceded the woman when walking or speaking. When a woman showed respect to her husband people would say that she was well-behaved. Our houses and lands were allotted by the government in return for the services rendered by a male family member, and were designated in his name. Whether a huge estate or a tiny farm, land was called *pashi*, or father estate.

While it may have appeared to the outsider that men were more powerful than women in our society, in reality this was not the case. In the family men and women were equal and discussed all important matters together before making a joint decision. On the other hand, it was considered that certain responsibilities naturally fell to men and others to women. Those appropriate to men included government service, the paperwork for household business matters, and the oversight of all outdoor work such as maintenance of the house, land and animals. Women's duties centered on the control of money and finances, keeping track of articles in storage, ordering from the market and entertaining guests. In addition, anything concerning wool was under women's domain, such as spinning woolen thread, weaving, dyeing, and making carpets. However, exceptions sometimes occurred, such as when a man or woman would take interest in work that was usually done by the opposite sex. In such cases, there was no social stigma attached, and although it was not a norm, there was complete acceptance of such exceptions by everyone. The only avenue not permitted to a woman was the government service.

When I arrived in the Yuthok family, I cared for my husband's clothing, dressed his hair, and showed him respect as a matter of course. All Tibetan men except monks wore their hair in long braids. In fact, the hair was never cut. Since I had seen my mother do these things for my father, I had a lot of experience from my own home and upbringing. Thus it was that I had to take on all of the responsibilities for a large household since there were no older women in the family.

It is easy to appreciate how a Tibetan noble household had many persons to feed. Besides about seven or eight family members, a dozen monks, and twenty servants with their relatives, there were often guests to be accomodated. There were two kitchens in the Yuthok house where all the food was cooked. One of these kitchens was larger than the other, the smaller one being for special cooking. Every day both of these kitchens were crowded while the cooks and their helpers prepared the meals.

From the estates and dairies owned by the family we used to receive grains, potatoes, radishes, meat, butter, and cheese. The deliveries were made to the family steward. First he would document the amount of produce he received from each estate and make a report to us. Thereafter we would sign a receipt and send it back to the managers of the estates. Any surplus grains were sold in those local areas and then the cash or goods received in exchange was sent to us. The money was stored in trunks and the goods in storerooms. The settlement of annual accounts of all the estates owned by the Yuthok family was done every year at Lhasa. The estate managers with the help of Tashi Tsering and Lobsang Chophel our secretary would settle the accounts and prepare new documents for the coming year. My husband and I both used to check the accounts and make the necessary corrections.

Among the Yabshi there was a big difference in the size of land holdings of the families. The Yabshi Lhalu and Yabshi Samdrup Photrang families had enormous estates. The other Yabshi families of Tagtser, Langdun, Phunkhang, and Yuthok had estates of almost the same size.

Only fifteen miles west of Lhasa we had a large estate, Phukpo-che in the Yamda area, where five medium-sized villages lay within a radius of two or three miles. From these we received potatoes, radishes, onions, peaches, walnuts, firewood, hay, tsampa, wheat flour, barley, and peas. The farms were like our storerooms, and since they were so near, it was easy for them to send things to us in Lhasa. Forty miles to the east of Lhasa we owned a broad grazing area called Chum, which was a vast pasture in a glacial plain below great mountain peaks. Two thousand animals could easily pasture there. We only kept about a hundred dri and yaks, but traders and nomads bringing a caravan of animals through would stop to rest them for a small fee.

Our remaining ten estates were mostly located to the west of Lhasa. In the east were two estates, about one hundred eighty miles from Lhasa. The products from these farms— dried yak and sheep meat, mustard oil, butter and wool— would be sent to us in Lhasa. As for barley and wheat, they would be sold at the estates and the revenue would be sent to us. The stewards of these estates would be selected from Lhasa and were chosen from amongst our most trusted servants. The yearly products that were sent to Lhasa never varied. Each year we would expect the same amount. However, in case of drought and poor harvest, we would make allowances so that the difference could be paid the following year. The position of the steward in these estates must have been profitable as some of them stayed in that capacity for well over fifteen years.

We had very few expenses since all of our staples were supplied by our estates. There were no income taxes in Tibet. All we needed to buy at the market was fresh vegetables in season, meat and a few luxury items from Europe brought via India such as soap, fine tinned foods, and beer and whiskey.

In Lhasa there were about twenty meat shops all situated in the eastern sector of the city. The majority of the shopkeepers were Chinese and Moslems, many of whom had Tibetan wives. *Yaksha* (yak meat), beef, and mutton were available all the time, but for pork, chicken, and fish the butchers had to be informed beforehand. Because these three items were taken only on special occasions, they were not included in the daily provisions available in the market. There was a vegetable market near the meat market where our cooks used to go shopping every morning. It was our habit for the cook to settle the bills every nine or ten days.

Half of our household income came from surplus agricultural crops including barley, green wheat, and peas that were sold or traded. Another ten percent derived from our own wool, which we sold in India; ten percent came from rents from pastures and farms; five percent from house rentals in Lhasa; and twenty-five percent from trading ventures, mostly buying Tibetan wool and selling it in India. Half of the total income was used by family members for their personal expenses, of which one tenth would be spent in charity for the poor. Forty percent of the total income went for religious offerings: half of this to the monasteries as gifts, one third of the remainder to our guru, and the rest for pujas and ceremonies performed by different lamas at our home, including the Beser monks who lived with us. About ten percent of our total income remained unspent, and this was kept in our storeroom. Extra cash could be converted to gold or gem stones, but was usually invested in trading ventures.

Although it is difficult to estimate in modern terms, our total income of 15,000 dotses converted in 1945 to 105,000 rupees or about 21,000 U.S. dollars, which today would presumably be at least ten or twenty times that amount. However, labor and foodstuffs were very cheap and not on a par with Western standards. To put this into another perspective, the dozen or so wealthiest families in Lhasa were probably about as wealthy as the royal families of Sikkim and Bhutan of that time. Part of our wealth of course lay in buildings, moveable furnishings and herds of animals which could be sold if necessary. The priceless antique religious statues, paintings and other ritual objects in the chapels in our Lhasa house and on our various estates were not thought of in terms of financial worth. Religious articles were never sold, but were treasured for their spiritual value. Whenever we traveled to India, we obtained cash for our expenses from our wool trading contacts in Kalimpong and Darjeeling by drawing from our reserves on account or borrowing by letter of credit. Many Tibetans from all levels of society engaged in trade, working both alone and in partnerships, as did the monasteries, which sometimes acted as banks by loaning capital.

On important family matters we had to consult Rimshi. It was already explained that he was not well and was confined to his bed almost all the time, so we had to find a convenient moment to consult him about any problems. The cook had to prepare separate food for him. After consulting him, the cook then would come to us every morning and ask what dishes we would like for our lunch. Sometimes I sent the cook to the daughters to see what special dishes they would like to have. Usually we rose at eight in the morning. First a maidservant would bring a kettle of hot water for our washing. After washing my face I always said prayers in my own room. Every day I used to offer fresh water in the silver cups on the altar, light the butter lamps, and then burn incense. After saying prayers for at least five minutes, followed by some prostrations, I would go for breakfast.

The servants used to bring breakfast for my husband and me to our own room. This consisted of tsampa and powdered cheese mixed with buttered tea to form a thick gruel, although sometimes we also had bread for breakfast. Tsampa, or roasted barley flour, was made in the following way: The barley was first washed and put in the sun to dry. Then a little sand was added to the barley and this mixture was roasted. After that the sand was sifted out by pouring the dry-roasted barley into another large pan. Next the barley was put into a bag and some hefty person, usually a man, would stamp repeatedly on the bag to separate out the husks. The grain was then poured in the wind to remove the husks. Finally the clean barley was ground between two stone wheels driven by a water wheel; after this it had to be sifted once more. I watched many a time how tsampa was made at our estate near Lhasa. From time to time the manager would send tsampa to our house in Lhasa for the cooks to use in preparing various dishes.

Lunch time was eleven A.M. For lunch again tsampa was served but it was not the same as the breakfast tsampa. This time it was made into *pak* (dough), which was served with a variety of other things such as dried meat and radishes, fried vegetables or sausages. Sometimes fried liver and egg dishes were also served with pak. Other times the cook prepared a different kind of dish called *thud* made from tsampa, cheese, butter, and sugar mixed together into a thick paste. It tasted a little like cake.

Dinner was served at six P.M. The two most popular main dishes were prepared with wheat flour. They were *momos* (meat dumplings) and *thukpa* (noodles in broth). Otherwise we had rice served with other meat and vegetable dishes. With this we had vegetable and meat curry and sometimes boiled meat with chili sauce. In Tibet there was no custom of taking dessert or fresh fruit after dinner, but Tibetans liked to have yogurt at the end of the evening meal.

We usually had our dinner in the dining hall where all the family members who could return from work or school dined together. When visitors came to see Rimshi we all took our dinner in his room. This was because his health was not good, and since he was unable to entertain guests in the usual way, he would ask us to join him and help carry out the duties of a host.

Because there were no telephones in Tibet our appointments were made through messengers, so of course visitors to the Yuthok family had to use that system. When called, visitors usually came straight away. Sometimes people came without an invitation. When we had no prior knowledge of a visit, we sometimes found it difficult to make arrangements all at once, especially if the guests had come from a long distance to stay with us.

Once Tsering Wangmo sent a message to Rimshi that she was coming to visit. Tsering Wangmo was the wife of the Prime Minister Yabshi Langdun Kungo Wangchuk, who was the nephew of the Thirteenth Dalai Lama.[3] Since she was the wife of such a high-ranking official, I naturally wondered how she would act toward us. Of course I was a bit excited when my husband and I received her for the first time. She had walked to our house accompanied by three servants.

She greeted us very politely. Although not beautiful, with careful make-up she looked elegant and dignified. We led her to the private chamber of Rimshi. Since he was sick he could not stand up but he greeted her warmly from his bed. Among the presents she gave to Rimshi there were biscuits brought from Europe and a bottle of foreign brandy. These things were much prized and very costly in Tibet.

From time to time the servants brought in tea and home-made cookies for us. When six o'clock came we all had dinner together in Rimshi's room. After dinner she came with my husband and myself to our room and presented us each with a small basket of dried peaches and dried cheese that had been brought from her own estates. She was a good conversationalist with a rich store of fascinating anecdotes, so the time passed very quickly. Just before dark a servant came from her house with a horse to take her back. At that time she was the same age as myself, twenty-three, and from that day until 1959 we kept in close contact. This was not the way we used to receive an ordinary guest. We showed special respect to her not only because her husband was the nephew of the Thirteenth Dalai Lama and now a prime minister, but also because she herself was a blood relative of the Yuthok family. In her own right she was much loved by all, and Rimshi had directed us to show her every possible courtesy.

These days could not last forever. In June, Rimshi died. Ten days before his death he called my husband, our family secretary, and a Moslem merchant named Adzi-la Ragamed to his room. My husband took me with him and there we saw three big boxes. Rimshi opened them in front of us and sold all the contents to Adzi-la. Among the contents were some very old Chinese porcelain bowls of various sizes, jade cups, and snuff bottles made with precious stones. There also were some bowls and ritual instruments made of silver. One of the boxes was full of brocade garments that looked very old and seemed to be very costly. The price of all those things was settled then and there. It seemed that he was thinking that after his death we might underestimate the value of those goods and let them go at an unnecessarily low price. Also he might have thought that we would want to keep them for his remembrance, and that they would lie untouched because the family members would hesitate to use them. So the three boxes were left to the care of my husband and we kept them in our room. Though his health did not seem to deteriorate further, a few days later the dreaded time came.

About one o'clock in the morning of the day Rimshi passed away his private attendant came and woke us up. He told us that Rimshi was breathing in a very labored way. My husband went immediately to see what was the matter, but returned soon. I could see right away that he was worried. He hurriedly gathered up some sacred relics and some other blessing medicines and returned with me to Rimshi's room.

Rimshi by this time was unable to speak. We gave him the blessing medicines mixed with water. These had been prepared by high lamas to be used in great emergencies, and their power is believed to be spiritual more than medical. In spite of all our efforts, he died within a few minutes. We asked the abbot from Beser Monastery who was staying in our house at the time to perform the death rites and to do the necessary prayers for the departed soul.

The year was 1933. Rimshi's death was a great loss for the family. The house now seemed suddenly empty. He had always been kind to me and treated me like his own daughter. During the six months before his death, I often used to visit him in his room. He did not have much strength to talk, but sometimes he told me stories about ancient times. Although he was only fifty-four at the time of his death, he looked much older, probably because of his prolonged illness. The next morning at seven o'clock we sent our messenger to tell the sad news to our relatives and family friends. A few hours later, after they had all assembled at our house, the arrangements for the final rituals were made. It was the custom in Tibet that the relatives and family friends should help the family of the deceased person arrange for the last rites. Our main servants along with other sympathizers joined in making the final arrangements.

About one month later I came to know I was pregnant and began to feel the same kind of discomfort experienced by expectant mothers around the world. I felt like vomiting whenever the servants brought food for me. Doctors in Tibet have no special medicine for this kind of sickness so we tried one diet after another. I took all sorts of sour things like yogurt and sour fruits that had been brought specially for me from the market. Since I was happy at the thought of having a baby, I did not mind the difficulties during those days.

Because this was my first pregnancy, my mother did all the work of consulting a high lama and having the prescribed prayers performed for long life (*Tse Drup*). My mother sought his advice on what particular rituals should be done for the baby, as well as what important things I should do during the pregnancy. I myself went with my husband to the Drepung monastery to get special blessings from Kyabje Khangsar Rinpoche, and requested him to find out what was to be done for the safe delivery of the child. He assured us that everything would be all right and not to worry. He did, however, advise me not to divert my mind from religion.

My fears were not unnatural because in those times about ten percent of the pregnant women in Tibet died in childbirth. It is said that walking is essential for pregnant women, so when

I was pregnant, I used to walk to Ramoche and circumambulate the temple there. Ramoche was the second most important shrine in Lhasa, housing the famous statue of Lord Buddha brought from Nepal by the Nepalese queen of King Srongtsen Gampo as a dowry. I took up the habit of walking around this holy place because my mother used to go there when she was pregnant.

Whenever I went to Ramoche I used to take along one servant. Ramoche itself was half an hour's walk from our home. There were two passages for circling the cathedral, the inner and the outer. It used to take me one and a half hours to make a hundred rounds of the inner passage. After I had finished my rounds sometimes a relative would come to meet me with tea and refreshments. It was our custom then to go to an open space nearby and sit together chatting sometimes for hours. For four months I went regularly to Ramoche to circumambulate the shrine.

When my delivery time approached I started assembling the things necessary for the birth. First I sent a small bottle of butter to be blessed by Kyabje Khangsar Rinpoche. This is called *jagmar.* I also requested special medicines from the Tibetan Medical and Astrological Institute. In 1916 the Thirteenth Dalai Lama established the *Mentsik Khang,* or Medical and Astrological Institute, and requested Khyenrab Norbu, the famous scholar of medicine and astrology, to formulate a medicine to benefit infants. In the same year, Khyenrab Norbu compiled a book called *Chipa Nyarcho* which dealt solely with the care of infants and their well-being. Among other things he recommended that the parents secure a small wooden plate on which was engraved the Sanskrit syllable *Hri,* to be placed on the tongue of the newborn along with a medicinal herbal powder so that the child should grow up to be intelligent. He also prepared medicines to be soaked in lukewarm water and given to the infant. These medicines were made twice a year. Khyenrab Norbu together with fifty of his pupils would pray for three or four days to bless the medicinal preparations. These would be sent to all the ninety-six Dzongs or districts of Tibet;

however, in Lhasa we were able to request them whenever the need arose.

The best medicine for quick delivery was believed to derive from a special dried fish caught from the Mapham Lake in the west of Tibet near the border with Nepal. With some difficulty we arranged to get this fish, and with it the cook made a special soup for me to take when the first pains were starting. My mother's private attendant Kyipa had also come to look after me and help at the delivery time. In this way everything was made ready for the important moment.

Finally one morning in the month of August I felt rather uneasy. A little later I felt some acute pains, which occurred several times. As luck would have it my husband was away that day. At about noon the pain became more intense. Tibetan doctors do not have any medicine to relieve this kind of pain, so my attendants gave me the blessed butter and the soup made from the dried fish of Mapham Lake. From time to time they brought tea with the soup but I could take very little. One servant was posted at the gate to tell visitors that we were not in the house. It is believed that if outsiders are allowed to come at that time, the delivery will be more difficult. That day I was very relieved that nobody came.

My maid Tseten Dolma and Mama Kyipa piled up some pillows and told me to lean on them with my face down. They said it would be easier for me to deliver that way. The pain gradually became so acute that I wished to die. The baby finally arrived about nine o'clock that night. It was a girl. Although by that time my husband had returned, he did not come inside the room. However, he looked in from the door again and again during the labor period.

Two midwives were there to help Kyipa do all the necessary things. The umbilical cord was tied with a woollen thread and then cut, leaving a short stub about three inches in length. When the child was washed it began to cry. Like any mother I inquired first if my baby was deformed or not. I felt happy and relieved when Mama Kyipa assured me that everything had gone perfectly and my little daughter was normal. Then my husband himself placed on the child's tongue the small wooden disk marked with the syllable *Hri*.

There was a strange custom in Tibet that we used to observe after a birth. Childbirth itself is treated as being very impure, so after a child is born a religious purifying ceremony is performed. In the case of a boy the ceremony is performed after two days and in the case of a girl it is after three days. The difference in time is because boys are regarded as being more pure than girls. Before the ceremony was performed, a separate kitchen was set up where meals for me and the baby were prepared by one of my private attendants.

When the news reached my mother, she was very happy and wanted to come at once to see the baby. I had a special reason when I sent a message asking her not to come. My mother had very weak eyesight and it was believed that visits to a new baby by people with weak eyesight would be harmful because of the contamination of childbirth. Since she also realized this, she was not too disappointed.

On the third day everything was taken out of the room in which I had given birth, and was thoroughly cleaned by the servants. A servant carrying a bucket of milk and water mixed with cow dung splattered the mixture over the room with a reed broom. You may or may not know that cow dung has a special quality of purification and acts as an antiseptic. After the cow dung mixture had been spread over everything, the room was thoroughly washed and the Beser abbot staying at our house gave *trusol*, a purifying blessing. In this ceremony the abbot chanted certain mantras during the final washing of the room. When this last cleaning was completed and the rites finished, the room finally was considered both clean and pure as before.

I was still very weak when this brief religious ceremony was being performed. Afterwards the child was wrapped in a small blanket and placed on a table beside us. After that relatives, friends, and servants came in for the first time to offer us greeting scarves and presents for the baby. A few days later we gave a small party and the guests who came joined in our happiness. This custom is usually observed in Tibet whenever a child is born.

Although I did everything I could to regain my strength, it took twenty days for me to return to normal. Actually I did not have much to do for my little daughter, since Tseten Dolma took care of nearly everything. All I had to do was breast feed the child. Since this was my first child I had a special feeling of happiness and I remember this time with much tenderness.

After one month the child was given a name by Kyabje Khangsar Rinpoche. She was called Mingyur Sonam Paldon. Since the youngest daughter of the late Rimshi was also named Mingyur we called our baby only Sonam Paldon. The next big event was to fix an auspicious date for little Sonam Paldon to be taken out of the house for the first time. Generally this date occurred about two months after the birth.

For this important occasion we had to prepare three small silver boxes each containing a tiny image of the Buddha. The covers of the boxes were of glass so that the images could look out. Through hooks on the sides of the boxes a heavy thread was drawn, and the boxes were tied by a special narrow cloth string around the shoulders of the servant who carried the baby in a blanket on her back. In this way the images of the Buddha were to rest on the back of our baby.

When the day arrived, the baby was dressed in beautiful robes of Chinese brocade. At the auspicious time she was wrapped in a blanket and our servant Tseten Dolma tied her carefully on her back. The three boxes containing the Buddhas were tied across her shoulders; then we were ready to start. With Tseten Dolma carrying my baby and with some other servants I went first to the Central Cathedral to perform special prayers. From there we went to the Surkhang house to visit my mother and family members, and we stayed for a few days before returning to the Yuthok house.

Another big change came in our lives that same year. Nang-karwa, the commander of the bodyguard unit of the Dalai Lama, resigned, and my husband was appointed as his replacement with the title of depon or general. My husband did not celebrate his promotion with a grand party but he did go for an audience with the regent Reting Rinpoche who in those days was the ruler of Tibet. After that, other junior officials of the bodyguard unit came to our house and offered him scarves. My husband did not find it necessary to stay in the commander's quarters in the army camp. Instead he kept a special servant named Nyima Tsering at the guard quarters to look after things there. In this way only the important matters had to be decided by him, and our days could go on almost as before.

By the time my daughter was nine months old, like any other baby of that age, she could do many things. She smiled a lot and two or three beautiful teeth appeared. We all watched eagerly to see her development day by day. We fed her *kyoma* until she was nine months old. This was a mixture of tsampa and butter made into a thin paste. After four months gradually we were to change her diet by adding meat soup, eggs, and sweets. Many babies got sick because the parents did not know what things were best for the child. However, Sonam Paldon never got sick because Tseten Dolma was a very experienced woman and looked after my child well.

A very strange and completely unexpected tragedy took place when Sonam Paldon was ten months old. One day a Moslem merchant by the name of Samadu, whom we knew well, had come to our house. He was a tall bulky man with a long white beard. When my baby daughter saw him coming, she got so frightened that she started crying hysterically. Even after three hours she did not stop. Samadu had to go away without doing his errand, for everyone was busy with the child and there was no one free to talk to him.

When the crying persisted we thought maybe there was some sort of pain, so a doctor from the Tibetan Medical and Astrological Institute was called to check the child. He said that there was liver trouble and gave her some medicines. These did not provide any relief. Next we called the private doctor of the Indian High Commissioner from Dekyi Lingka in Lhasa. In spite of all these efforts, her condition did not im-

His Holiness the Thirteenth Dalai Lama of Tibet. Photo: Sir Charles Bell.

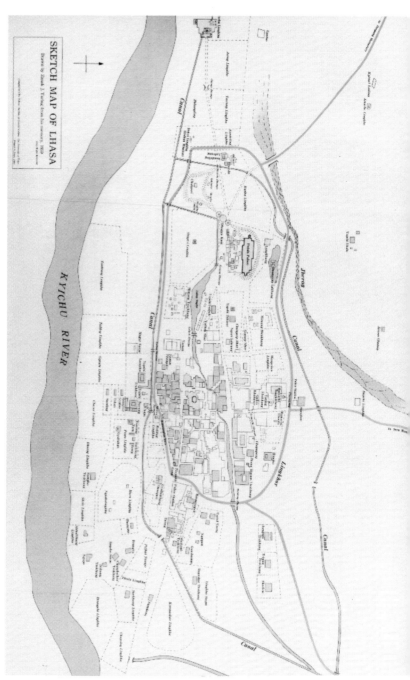

Map of Lhasa and surrounding area, 1959. Drawn by Zasak J. Taring. (Tokyo: University of Tokyo Press, 1984.)

The Potala during procession for the New Year's ceremonies, Lhasa, ca.1910-20. Photographer unknown. Photo courtesy of the Newark Museum.

View of Lhasa, ca.1935-37. Yuthok house and bridge in middle ground. Photo: C.S. Cutting. Photo courtesy of the Newark Museum.

Author's parents, ca.1926. Photo courtesy of Dorje Yuthok.

Area of Lhasa known as Yuthok Khor (Yuthok's area). Yuthok Bridge is visible at the far right. Photo: C.S. Cutting. Photo courtesy of Newark Museum.

Sakya Dolma Photrang Dhakmo with two servants. Photo courtesy of Dorje Yuthok.

Yuthok Bridge, Lhasa. Photo courtesy of Dorje Yuthok.

Author's brother Wangchuk Dorje. Photo: Heinrich Harrer.

Author's sister Lhawang Dolma with husband and
children. Photo courtesy of Dorje Yuthok.

The Tsuk Lhakhang in Lhasa, with His Holiness' chambers in the foreground. Photo: Peter Gold.

Author's brother Lhawang Topgyal in ceremonial robes called *gyalu-che*. Photo courtesy of Dorje Yuthok.

The third incarnation of Kyabje Yongzin Trijang Losang Yeshe Tenzin Gyatso (Trijang Rinpoche), ca.1956. Photo courtesy of Dorje Yuthok.

The Fourth Kyabje Trijang Rinpoche Tenzin Lobsang Yeshe Gyatso, ca.1987. Photo courtesy of Dorje Yuthok.

Palden Tsering, Treasurer of Trijang Labrang.
Photo courtesy of Dorje Yuthok.

Kyabje Khangsar Rinpoche Ngawang Yangchen
Chokyi Wangchuk. Photo courtesy of Dorje Yuthok.

At a party at Tsarong House, ca.1937. Mrs. Pema Dolkar Tsarong is the third lady from left; author is fourth lady from left. Author's husband is standing at extreme right, last row; author's son Gyalten Wangchuk is child in white in front row, extreme left; Tsering Paldon (author's neice) stands behind him. Photo courtesy of Dorje Yuthok.

Author (with hat and glasses) on a journey to India, ca.1950. Photo courtesy of Dorje Yuthok.

Author, 2nd from right, with relatives, ca.1937. Photo courtesy of Dorje Yuthok.

Children of the Surkhang and Yuthok families, ca.1942. Front row, left to right: Rongdak Norzin Dolkar (author's neice), Tashi Paldon (neice), Thubten Choden (daughter), Zeshim Norzin Dolkar. Middle row (seated): Chundhen Dolkar (neice), Dondul Wangchuk (son), Gyalten Wangchuk (son), Nuchin Thinley (nephew). Back row (standing): Tshering Norbu (servant's son), Sonam Namgyal (servant's son), Penpa Wangdu (servant), Tshering Dondup (servant's son), Jigme Wangdu (servant's son). Photo: Heinrich Harrer.

Generals in the Tibetan army. Author's husband, left, with Taring Jigme, ca.1931. Photo courtesy of Dorje Yuthok.

Khenrab Norbu, the famous doctor of Tibetan medicine and astrology. Photo courtesy of Dorje Yuthok.

Author's brother Surkhang Wangchen Gelek with
his wife and daughter. Photo: Heinrich Harrer.

Author's uncle Khemed Sonam Wangdu with Heinrich Harrer, ca.1947.
Photo courtesy of Heinrich Harrer.

The author's half-brother Ngawang Jigme Surkhang with his daughter Diky Palmo, 1985. Photo courtesy of Dorje Yuthok.

Tibetan boat, made of yak-hide. Photo courtesy of Dorje Yuthok.

Ceremonial beer-servers, Lhasa, ca.1942. Photo:
Ilya Tolstoy/Brooke Dolan.

Nomads of Northern Tibet and their tents. Photo courtesy of Dorje Yuthok.

Ladies wearing dresses from different parts of Tibet. Photo courtesy of Dorje Yuthok.

Drawing of a Tibetan kitchen by Mr. Taring Penor. Courtesy of Dorje Yuthok.

The Raja Mata of Nalagarh (left) with the Raja Mata of Patiala. Photo courtesy of Dorje Yuthok.

Mrs. Marge Ranney. Photo courtesy of Dorje Yuthok.

Author's oldest son, Gyalten Wangchuk. Photograph
courtesy of Dorje Yuthok.

The author's daughter, Thupten Choden
(seated), with her niece Choden Dolkar
Goldstein, 1952. Photo courtesy of Dorje
Yuthok.

The author, 1988. Photo: Christine Cox.

Author's son Dondul Wangchuk, with his wife Tsering Choden and children. Photo courtesy of Dorje Yuthok.

His Holiness the Fourteenth Dalai Lama of Tibet, 1989. Photo: Don Farber/ Thubten Dhargye Ling.

prove. By this time we began to realize that it was not a simple matter. Then for eight days we performed special rituals with the expectation that some relief would come. We all searched our memories wondering what could be the cause of my baby's disturbance.

Some members of our family were of the opinion that the trouble was caused by a Dharma Protector called Dorje Shukden who was displeased by our acts. It is said that this protector obeys the Dalai Lama's Junior Tutor, Kyabje Trijang Rinpoche. Our family's changtzod Tashi Tsering and his brother Kalsang Lhundup had good connections with Trijang Rinpoche so they brought him to our house. Although at that time Trijang Rinpoche was only about thirty-five years of age, he had such a great personality that instantly our faith was drawn to him. He would be able to contact the Dharma Protector. This was my first personal contact with this Rinpoche who later became my root guru.

It is interesting to know how these Dharma Protectors were approached. The medium for the protector Shukden was a monk who lived in a shrine called Trodhe Khangsar, located in the southern part of Lhasa. First this monk was called to our house to perform the oracle ritual. After doing the rituals of the protector, the oracle fully possessed the monk who seemed to become very angry. Trijang Rinpoche then requested him to save the life of the child. In reply the oracle said, "This time the sun has already set and I cannot turn it back. Next time I promise that Yuthok's children will be saved from the sudden danger of death." After saying this the oracle withdrew its possession and the monk became normal again. Then Trijang Rinpoche came into the room where the baby was lying and blessed her by placing his hand on the child's head.

When death comes it enters like a rushing river and no one can stop it by any method. In this way my first child died in the evening of the following day while my mother was holding the baby in her lap. Great sadness crept into everybody's mind and I myself fainted. When I recovered consciousness, I tried to console myself with the thought that there was nothing we could have done to save her from being taken away. After birth, death is inevitable and everybody must die in his own time. Even Lord Buddha cannot save people from death. I tried to remember all these things.

According to the custom the body was not taken out of the room for three days. During those three days there were many things to be done to help the soul. High lamas were invited to do a special prayer called Phowa, which is to help the transmigration of the departed soul to a higher realm. In our tradition we don't perform the usual elaborate rituals and prayers when a child dies. For an adult the death rituals and prayers go on for as long as seven weeks, while for a child they last only one week. During this time donations were to be given to all the monasteries and nunneries in Lhasa to pray for our baby. Alms were distributed among the beggars in the streets. Thousands of butter lamps were to be filled in the great temples. My husband and brother made all of these arrangements while my mother sat by me all the time to console me.

On the third day the body was taken out of the room. Usually the dead bodies of small babies were thrown in the river, but if the death was caused by an infectious disease, then the body was buried. In some cases if the first child died, the body was kept in the house for the safety of the next child. It was believed that if the first child's body was preserved in the house, the next baby would survive longer. For that reason they kept my child's body in a storeroom on the ground floor. This I came to know later. They said the body had been wrapped in a white cotton cloth and put in a clay pot. Certain herbs were added in order to fill the space and make the smell nice and then the pot was put in a secret place in the rafters of the storeroom.

Later, when I came to know that my child's body was in the house, I wanted to see it very much and asked my husband and servants several times to show it to me, but they made many excuses and pretended they didn't know anything about it. As new babies were born to me later, the desire to see the body vanished gradually. Later I always visited the shrine of

Shukden in Lhasa during my pregnancies, which I had not done the first time.

The body of my child was kept in the house until 1943. At that time we were in contact with a spiritual adviser, Geshe Jinpa Ngodup of Drepung Monastery, whom I asked for advice as to what should be done with the child's body. He told us that it would be best for the body to be cremated. So at long last Geshe Jinpa and others took the body to the Beser monastery where it was cremated. Geshe Jinpa and twenty other monks from the Beser monastery did the cremation rites and offered prayers for the baby. Later Geshe Jinpa told me that the body of the child had become tiny and shrunken and the clothes that were used to wrap her body had so decayed that they turned to dust when touched. Hearing all this made me remember her so vividly that my grief seemed to become fresh once more.

In 1936 I became pregnant again, but this time the pregnancy caused much more discomfort. Even so I made daily visits to the Ramoche temple to circumambulate as before. Just before the delivery I went to the Surkhang house so that I could get help from my mother and her servants. This time it was an easy birth for me, and the baby was a healthy boy.

There was a special Tibetan practice of getting a child's name long before birth. Since high lamas knew whether the child would be male or female, they could give the right name. When I was pregnant, in the interest of my own safety and that of my child's, we had invited a great lama of Drepung Monastery named Mokchok Rinpoche to perform some rituals that lasted for a week. During his stay at our house we asked him for an appropriate name for the unborn child. He said since he thought our child would be a son he would give the name Yeshe Lodoe and for several years we called our new son by that name.

Tibetans do not always keep their given names throughout their whole lives. For example, sometimes a name would be changed when a person became seriously ill. We believe that by changing the name of a person some obstacles in his life might also be changed. When monks or nuns enter the religious life they always change their name at the time of ordination. In some cases people would change their name after meeting a holy lama in the belief that a new name with the lama's blessings would bring betterment in life. My son Yeshe Lodoe was not having any special problems, but we just felt that he would gain something if he took a new name from our guru Kyabje Khangsar Rinpoche. This he did and our son's new name, Gyalten Wanchuk, has not been changed since.

In any event, after the birth of my son, life went on. One day in 1937 the regent Reting Rinpoche sent a sudden announcement to my husband that he was being transferred to the civil service; Zomphud was appointed as the new commander in his place. At that time Reting Rinpoche clearly did not favor the Surkhang family. Zomphud Theji was my mother's half brother. Their mothers were sisters from the Tethong family. The elder married Lhagyari and the younger Thonba. The younger sister had had an affair with Lhagyari from which a son was born who later went as a makpa to Zomphud. My husband had to report to the regent immediately to receive his new rank, that of *theji*. Friends and relatives gave my husband well-wishing scarves and a shower of presents. In return he had to give a medium-sized party lasting three days for the officials and the other well-wishers to celebrate his promotion.

Though the theji title is higher than the depon or commander of the guards, we viewed it as a doubtful honor. It seemed to be a sort of humiliation because a commander is an active or responsible position while that of theji is rather inactive. You can well imagine how mixed our feelings were as we took part in the many functions that were associated with this promotion. From the very day my husband was promoted, my family members as well as outside people started calling me Lhacham. This title was given as an honor to the wives of officials whose rank was theji or higher.

My husband's older brother Rimshi had a daughter named Tseten Dolkar by his wife Chime Yudon, the Thirteenth Dalai

Lama's niece. She had a secret affair with my younger brother Lhawang Topgyal and became pregnant, which we discovered about four months later. I was worried that Tseten Dolkar's older sister Dekyi Lhaze, who was married to both Lhawang Topgyal and our elder brother Wangchen Gelek, would find out and that this would affect their marriage.

Then suddenly one day Zeshim Cham, the widow of a former official, came to visit me with a small gift and kata of excellent quality. This was my first meeting with her in private. She asked me for the hand of Tseten Dolkar for her son Pema Senge. I was very happy at this prospect, but was uncertain how Tseten Dolkar would accept this proposal. I told Zeshim Cham that Tseten Dolkar was pregnant, but she said that she already knew about this and that her son wanted very much for her to be his wife. I therefore agreed to discuss the proposal with my husband. After my husband and I spoke, we consulted with Tseten Dolkar about the proposal and she agreed to the match. We sent word to the Zeshims through our steward that the proposed marriage had been accepted. Since Zeshim's father had died, his mother visited my husband and me the next day requesting that the marriage take place as soon as possible. In great haste we made plans. At the time of her marriage in 1938 she was eighteen years old and seven months pregnant. Soon afterward a girl, Tashi Paldon, was born. A few years later they had another daughter named Norzin Dolkar. To our great grief the mother, Tseten Dolkar, died a few hours after giving birth when the doctors could not stop the bleeding.

That same year Tsering Paldon, my husband's neice and the sister of Tseten Dolkar, also received a marriage proposal. This was from the family of my father's cousin, who was the wife of Nangjung Shapey. They had three daughters and one son, of whom the boy was the youngest. The middle daughter Sonam Dekyi had taken a makpa or bridegroom into the family. They were of the gerpa rank.

One day Sonam Dekyi came to see me and said that my husband's niece Tsering Paldon would be a good bride for her younger brother. She asked if my husband could present her horoscope to them. After I spoke to my husband, he agreed, as did Tsering Paldon, whereupon I gave her horoscope to Sonam Dekyi. Out of several girls being considered, Tsering Paldon's planets were the most suitable for the groom. It was then agreed that the marriage should take place in 1939. Nang-jung Shapey soon had to leave for Kham where he was to be governor. His son Tsering was a secretary in the Kashag or Cabinet. The makpa (Sonam Dekyi's husband) had not become a government official since he had assumed the duties of running the Nangjung family affairs and estates as if he were the changtzod. This enabled the rest of the family to move to Kham with the father.

In the year 1938 I was again expecting another baby. Since the previous delivery at Surkhang house had been so easy, I thought being there would bring me luck. Therefore I told my mother I wanted to be with her during my delivery. She said she would be very happy to take care of me and that I could come as before. Thus I moved to Surkhang when the nine month period had passed and remained there waiting for the birth.

I had breast fed my first son until there was no more milk. This had happened only six months after his birth. I couldn't bear my son missing this comfort and thought it necessary for him to be breast fed. At that time one of my favorite cousins named Tsering Yudon Drumpa was staying with us as my guest. She had a child named Lobsang Phuntsok who was the same age as my baby. Since she had enough milk to feed two children, I asked her if she would nurse my son Gyalten Wang-chuk along with her own child for a few months. In our country many people observe this custom. When a child's mother is ill or if she dies, her family members try to find some relative to breast feed the baby. Only when it was impossible to find a wet nurse would we feed the infant with cow or yak milk. When I went to Surkhang for the delivery, I left my little son at Yuthok in the care of Tseten Dolma to be nursed, but every day she brought him to see me.

In mid-winter of the next year a second son, Dondul Wang-chuk, was born at noon without much difficulty. Shortly after the birth of this child, my first son saw me breast feeding the new baby and became very jealous. With dreadful wrath he tried to stop the little infant from suckling my breast.. We were all amused by Gyalten's reaction and tried to console him with a show of extra love.

When the new baby was born, there was nothing wrong with his eyes as far as I remember, but when he was only a few days old we noticed that he had developed a painful eye disease. Tibetan doctors told me that newly born babies should not have any medicine applied to their eyes, even when there was a disease, because they are too tender for any foreign substance. So I rinsed a white silk cloth in warm water and now and then cleaned the baby's eyes. Naturally I worried a lot at that time for fear my son might go blind. Usually when people had eye disease Tibetans pray to Chenrezi for a cure. A Mani mantra was to be repeated several hundred times. Then the person would blow his breath to his own eyes or would ask someone else to blow the breath for him. I did this for my child. When after three weeks they cleared, I was greatly relieved to find that his sight didn't seem to have been affected.

Now that I had two children instead of one, we needed an extra mama for the elder son. This matter I had discussed with my mother. She suggested one of her cousins, named Tashi Yangzom, who had separated from her husband. Tashi Yangzom had been staying with Mother for the last few years, but there was not much work for her to do besides keeping Mother company and helping her to do a few odd things. When I asked Tashi Yangzom whether she would like to be a mama for my new son Dondul Wangchuk, she said she was willing to help. Tashi Yangzom was certainly a kind person, but she was not as good as Tseten Dolma in taking care of my child. Sometimes she would overfeed my son, and she did not keep my standard of cleanliness. Nevertheless my baby's health was good and his development normal.

In 1941 I was pregnant, and had no problems until two weeks

before I gave birth to a girl at Yuthok house. Since I already had two sons, I was very happy that this was a girl. We requested my guru Kyabje Trijang Rinpoche to give her a name. The name he chose was Thupten Choden or Thupchu for short. After her birth I slept with her every night on a low bed and was very careful with her. I got up every morning about seven o'clock to breast feed her and change her diapers. Tseten Dolma was her mama, although she also helped look after our older son Gyalten Wangchuk.

My husband's servant Lhakpa Tamdin took care of Gyalten Wangchuk for the most part, and was much loved by him. During the day I saw to it that the other mamas took care of the boys' clothing and meals. When I had the new baby, she slept with me while her little brother slept separately in his own bed in the same room. When they were four or five years old they began to stay in their own room with their mamas looking after them. When I was not busy and there were no visitors, the children would come to my husband's room for their meals and also do things like learn the alphabet.

After Thupchu was born I had no more children. Tseten Dolma looked after her like her own child until 1959. The bond between them was like that of mother and daughter. Now that we had three healthy children—two sons and one infant daughter—our family routine was happily established in the Yuthok Lhasa house. But life however pleasant or however miserable is never permanent; change is always just around the corner. Even though we knew this fact very well, at that time we never imagined the drastic changes that were so soon to follow one after another.

9 Jewels and Finery

In Tibet the jewelry, dress, and make-up of ladies differed according to their station in life and according to the region, but there were still basic similarities that they all shared. Sixteen different types of jewelry were worn by women of Lhasa and Central Tibet.[1] The jewelry was made from gold and silver set with semi-precious and precious stones like turquoise, pearls, jade, and sometimes with diamonds. Frameworks made of wood or leather were needed for the *patruk* or headdress and the *mutig thugkog*, which was worn on the top of the patruk. These forms were purchased ready-made in the market and later decorated with stones by a jeweler. Other pieces of jewelry were made either in our own homes or purchased from a shop. Some of the pieces were inherited from ancestors but in affluent families there was always the desire for a new piece. Whenever the ornaments were not being worn, they were stored carefully in soft cloth and kept safely in a locked trunk in a special storeroom with the other treasures of the house.

Not all sixteen types of ornaments could be worn at the same time. On New Year's Day and at the time of one's own wedding, as many as twelve pieces were worn. On the occasion of promotion of government officials to the higher rank of sawang and so forth, the *trungshuma* (women who offer the ceremonial *chemar* and *chang*) also wore twelve kinds of jewelry. For a party women wore no more than five kinds of ornaments.

Women in general, of course, always preferred jewelry made of gold with precious and semi-precious stones, but those who could not afford gold would wear jewelry made of silver, set with semi-precious stones according to taste and what they could afford. However, it was a must for every woman including the villagers to possess a patruk or some other kind of headdress and an *agor* (a long earring attached to the headdress), *gau* (a jeweled pendant box), and *trakey* (a string of pearls for the hair). In olden days Tibetans never liked to use any imitation jewels. They preferred to wear real ones even if they were small in size. Sometimes mother-of-pearl was substituted for real pearls.

In addition to the sixteen traditional ornaments, ladies loved to wear extra beads, bracelets, and finger rings. In fact, there was a superstition about this which said that foods cooked by a woman who was not wearing bracelets or rings was always less delicious. This superstition encouraged the women to wear at least some jewelry on their hands and arms. Finger rings were usually made of gold or silver set with turquoise, jade and other precious jewels and some kind of ring was worn by almost everyone, both men and women, from olden times till today.

In earlier days bracelets were also worn by everyone, rich or poor, but gradually this custom dropped away. Most of these bracelets were made from gold, silver, or brass, and sometimes a combination of these. There were also bracelets made of jade imported from China. Bright colored plastic bracelets, although inexpensive, were brought from India and were very popular with the younger girls and women. Even children wore these.

Around 1930 a bracelet made from gold might weigh as much as five and a half ounces. Some were even heavier. Later the style changed and ladies preferred lightweight gold bracelets. At that time I wanted to follow the fashion, so I had a gold bracelet made for me that weighed only one ounce. Some ladies began to wear this new kind of bracelet all the time and not just on ceremonial occasions.

Since olden days there was the custom of wearing bracelets made of conch shells on the left wrist. Unlike other bracelets, the conch shell bracelet was not to be taken off once it was put on the arm. When I reached the age of thirteen, a conch shell bracelet was fitted to my wrist. At first I found it very uncomfortable, but finally I got used to it. About two years later my arm was badly cut. Because the bracelet made it difficult to apply the proper medicine and bandage, it was necessary to break the shell. After that I did not wear another conch shell bracelet. Besides, they had gone out of fashion.

There was also a fashion of wearing rosary beads wrapped around the arms at the wrist. One hundred and eight beads, the number necessary for a rosary, were made from coral and turquoise. Sometimes some smaller beads made out of coral or even glass or plastic would be added to the one hundred and eight beads just for decoration. I saw women wearing these ornamental beads wrapped around their arms even when I was a little girl, but after I had to leave Tibet in 1959, I have not seen a single refugee Tibetan woman with these ornamental beads.

By the time I was nine or ten years old, very few women in Lhasa had wrist watches. Later, about the time I was ready to go to the Yuthok house as a bride, the traders were beginning to bring them from India. At that time I became the proud owner of one and was very happy wearing it.

I have been describing the jewelry that was used in Tibet during my lifetime. Until early in the nineteenth century the ornaments were small and of exquisite design and craftsmanship. The goldsmiths of that time were very skillful. Their work was done in fine detail and with beautiful artistry. The sixteen traditional types of ornaments were popular for at least two or three hundred years. However, the young ladies of Tibet failed to appreciate the craftsmanship and exquisite beauty of the small pieces, and gradually they fell out of favor. In fact the old ornaments were smaller by half compared to the agor and gau worn in my day. I used to ponder over this change of fashion and thought that in olden days the ladies felt much less discomfort with their jewelry.

My mother would tell me how when she was a child my grandmother Tashi Gyalmo would never take off her *lentze* (hair wig), which was tied to her head even when she went to bed. Only when it was time for her to wash her hair were these long hair pieces removed. However, she would remove the other ornaments each evening and would put them on again first thing the next morning.

By the time my mother came to the Surkhang house as a bride, the custom had changed. She no longer wanted to wear the lentse except on ceremonial occasions since by that time a more convenient hair piece had taken its place. Nevertheless, she still had to wear the other ornaments like the patruk, agor, gau, and *trakey* (a string of pearls that held the braids in place) whenever she went out or when guests were coming. As the fashion changed and ornaments were becoming larger and larger, the custom of keeping the jewelry as a memory of ancestors was dropped. Often the precious and semi-precious stones were removed from these beautiful pieces and used to create new ones. In this way the old ornaments with their precious and semi-precious jewels disappeared and were forgotten. However, ornaments made only out of gold or silver were usually kept as they were. These exquisite heirloom pieces were used to adorn the religious images.

By the time I joined the Yuthok family, I had a complete set of jewelry in the style worn by Tibetan women at that time. In those days women of our class traveled to India and developed a fascination for diamonds. It was no different for me, so whenever I went to India, each time I would buy some small diamonds and a few big ones. I had these made into a beautiful pendant with earrings to match.

As late as 1928 before I went to the Treshong estate, the practice in Lhasa of wearing lentse and patruk had not changed. Gradually after that time the custom changed and women started wearing less and less jewelry. I followed this fashion and wore only some of the jewelry when I went out to worship in a temple or to see my mother and friends. Only at parties and special occasions did I wear a full set of jewels.

About the year 1929 His Holiness the Thirteenth Dalai Lama passed a decree stating that women were not to keep or to wear so many kinds of precious and expensive ornaments because he observed that the fascination for ornaments was driving many families into debt and hardship. Naturally, buying and selling them began to be restricted, which directly affected the economy of most families. Most Tibetans had a great fascination for ornaments, and before this all families, rich and poor, invested great sums in jewelry. His Holiness further stated that women from families of the fourth rank or above should wear only the *mutig* (pearl) patruk and jewelry worth no more than five hundred dotse, while the lower class women should wear only a plain patruk and should not wear jewelry exceeding two hundred fifty dotse in worth. Thus, the wives of big traders were not allowed to wear the mutig patruk at all because it was made with expensive pearls. However, they were allowed to wear patruk of turquoise and coral. Tibetan jewelry was very costly; each kind of patruk, whether it was pearl or turquoise and coral, was worth about two thousand dotse. To put this into perspective, at that time an ounce of gold could be bought for about six dotse. Most types of jewelry cost only one thousand dotse but some pieces were worth as much as three thousand dotse. Even an inferior quality of patruk was worth about five hundred dotse. Thus the wife of a high official might wear six thousand dotse of jewelry to an important celebration while wives of traders wore even more than the nobility.

My mother had always felt strongly about women maintaining the tradition of wearing their ornaments when going out. So when the new order came from the Dalai Lama she faced the problem that many women in Lhasa did of trying to break away from the old tradition. Most well-to-do people were unhappy about the new law since wearing jewelry had become so much a part of their everyday life. The women folk of traders were also sad because now they could not wear the mutig patruk. For a few years after the decree was issued, women did not wear or buy any new jewelry and had to be content with only the simplest ornaments from their collections, even when going out for parties, gatherings, and the market.

Some women even borrowed inferior jewelry from the servants or from friends who were not so rich, because they felt too uncomfortable when they went out without any. They were really trying to follow the decree, but the custom of wearing elaborate ornaments was so longstanding that they felt awkward and not properly dressed when they were restricted to wearing only a few simple pieces.

The people complied with the order of His Holiness for only a few years. After His Holiness passed away in 1933 the people's craze for elaborate jewelry instantly revived, and the work of goldsmiths was once again in demand. They made the more popular pieces such as the agor and gau in their workshops according to their own designs, and then sold them for profit to customers who wanted to buy ready-made ornaments. Many, however, used to invite the goldsmiths to their own houses to make custom jewelry.

The goldsmiths who came to our home worked from nine o'clock in the morning until five or six o'clock in the evening. We would have the materials ready for them in advance and would assign a servant to look after their personal needs during the day. Besides breakfast, lunch, and dinner, refreshments like chang and tea were to be served to them unceasingly. They would be paid for the job rather than for the time it took to make the ornaments. Only after they finished their work would I ask their charges. One time for making a pendant they charged twenty-five dotse. At the time I thought this was very high but since the quality of their work was so exquisite I added one more dotse for a bonus.

In 1946 there was a fashion for a gau in a new design. I called two goldsmiths and ordered two to be made out of five ounces of gold each. In addition twenty-four pieces of turquoise and many other jewels were needed for each gau. I produced the gold and turquoise from my own supply, but the other jewels I had to purchase from the goldsmiths who usually kept gold, silver, semi-precious and precious stones for sale to the customers. These two pendants took them twenty days to complete. I kept one for myself and gave the other to my mother. She liked this new design so much that she often wore it.

Gold ornaments were usually made from gold mined in Tibet itself. Although gold is found in many parts of Tibet like Stod, Eh, and some places of Kham, the gold found in Nyarong in Kham was regarded as the best quality. The demand for gold was so great that there was not enough mined in Tibet. Very often gold had to be imported from India and China.

Turquoise made up about seventy percent of the jewels and precious stones used in our ornaments. The remaining thirty percent was comprised of other jewels like corals, rubies, emeralds, sapphires, and jade. Turquoise (which is called *yu* in Tibetan) is found in small quantities all over Tibet. It comes out of the earth in various sizes and shapes. During my time, when I needed extra stones they were bought from the jewelry shops in Lhasa. Most of these had been brought from other countries such as India, China, and Iran.

Gzi is a special indigenous stone found only in Tibet, mostly in the region of Kham. This stone is unknown to the people of other nations and I have not found any corresponding English name for it. The nearest stone to it is onyx but the real gzi is quite different from it. The gzi has many eyes and the most popular and auspicious gzi are the three- and nine-eyed ones. It is believed that wearing these two kinds of gzis prevents the evil effect of devils and planets. Both men and women will often wear a piece of gzi on a string under their robes.

The gzi was especially appreciated by the people of Kham. Both men and women wore beads of gzi and coral combined in various lengths hanging around their necks. Some persons had the superstition that wearing gzis with six eyes would bring bad luck so these were usually avoided. There were many mysteries about the gzi. It was said that they were always alive in the earth like bugs until touched by a human hand, which killed them. If found by anyone, on the ground or in a stream, they would seem to move slowly like a beetle. After they were caught, people drilled holes through them to string them on a necklace. It was further believed that the gzi was a special creation of the gods and demi-gods. It is strange to note that no matter how many pieces are compared, even a thousand or more, no two have ever been found to be at all alike. Their colors vary from shades of black, brown, and white with contrasting markings.

I have always admired beautiful jewelry and felt pride in the possession of so many ornaments. Of course there was the problem of safe storage when they were not being worn. When in 1959 I had to flee to India, luckily I managed to bring all of my jewels with me, which proved to be a great blessing. Later, one by one I had to sell them to provide an income. Even though I had had these ornaments for many years and had felt the pride of possession, I was never sorry when I sold them. I felt a sense of satisfaction that by using my ornaments in this way I was a burden to no one. I feel no regret that I no longer have my precious jewelry. What I once cherished and loved I was able to use not only to take care of myself and my family, but also to donate to charity.

Until now I have been describing the jewelry worn in Lhasa by the women in noble families and those who belonged to the trader class. Of course families belonging to these classes were affluent and much of their wealth was invested in jewelry. There is no doubt that Tibetan jewelry has a special style that is unique to our culture. The same is true of the Tibetan dress. One might then wonder how the Tibetan dress is basically the same all over Tibet, while the jewelry differs so much from place to place within Tibet. There is a story that gives the answer. It goes like this:

The thirty-sixth king, Tridey Tsugden had two queens— one Tibetan, the other a daughter of the Emperor of China, whose name was Chin Ding Kongchu. The Tibetan queen had no issue, but a boy was born to the Chinese queen. This child was to be the prince who would one day inherit the throne. The Tibetan queen was so jealous that she abducted the newly born prince and claimed him as her own. At this turn of events the Chinese queen was so shocked and distraught that she became mentally unbalanced.

In her madness she set out to destroy the Tibetan way of life. Even at that time Lhasa was recognized as having many auspicious signs in the environs. The queen tried to ruin them so as to remove the blessings that were radiating from them. Then out of madness, to divide the womenfolk, she went to all parts of Tibet and at each place showed herself with a different style of headdress and jewelry. Legend has it that the differences found today started from the frustrated Chinese queen.

Tibetan women always wore something on their heads. They used an elaborate headdress, either a patruk or something similar to a hat, or an elaborate hair-style, or simply some jewels fastened to the hair. The women in the Tsang area west of Lhasa wore a headpiece called *pagor*, which was similar to the patruk worn around Lhasa but much more elaborate. This piece was very large and semi-circular in shape. Both its design and shape were very different from the patruk. The pagor was made with bamboo about the thickness of two fingers bent into the shape of a bow. This bow form was covered with red cloth and then decorated with pearls, turquoise, and corals. Some gold lockets studded with jewels were strung together and then fixed to it. This headdress looked so very cumbersome that I used to wonder how the women managed, but I guess they were accustomed to the inconvenience.

The headwear of the women of the Kongpo region which lies to the east of Lhasa was much more practical. First the women of this area would make their hair in two plaits hanging down on each side. After they had fixed their hair in this fashion, they put on a circular cap made of dark woolen cloth and decorated with pieces of silk stitched together in a special design but with no jewels attached to it.

The women of Kham in eastern Tibet wore their hair hanging down in a single plait. To the hair on top of their head they attached some small pendants which were strung together with a strand of corals and turquoises. The delicate designs of the pendants were made from gold or silver beaten into threads. There were a few precious or semi-precious stones added to these beautiful designs.

The only Tibetans living in the cold northern regions of Tibet were nomads. The women of these regions wore their hair in a most peculiar fashion. They would twist the hair into very fine braids long enough to reach down to the waist. Forty or fifty braids would then be plaited into one plait and thrown down the back. Just above this one large plait a piece of red and green woolen cloth was tied. This cloth was adorned with many huge pieces of turquoise and amber that had been stitched to it. On the end of this cloth some silver coins were fixed in a very beautiful way. To make the hair into braids was no small matter. It took about twenty-four hours in all just to plait the hair of one woman into braids. If there was only one person to do this, she would have to attend to this braiding for eight hours a day for three consecutive days. If the lady doing the braiding was not a friend or relative, she would be given a yak for her work and of course she was given her meals and refreshments on the days she worked. However, usually the ladies were helped by members of their own family or by friends who would help each other in turn. One such coiffure would last for six or seven months. The hair of these nomads was the most elaborate of all styles.

All over Tibet from ancient times until today the general style of a woman's dress has been the same. The dresses are made either with or without sleeves. Under the dress there was always a long sleeved blouse made of light-weight silk, the sleeves of which extend far below the hands and are kept rolled up above the wrist. The dresses for special occasions of pomp and show were made out of silk brocades in a style something like a robe. The silk brocades were imported from China and were very colorful with designs of beautiful flowers all in soft tones. There was a *tangtsag* or overdress which was sleeveless and worn over the regular dress whenever the traditional seven sets of jewelry were worn. This was very necessary when the *tsigyu thakpa*, *norbu gakyil*, and *dikra longtreng*[2] were worn, because these ornaments had to be fastened with special ties that were sewn onto this overdress.

The overdress was also made out of printed Chinese brocade or Indian silk, and was decorated with three panels woven in a special design. There were two panels, each six inches wide, going from top to bottom on each side of the front, and another wide panel going down the back. These panels were of the same colors and design found in the traditional aprons worn by married women consisting of narrow, brightly colored horizontal stripes. The overdress was seven or eight inches shorter than the traditional dress worn underneath. Such traditional clothing could only be worn with the other ornaments, patruk, agor, and gau. It was permissible to wear the gau alone without the other dresses and ornaments—often during informal visits or when one went out to the market. This custom was adopted around 1930 or thereafter.

The traditional dress for girls and ladies all over Tibet was a long robe-like dress that crossed over in front and reached to the ground. This dress was used from the age of four or five onward. Sometimes it was made with a very full skirt and sometimes it was almost straight, but it always crossed over in front like a bathrobe and was tied at the back by a belt made out of different material. Although the design of the dress has not changed from ancient times until today, from time to time the traditional colors have altered slightly. For example, I remember how around 1925 the dresses were mostly solid dark purple, dark brown, dark blue, dark green, and maroon. At that time no one liked other colors but gradually the style changed to medium tones of these colors. The women never liked bright colors or patterns such as is found in Chinese and Indian women's fashions.

In the various provinces there were some minor variations. For example, the ladies in Kham gave much attention to the materials out of which they made their dresses, which they wore very loose. The women in the central and Tsang provinces also made their dresses in this style. The ladies in the Kongpo region added a very beautiful belt called *chama* made out of a piece of thick cotton cloth especially woven and then adorned with silver or bronze sometimes engraved with gold in a beautiful design. This belt was fastened with a pair of decorated buckles. By far the most usual dress worn by the rich and poor alike was made from black wool woven by Tibetans from native sheep. The wool was of different weights, some thin and some heavy, some fine and some coarse.

In ancient times until 1959 when a girl reached the age of sixteen, she was considered mature enough to wear both the patruk and the *pangden* (apron). At the time the girl was to start wearing these, there would be a special ceremony to signify that now she was a young woman. In some instances this ceremony would be performed at an earlier age. Because I was so tall, I was only fourteen years old when my mother decided that the time had come for me to wear the dress, apron, and jewelry. This made me feel very proud and grown up.

Probably in olden days the apron was first worn to avoid getting the front of the dress dirty while working. Gradually women of all classes came to wear the colorful aprons. It was soon discovered that it had the additional benefit of keeping the lap warm. The apron was made out of heavy silk or light weight wool that had been woven into brightly colored horizontal stripes. All aprons must have the seven colors of the rainbow. Wearing the apron was the fashion throughout Tibet except in the northern region where the nomads lived. Even today these aprons are made by Tibetan refugees who still like to wear them. The weaving of the cloth used in these aprons was always done in Tibet. Heavy silk thread or thin woolen yarn was imported from China or India. After it had been dyed in many bright colors, it would be woven into a special design of horizontal stripes. Tibetan wool was also used for aprons and was prepared in the same way as the imported yarns.

The finest quality of woolen cloth was called *nambu*. The wool came either from sheep or the soft hair of goats, and it was dyed for use as clothing. Natural dyes were made from certain plants and rocks found in Tibet. Dark purple and red dyes came from plants that grew in the southern parts of Tibet. Blue and green dyes came from rocks found in Nyemo on the mountain, and a yellow dye was made from the leaves of a plant called *churchur* (rhubarb) found in the hills around Lhasa. Whether the raw materials were imported or Tibetan, the weaving and dyeing were done in our own home in Lhasa. The wool would be brought from our estates. My mother would arrange for someone to come to the house and spin the wool into a thin yarn. Others came to dye this yarn bright colors, and lastly the weavers came to weave it into the special horizontal stripes characteristic of the aprons. The wool used by the more affluent families was very soft but that used by the peasants was coarse but light weight. They also did the dyeing and weaving in their own homes. There was never any shortage of Tibetan wool because the estates, the villagers and nomads all kept flocks of sheep.

Regardless of all these variations there was always a long-sleeved blouse worn under the dress. It also was made to cross over in much the same way as the dress but the blouse crossed high at the neck. These were usually made of some light weight silk imported from China or India; the ordinary people made their blouses from a cotton imported from India. The blouses were always made in the same general style but the colors depended on the fashion of the day. In olden days the blouses would be of medium or light shades of solid red, green, blue, or orange and some were brown or white, black or purple. Then in about 1927 some ladies started a new fashion by wearing a new color, pink, which soon became popular. Since everyone liked to wear this color, both my mother and I wanted to follow the fashion. My mother went to the Lhasa market three different times to search for some imported pink colored Chinese silk. Finally on her third try she managed to purchase a roll of silk of the color she wanted. She called two tailors to the house to make one blouse for her and one for me. We both felt very elegant when we wore our blouses, but before long the color fashion changed and again we followed it.

The items imported into Tibet were more than balanced by the many things that were exported. Large quantities of sheep's wool, yak hair, yak tails, skins of tiger and leopard, deer horns and musk were among the more exotic exports. There were many professional traders as well as owners of estates who exported their products and imported items that they could sell at a profit.

Although the silk and wool imported for the aprons was in the form of thread and yarns that were dyed and woven into cloth inside Tibet by Tibetans, the silk and wool used in the dresses were imported in the form of cloth ready for use. Our family used to purchase this fabric by the bolt and then keep it in our storerooms waiting to be made into clothing. Imported Chinese brocades and silks and Indian silks and woolen material could be purchased in the market. But Tibetan wool was made into yarn at the estates from the sheep's wool and then brought to the house of the estate owners in Lhasa for dyeing and weaving. Making wool into yarn and weaving the yarn into cloth was also done by the villagers in their homes.

There were special dresses for the extreme cold. In Lhasa we wore very heavy woolen dresses and sometimes dresses made out of tanned sheep skins covered with silk brocades or soft woolens. The nomads also wore dresses made from tanned sheep skins, but they did not put a cover over this. The natural wool was always left on the skin and worn inside. Whenever the weather was too cold and the heavy woolen dresses or the sheepskin dresses were not warm enough, the women would wear two dresses at a time. The outside one would be without sleeves.

Even in Lhasa ready-made dresses and blouses were simply not available in the markets. All of our clothes had to be sewn at home. Sometimes my mother would call as many as eight or nine tailors at a time. These tailors, like the jewelers, had to be paid a set sum for their labor. Besides this, they expected food, refreshments and some gifts. Even shoes had to be custom-made by cobblers who came to the house because there were no shoe shops in either the cities like Lhasa or in the villages. Although the style of shoe differed a little in the various regions, still they were basically the same. The sole of the shoe was made either from thin strips of leather that had been sewn together, or sometimes it was made by layers of coarse wool sewn in small stitches in an all-over pattern with a strong cord-like thread. The top of the shoe resembled in shape the top of a heavy bedroom slipper as worn in the USA. For the upper part of the shoe there first was a strip of red woolen material sewn with a heavy blue thread in a close over-stitch to the sole. Another piece of green wool was sewn at the top of the red wool to cover the foot. Sometimes an embroidered pattern extended from the toe to the top of the instep. There was a tall woolen legging sewn to the green piece of wool, which was open down the back and tied at the top, thus giving the shoe its boot-like shape. The cobblers who were called to our house to make these shoes worked under the same general plan as the jewelers and the tailors.

Like women all over the world, Tibetan women loved to make their faces beautiful. From ancient times until about 1940 a paste called *todcha* was used by all women. Applied heavily, it served as a protection for the faces of the peasant women and the nomads who had to do their work out of doors exposed to all kinds of weather. More sophisticated women would wear this paste as a cover-up for blemishes and for softening the skin, to make their faces beautiful. The village women were using todcha up to 1959 but the sophisticated women were by this time using imported creams. Todcha was made from the roots of the *sal*, a tree about seven feet high with lots of thorns. These roots were boiled together in water until they formed a thick paste, which was combined with certain medicinal herbs and then put into small wooden cylinders to be sold all over Tibet. It produces a beautiful reddish yellow color. It was usually made in villages in Kongpo and Dakpo in the south-eastern regions near Lhasa. As Tibetan women came more and more into contact with the rest of the world through the imports coming from India, they began to use western cosmetics. By 1920 powder, lipsticks, and rouge were used by many of the young ladies in Lhasa. Even a few older women adopted this practice.

I have described in some detail the changing fashions observed by Tibetan women until we lost our country in 1959 so that young refugee Tibetans growing up all over the world can have a glimpse of their own past and the rest of the world can appreciate the unique style of dress among Tibetan women. The dignity of womanhood and motherhood is reflected in the Tibetan style of dress and the natural elegance of women was enhanced by the use of ornaments. Today the Chinese have almost wiped out this rich Tibetan tradition of dress. They have systematically wanted to stifle the individuality of the Tibetan way of life. In place of our beautiful and durable handicrafts, which are part of our traditional culture, they have endeavored forcefully to substitute cheap factory-made goods from China that are expensive, quickly fall apart and do not even keep people warm in our cold climate. Nevertheless refugees all over the world are carrying the culture of their ancestors in their hearts and are preserving their dignified customs. However, the practice of wearing ornaments has been lost.

10 Life In Lhasa

Lhasa was known all over Tibet for its easy-going and care-free way of life. All Tibetans enjoyed a slow pace and had a happy outlook on life, but the presence in Lhasa of the Dalai Lama, many large monasteries, and the aristocratic families enabled the national and religious festivals to be celebrated there with great pomp and ceremony. Everyone who lived in Lhasa, both high and low, could speak polite or honorific Tibetan, a special language not always understood by people from the provinces. Proud of their speech and polished manners, the people of Lhasa were by simple Tibetan standards sophisticated. The population of Lhasa totaled about twenty thousand, including those in monasteries.

Religious festivals have always been very important in the lives of Tibetans. There was a special festival for women which fell on the fifteenth day of the tenth Tibetan month. This ceremony was called Pellhai Duchen. On that day the image of Pellha Dragmo, which was kept on the third floor of the Tsuglak Khang (Central Cathedral), was carried in procession around the Barkhor or main street in Lhasa by monks of the Meru Monastery.

Pel Lhamo is the manifestation of the Divine Mother. She was first introduced to Tibet by the Buddhist Indian Pandit

Sangwa Yeshe around the eleventh century and was his Dharma guardian. She is worshipped under many different names and manifestations. When Tibetans go to Calcutta, they always go to the Kalighat to worship Mother Kali there. According to Tibetan custom Pellha Dragmo stays in the temple in Lhasa all year, until her festival day when she is taken in procession around the Barkhor. This procession symbolizes her going to Mount Sumeru, from where she can see the sufferings of all sentient beings and thereby give them relief.

In association with this festival relatives and friends would visit each other for fifteen days starting the first day of the tenth month and ending on the fifteenth. The visitors would always give some money to children and servants. Of course these were happy days for children. The money given was a special luxury since it was usual to purchase goods on credit and pay afterwards. Since customers were very honest about paying their bills, there was no necessity for daily cash transactions. But on that fifteenth day we had to carry money with us wherever we went. This day was a time for merrymaking.

The special worship of Pellha Dragmo began early in the morning of the fifteenth day of the tenth month, when all women in Lhasa were expected to go to the temple for worship. On that day about twenty *Pelsolmas*, women who had been appointed to make special prayers and offerings on certain specified auspicious days, would be there chanting the ritual prayers. Previously the honor and responsibility of being a Pelsolma was given to some of the wives and daughters of the noble families with the rank of yabshi and sawang. My father used to tell how once our cousin Yangchen Dolkar had been chosen for this honor when our grandfather was holding the rank of sawang. Pelsolmas were required to wear special dress and jewelry that were to be worn only for the prayers. The system of appointing these women had changed over the years so that in my day it was customary to send our servants to perform this duty. We would supply these servants with the proper costume which was not as expensive as ours but was of similar design. The responsibility of the Pelsolmas was not easy because they had to memorize many special prayers to be offered for one week prior to the main celebration. On the last day they would begin very early since the procession could not begin until they were finished.

I wanted to follow the custom of visiting the temple before their prayers had finished, so when I was living at the Yuthok house, I had to get up very early in the morning and put on my best dress and jewelry. Since it took about half an hour to reach the temple on foot, I started by three o'clock with six male and female servants carrying the various offerings. One servant carried a torch for lighting the way. After making the prayers to Lhamo, I would return, but never felt any fatigue from the heavy dress and jewelry because of the happiness I felt from the worship of this deity. We used to return home so early that there was still time to go back to bed to sleep some more until dawn.

After the Pelsolmas had finished the religious ceremonies in the Tsuglak Khang, the deity was taken off the altar and carried in a procession around the Barkhor by one monk of Meru Monastery. He would do this by "wearing" this ten foot image which, however, was hollow and not too heavy. First the monk was to purify himself for some weeks by doing religious rites in a retreat. Once I was told that one monk who had not done this suffered much difficulty on that day. When the time came to start the procession, the monks helped put the image on the head of the chosen monk. Other monks playing musical instruments would lead the way. From time to time the procession stopped and the monk carrying the image would sit down on a special chair carried for the purpose. Then the people who lined the roadside to watch the procession gathered around him to offer scarves and beer appropriate for a wrathful deity. This procession used to halt at a place near the Surkhang family house.

The Pellhai Duchen festival marked the formal end of the warm season. After that day it was the custom for the women of Lhasa to change from their summer light-weight dresses to heavier winter ones made of sheepskin covered with silk or woolen cloth. After ten days there was another very important religious festival called Ganden Ngachod. On that day the government officials would change their summer robes for winter clothing.

Tibetans have reason to be proud of their capital city. From the time of the Fifth Dalai Lama the city was carefully managed by a special municipal council called the Lhasa *Nyertsang*, which attended to both secular and religious activities. There were two officers who were jointly in charge, one monk and one lay official, both of the fifth rank. Our father once held the head position as the lay official. One of the responsibilities of the Lhasa Nyertsang Council was to oversee new construction. Whenever anyone intended to build a house within the city, first they had to submit a plan to this office. The most important points for it to investigate were objections by neighbors to building a house on the site; whether the building would detract from the general beauty of the city; which direction the rain water on the roof would drain off; and where the tunnel door of the new latrine should be, so as to remove the refuse in a proper way. The underground channel for refuse water had to meet certain specifications.

These officials originally had the duty of reporting daily births and deaths in Lhasa and transcribing them in the main record book. The Lhasa Nyertsang office made presentations to all parents of newborn babies both rich and poor consisting of a scarf and piece of white woolen cloth sufficient for a garment for the new infant. The office kept a daily record of all events occurring in Lhasa. Recording births and deaths was discontinued around the end of the nineteenth century during a big political upheaval in the country when the Dalai Lama was too young to run the administration. However, the other duties of the Lhasa Nyertsang kept functioning until 1959.

The cultivation and harvest of crops in the Lhasa area were coordinated by this office. Government estates and district farms in the area around Lhasa as well as some distant areas were required to send cash in addition to consumer goods to the

Lhasa Nyertsang office, which arranged for their storage. The funds were used to meet the expenses of various activities of the office. It maintained records of all of the other government departments and sponsored many of the traditional celebrations of the monasteries in Lhasa.

Another duty of the Nyertsang was to distribute daily a quantity of butter sufficient to fill the thousands of lamps which burned continuously in front of the many deities in both the Tsuglak Khang and the other temples in the Lhasa area. The Lhasa Nyertsang officials also had to provide the daily rations for all the caretakers of the Tsuglak Khang and see that the monks supervising the worship in the many small chapels within the cathedral were properly maintaining all the religious treasures. A supervisor and steward were sent to each chapel every evening at about nine o'clock to watch the butter lamps be extinguished. Both a religious ceremony and a fire prevention practice, this duty was so important that frequently the head of the Lhasa Nyertsang office would go personally for the inspection.

Since this office could not do everything, another organization called the Lhasa Welfare Association, or Lhasa Tsokpa, was formed to help. This association had existed for many years and was made up of about thirty members, mostly Lhasa merchants and landlords, and a few government officials. Special privileges were given to these members for performing duties which included handling the details of special celebrations and reporting the news occurring within the city.

The annual festival of farmers called Lhasa Wongkhor which took place in late summer was sponsored by the Lhasa Welfare Association. They invited the Lhasa Nyertsang officials and their staff to take part in this festival along with about twenty monk caretakers from the Meru monastery of the Tsuglak Khang. All of those invited would assemble at the appointed time in their best dress on horseback. When all of the participants had arrived, they marched in a grand procession around the crop fields nearby. This festival was essentially religious in nature. There were also special prayers for a good harvest season offered in the Tsuglak Khang. Some of the staff from the Central Cathedral walked in front of the procession blowing horns, trumpets, and conch shells, while others played drums and gongs. After circling the fields, the procession returned through the marketplace to the Lhasa Nyertsang office, where ceremonial tea and refreshments were served to all.

Nearly everyone in Lhasa belonged to one or more religious or social associations called *tsokpa,* one of the principle purposes of which was to enable members to join with many friends in week-long parties and picnics. Among these the most important religious associations were the Yonchap Tsokpa (Water Offering Association) and Shitro (Prayer) Tsokpa. Besides these religious organizations there were many social clubs like Drokmo Tsokpa (Friends' Association, for women only), Lhadri Tsokpa (Artists' Society), Shingzo Tsokpa (Carpenters' Association), Dhozo Tsokpa (Masoners' Association), Lhamzo Tsokpa (Cobblers' Association), Ngozo Tsokpa (Association of Leatherworking Tailors), and Tsemzo Tsokpa (Tailors' Association). Each of these associations had many subgroups and chapters that were not in any way associated with the government. The Shitro and Yonchap Tsokpas had small memberships of about ten to fifteen families each. All of the others had memberships of sixty to one hundred families each.

When the day came for them to convene, the members would assemble early in the morning wearing their best clothes and jewelry and proceed to the Tsuglak Khang carrying religious offerings. The members of the Yonchap Tsokpa had the responsibility of changing the water offerings in the temple. They would prepare the water by adding a little saffron and then place the container in front of the Jowo Rinpoche, the most holy image. Although they prepared the water during holy or auspicious days, it was the custom to keep water offerings in bowls made of silver and gold in front of the Jowo Rinpoche statue at all times. On special religious days the members would wash and polish the bowls and then arrange the offerings of water in the same way as before. The Shitro Tsokpa was also a religious association which had a special place in the temple to hold its gatherings. They would invite lamas and monks to come so that the members could join them in saying prayers. There were many important religious days during the year when the members of the Shitro Tsokpa were busy with their activities.

The social tsokpas held their meetings only once or twice in a year. Since their membership was large, they needed a huge hall for their gatherings. For this purpose they used the houses in the government parks of which there were several such as Changzo Lingka, Tsedrung Lingka, and Drungchi Lingka. These houses had been built for the gatherings of the government officials, and the tsokpas used to hire them for their own meetings. Picnicking and merrymaking would continue for several days, and on the last day they would elect their next working committee members. All associations met their expenses from contributions made by the members. Sometimes in order to raise extra funds they would give loans on interest. Those handling these funds had to give a yearly audit and accounting report to the organization.

Party making was not the main purpose of these associations, but rather helping one another when any members were in distress. They also gave support whenever any of the members had disputes and even tried to negotiate when couples were in disagreement. They also used to help in the event of sickness or death and console the bereaved. Besides supporting their own members they also offered help to the poor of the community by providing financial assistance. In this way different social associations had many roles to play in the Tibetan way of life. The members came from middle class families, not unlike the Masonic organizations of fraternal orders in the West.

The government under the inspiration of His Holiness the Dalai Lama did not turn its back on any segment of the population, including the non-Tibetans. In 1950 there were more than fifteen hundred Tibetan Moslems living in Lhasa, the descendants of merchants who had come from Kashmir at the time of the Fifth Dalai Lama. When they came they had brought their own wives, but later many had married Tibetan women so that gradually a Tibetan Moslem community was established. Upon marriage the Tibetan girls were given a new Moslem name and were never called by their Tibetan names again. These wives followed the same Tibetan tradition of dress and jewelry. The men wore Moslem style robes and bands of white cloth on their heads called *leythod*. They also wore thick belts at the waist, quite different from the usual Tibetan dress.

The Fifth Dalai Lama had been especially kind to the Moslems. He gave them a huge area for a park, called Wild Ass Park (Kyangthang Naka), more than a mile away from the western sector of the city. The Tibetan Moslems reserved one part of this park for the burial of their dead in coffins. Another section was used for picnic grounds. They kept their own religious practices by maintaining two Mosques, adjoining which were schools that had been established for their own community. In general these Tibetan Moslems were professional businessmen and as such they were law-abiding and respected by all. They had been given citizenship several centuries back and as citizens had to pay a small amount of tax per head annually. These taxes were collected by their own headman who was chosen by the local Tibetan government, and were paid to the Lhasa Nyertsang office. The relationship between the Moslems and this office was very good. On the occasion of their New Year festival the headman and his assistants used to present the government office with some of their special dishes. In return the Lhasa Nyertsang office would send back with the bearers gifts of butter wrapped in a yak hide and some sacks of flour. This custom had been going on for centuries.

It was the custom for the officials in the government and their families to organize grand parties during the late summer or early autumn when the weather was nice. There were four such grand parties: one was hosted by members of the Kashag (Cabinet), called *Kashag Thuktro*; one was hosted by the lower lay officials and called *Drungchi Yarkyid*; and there were two parties hosted by monk officials. These parties were called *Yigtsang Trochen* and *Tsedrung Yarkyid*. Each lasted five to seven days and was considered a holiday to be spent with friends. Individuals from these groups used to take turns as hosts, helped by their friends. Lay and monk officials from both the higher and lower ranks were invited to the Kashag Thuktro party. Higher rank officials were invited to the Drung-chi Yarkyid. The hosts also invited some of their friends. Monk officials were invited to the layman official's parties and vice-versa, but there were restrictions. Since the gaiety of laymen's parties included drinking barley beer, the monks did not attend much. The monks in their turn did not invite women or children who, however, were included in the laymen's parties. A beautiful house was specially constructed for these parties in the Drungchi Lingka about 1943 from donations given by the lay officials together with some help from the government. Special furniture was made for the interior, so that every convenience for giving grand parties was available.

At the Kashag Thugtro party for laymen there numbered about one hundred fifty guests and one hundred fifty servants who accompanied their masters. The cost of the most elaborate party given by the Cabinet members totaled about three thousand dotses. The government furnished some foodstuffs like butter, grains, and money, but the hosts had to make up the difference. One of the four cabinet ministers had to host the Kashag Thugtro every year.

Parties were similar and varied only in that some were more elaborate than others. My elder brother Wangchen Gelek was a sawang for many years and thus had to host the Kashag Thuktro several times. My mother told me that over and above the money provided by the government, the party would cost him about three thousand dotses. A day was chosen when the weather was expected to be nice, and about three days before the party the guests would be invited. The host was responsible for sending the invitations, which were delivered by his servant with ceremonial scarves to each of the families invited. The scarf was offered and then returned while the invited persons would verbally make their acceptance.

The guests would begin arriving at about eleven o'clock. The highest ranking guests arrived on their horses with their servants. Those who lived close enough would walk, followed by their servants. The host and some of his friends would be called to greet the guests as they arrived. When women from a high family arrived, the women folk of the host family came personally to greet them. All the time there would be two servants stationed at the gate to welcome everyone and direct them inside. About twelve cooks and ten helpers had to prepare two main meals and one special tea with hors-d'oeuvres, in addition to serving tea and drinks with small refreshments throughout the day and after dinner. Most of the guests stayed until ten P.M. but a few stayed for the night. Many kinds of foreign liquors were served as well as the Tibetan barley beer.

The guests arrived in time for the noon meal, so many tables were set up in the rooms of the party house, each of which could accommodate eight to ten persons. The tables would be set with the cold meat dishes that made up the first course. The guests were then asked to take their seats. After a little while the servants would bring hot foods, including dishes made with lamb, pork, chicken, beef, fish, and seafood imported from China along with some vegetables. After some time noodles with soup would be served as a last dish. The evening meal at seven o'clock had a similar menu except the dishes were more elaborate and varied. Instead of noodles, rice and momo were served. This evening meal lasted for about an hour and a half.

When the tables were set with food, the hosts would invite all of the guests to be seated and start eating. The men always sat in separate rooms from the ladies, and while there was not much trouble in encouraging the men to start eating, the ladies were usually quite shy. It was the duty of the women of the host's family and their friends to encourage the ladies to begin. Usually this urging went on for some time until finally the eating started. Often the women who were acting as hosts had to forego their own dinner because they themselves could not start before their guests. The hostesses often had to wait until they returned home to eat.

Besides these two elaborate meals, Tibetan tea made with butter, salt and a little milk all churned together was served throughout the day. At about four o'clock in the afternoon an English style tea was served along with elaborate hors-d'oeuvres. Drinks were served continuously. All day there would be games, dancing and singing programs, and walking in the woods. Like one big house party, these parties lasted five to seven days in this way.

Naturally there were many details involved in the management of these affairs. The families and friends of the hosts were always glad to help. The main work was handled nicely by the servants, who had come along with their masters and were given special rooms for their eating and entertainment. Although their food was less elaborate, it was also festive. Whatever food was left over was given to the beggars, who always knew the time of the parties and waited outside the main gate. Sometimes they would get enough food to take back to their dwellings, the tents on the outskirts of town.

The parties hosted by monk officials, Yigtsang Trochen and Tsedrung Yarkyid, were also very elaborate affairs for one hundred fifty or two hundred guests. They held these parties in Tsedrung Lingka. Usually the parties lasted for seven days, but at the end if food still remained, they would sometimes extend the party a few more days. Yigtsang Trochen and Tsedrung Yarkyid were always on a different date from the parties of the lay officials, who would be invited as guests. No alcoholic drinks or chang were served at the monks' parties since they were never allowed to drink. Like the parties of the lay officials theirs were full of activities. They spent their time playing games and performing religious dances. In the evening there were operas. In fact, whether lay or monk parties, everybody enjoyed themselves playing, singing, and walking about doing whatever they wished.

Everyone in Lhasa looked forward to picnic time. The first picnics started when the trees began to sprout new leaves in the month of April. The most popular time for picnics was from about mid-May until the end of autumn when the days grew cooler and the leaves started to drop to the ground. Most of the favorite picnic spots were on the southern side of Lhasa near the river. Some of these parks belonged to the government and some to private individuals. Whoever wanted to arrange a picnic had only to ask the caretaker for permission; no fees were required.

Not only the people of Lhasa, but also the villagers and the townspeople liked picnics. Although in the villages there were no parks kept by the government, there would be some suitable areas nearby where the villagers could enjoy themselves and relax. If there was a river, they would play in the water.

Most Tibetans didn't swim but liked to play in the water of the river. Sometimes we just sat on the banks and watched the river go by. On all family picnics we would take our clothes for the servants to wash. Otherwise we walked here and there, played games, and just relaxed in the nice atmosphere.

There were several picnics every summer for our family to enjoy. If the picnic was a small one, the servants prepared the food at home and carried it along with tea to the picnic ground. If a family picnic were to be very large, several families might join together in the planning. Often several friends and relatives would share the expenses to make a big picnic that would last seven, eight, or even nine days. For this kind of picnic many tents would be needed. One was arranged for eating and others would serve as separate rooms for each family for sleeping. Even the servants would have their own eating and sleeping tents. A big tent would be set up as a kitchen and another just for storing the food supplies. A few days before the picnic was to begin, the servants were sent ahead to set up the tents and make all the other arrangements.

This love of tents and the outdoors, like the practice of traveling on lengthy pilgrimages, was no doubt a reflection of Tibet's nomadic heritage. Both rich and poor went on picnics, and though not all had servants to make the preparations, everyone had fun getting ready and enjoyed picnics in their own ways.

11 Wife of the Governor of Kham

Since ancient times, Tibet was divided into three large regions: Ngari in the west, U-tsang in the center, and Do-Med in the east. Each region was further composed of provinces, of which there were three in Ngari, four in U-tsang, and six in Do-Med. For four years beginning in 1942 my husband was the governor of Do-Med.[1]

The governor of Do-Med or Kham was called the *dochi*, and his office was located in the town of Chamdo. The dochi oversaw all matters of administration for both the region as a whole and the separate provinces and districts, and reported all important matters to the government in Lhasa. The region was further divided into many small sub-districts each headed by an appointed tax collector or district officer. These officers were to report any unusual happenings or local problems that they could not solve to the dochi. The office of dochi was an important position with many responsibilities, so naturally much respect was paid to the holder of this title. This system of appointing a dochi to supervise the existing district officers was instituted in 1912 when His Holiness the Thirteenth Dalai Lama appointed Kalon Lama Jampa Tendar, the monk cabinet minister, to act as the first dochi of eastern Tibet.

In the year 1942 Kalon Nangjung[2] was about to finish his

term as dochi. The post of dochi terminated every four years, so the time had come for him to return to Lhasa. Since we knew that the shapeys or cabinet ministers would be compiling a list of candidates for his replacement, and since my husband did not have any special assignment, I suggested to my husband that he request that his name be submitted along with the other candidates being considered. On inquiry we discovered that the list had already been finalized so I made the further suggestion that my husband go personally to the regent's changtzod to put forward his recommendation. He decided that this was too indelicate and requested me to approach the regent's changtzod on his behalf, which I did after further consultation.

Though this was not really customary, this step was necessary if my husband was to have a chance for the post. So I approached the changtzod, the treasurer of the regent. Through him I laid down the usual offerings of *mentral tendod* for the regent and explained the purpose of my visit. The mentral tendod or mandala offering is intended for lamas or the head of state. The offerings included the traditional scarf, and three dotse. There were also sixteen gold coins for the *changtzod chenmo* or grand chamberlain of the palace, which were not actually part of the mentral tendod. It was customary to make some such offering to a lama whenever a person went to seek his blessings.

It so happened that our friend Lobsang Yeshe was with the changtzod that morning. Lobsang Yeshe was not only a great favorite of the changtzod but was also a very close friend of my youngest brother Wangchuk Dorje. That day Lobsang Yeshe in my presence spoke in favor of my husband. I left the changtzod optimistic that all would go as desired. Although the changtzod agreed to relate our request to the regent, when I returned after one week to see what had been decided, I was disappointed to learn that no such order to recommend my husband for the post had yet been given.

However, to our surprise some days later we learned that the regent Taktrak Rinpoche had ordered the Cabinet to inform my husband that he was to be appointed as the new dochi with the title and rank of dzasa. I had never before known or talked to the changtzod of the regent, but because of my brother Wangchuk Dorje and his friend Lobsang Yeshe he had helped us. People used to say that the regent would always listen to the words of his changtzod, which this time certainly seemed to be true. As a result of this unusual favor to my husband, much to my embarrassment, it was later rumored in Lhasa that I was having an affair with the changtzod, which was totally untrue.

Soon we were making preparations for my husband to go to Chamdo. There used to be at least ten government officials appointed to accompany the dochi when he was ready to leave for his new office. Since there were already some officials staying in Chamdo whose terms had not been completed, only six newly appointed officers accompanied my husband on the long journey. As a rule only those who were willing to serve in that region under the dochi were selected. Upon acceptance as candidates, they had to report to my husband. He would then confirm their appointments, depending upon their attitudes.

A few months before my husband was to leave for Chamdo a government official by the name of Marlampa made haste in seeking the hand of Mingyur Dolma, the youngest daughter of my husband's elder brother Rimshi, for his son's bride. After everyone, including Mingyur Dolma herself, discussed the matter, she agreed to his proposal. Naturally there were many arrangements to be made. Following a brief ceremony she was sent off as Marlampa's bride. She took with her as dowry her rightful share from the Yuthok family. It was fortunate for us that the Marlampas' house was situated inside Lhasa city, so that all the marriage ceremonies could be completed within the short time left before my husband's departure.

At that time my stepsons Rinzin Tseten and Jigme Dorje were studying in the St. Joseph School in Darjeeling. During their winter vacation we used to bring them back to Lhasa by sending six servants with some riding horses and mules. This time, instead of spending the vacation in Lhasa, they were to accompany my husband to Chamdo in order to have the experience of visiting a new place. Thus, many things had to be accomplished within a brief time. Though I could have assigned our senior servant all of the remaining details, I felt it my duty to settle our financial affairs in Lhasa. I explained all this to my husband, and we agreed that I should stay behind to finish the remaining work.

Since the newly appointed dochi has the right to take one good doctor from the Tibetan Medical and Astrological Institute for his private use, he chose our family physician Tenzin. None of us therefore worried about not having good medical care in Chamdo. Finally in the middle of 1943 everything was ready, and my husband together with his sons and newly appointed colleagues left for Chamdo to take up the duties of dochi in eastern Tibet.

Back in Lhasa I gradually put all of the financial affairs of the house in order, including the accounts for all of our estates and trading activities. My husband had been extremely busy with the wedding of his niece, making new staff appointments, and meeting with government officials, so he left me to take care of all the family's business affairs. This included settling accounts with many people. First I converted all the grain lying in storage in our estates into cash. I also sold some of my extra jewelry. Although we were not short of money, I thought it was better to turn these things that were not needed now into cash rather than try to arrange for their safekeeping in our absence.

We had a very sincere and industrious servant named Tsewang Namgyal who always dealt with our family business affairs. I had sent him two times to Kalimpong in India to attend to our business transactions there. At that time Kalimpong was a very busy trading center for both Tibetans and Indians. Most of the Tibetan traders went there for trading and buying merchandise needed in Tibet. I decided to take advantage of this market. After my husband left for Kham,

I sent Tsewang Namgyal to India with an order to buy four hundred loads of white and blue cotton yarn. At that time in Lhasa we had learned that there were five or six Chinese traders from Yunnan in China who had purposely come to Lhasa to buy Indian cotton yarn since this had become very scarce in China. Knowing all this I instructed our servant to bring back the loads of Indian cotton yarn, half of which we would sell in Lhasa to the Chinese traders. The rest I would send to Yunnan on the northern China border to sell.

From time to time this cotton yarn trade was very profitable for both Tibetan and Chinese traders. The idea for this business had been suggested to me by my elder brother Wangchen Gelek and I had simply acted on his advice. This was the beginning of my trading ventures, and I repeated it at least every two years. My interest in trading and business had been encouraged by my parents when I was a child. When I was eleven or twelve years old, I knitted socks for my father which my mother embroidered by copying a simple Indian floral design on the top. My father liked them so much that he said he wanted to pay me for them. Then I knitted two more pairs and sold them to him. With that money I began to buy coral beads in the market, until I had collected a string of rather nice ones. When my mother bought these from me, it gave me a profit. I then purchased one large piece of coral of good quality. In this way I began to learn about trading and making money. I always enjoyed doing business after this.

There were no restrictions placed upon government officials doing business, but it would be illegal and unethical to use a government position to force the people to buy any merchandise or to charge them high prices. Whenever this kind of activity was discovered by the government it was considered a serious offense. But government employees were free to engage in legitimate business transactions while they were on official duty or tour.

While attending to these business details, I felt very much separated from my husband. Since there was no post or telegraphic link between Chamdo and Lhasa, the exchange of letters was very difficult. The dochi however had the authority to send by special messengers any political news to the central government in Lhasa. These messengers were called *adrung* and were chosen from the personal bodyguard unit of the dochi. The government officials also were allowed to send personal letters through them. Whenever the political situation in Chamdo became tense, the frequency of such messengers increased. Sometimes we sent letters as often as three or four times a month. Even so the distance and separation seemed great to me.

My two stepsons returned to Lhasa after staying four months in Chamdo with my husband. Two months later they again left for school in Darjeeling. The outgoing dochi Nangjung, along with his son and daughter-in-law, returned to Lhasa after the completion of his tenure in eastern Tibet. At that time his son's health was not good. Naturally the son's wife Tsepal, my husband's neice, was very worried. He was taken to many Tibetan doctors in Lhasa, and when no improvement came they even consulted the private doctor of the Indian High Commissioner at Dekyi Lingka on the outskirts of Lhasa. Despite all the medical treatment given to him, his health kept deteriorating until finally he died.

The illness was cancer. On the day of his death I was with Tsepal at Dekyi Lingka. After her husband died we came back together to the Yuthok house. She stayed on with me most of the time until I left for Chamdo. Four years later she again married into one of the noble families in Lhasa named Samdupling. Remarriage after the death of a husband was an acceptable custom, and hers was arranged by her relatives in consultation with her. Even though my relationship with all the Yuthok family members always remained good, Tsepal and I had a special love for each other. She was very impulsive but I did not mind. She always said abruptly whatever came to her mind so that in the eyes of people who did not know her she might have appeared too bold.

To cite one such instance, I went one time to stay overnight a little distance from Lhasa at an estate called Phupo Chi. Taking advantage of my absence from the house that day, my husband sent a servant to fetch a very young and beautiful prostitute by the name of Dhondup Tsomo to our room. My husband planned to be home later in the evening, but before he arrived, Tsepal discovered that the woman was there. Tsepal scolded her, demanding to know what right she had to come there to the house of a respectable married man when his wife Dorje Yudon was still living with him. Dhondup Tsomo was very frightened and jumped out of a window. She thought she was quite high up and was going to be killed. But instead she fell down only half a storey and crashed onto the big wooden lid of a great vat of horse urine in the stable yard below. Inside the vat a ceramic pot containing wool to be dyed was smashed by the impact of her fall. This made a big noise, but she was not hurt. She jumped up and fled away. When my husband came back he was furious to know that Dhondup Tsomo had been driven away by Tsepal. He scolded his niece saying that even though she was his relative, she had no right to interfere with his affairs. I only came to know of these events long afterwards.

While I was still in Lhasa attending to family business, I was not too surprised to hear from one of our relatives that my husband was having an affair with Yungdrung, the wife of one of his colleagues named Dhemon. I knew Yungdrung. She was about my age and had a sweet manner. Of course this news made me very unhappy. On hearing this I wrote repeatedly to my husband asking if he really was having an affair with another woman. In reply he wrote a reassuring letter telling me not to believe such talk. He further said that he was living like a celibate monk. Even though I thought he might not be living like a monk, this reassurance from him gave some relief to my heart.

Thinking about all this from every angle, I realized that now I must leave as soon as possible for Chamdo to join my husband. It was not easy to leave the five small children so suddenly when there was still much to settle, but I started making preparations for the long journey right away. It had been one year and four months since my husband had left Lhasa. Even up to this time I was still unable to join him. Now in the last days before leaving for Chamdo I had to brief my servants and then delegate all the unfinished and future tasks to our senior servant Tashi Tsering. I put the storeroom in the charge of a servant named Thinley. Among the children our two sons were to come along with me, but our daughter Thupten Choden and nieces Tashi Paldon and Norzin Dolkar were to stay at home. Though I knew that they would be looked after nicely by our servants, I asked my mother to take special care of them during my absence by keeping them at her house. Although there were special nannies to take care of all the children, Tseten Dolma was specially delegated to take care of our daughter because she was the youngest.

Two days before we were to leave Lhasa, I went with my children to an audience with our root guru, Kyabje Trijang Rinpoche. As was the custom we took offerings of scarves and a gold coin. After my children also offered him scarves, we all prayed for his long life and that we might meet him again. When we took leave of him, we again prayed that our wish be fulfilled. He blessed us with his own hand and put a scarf around each of our necks. He wished my sons and me a safe journey and assured us that we would see him again.

The following day we went to the temples in Lhasa to pay homage and make special offerings to the protector deities for our safe journey. It is our ancient Tibetan custom to do this ritual whenever we take a trip. Later that day we went to see my mother and had dinner with her. That night I left my daughter Thupten Choden with Tashi Paldon and Norzin Dolkar at the Surkhang house in my mother's custody. When the time for departure came, I was very sad to leave my mother and the children behind and could not control my tears. On seeing me cry, my mother also began to cry. My elder brother consoled us jokingly, saying "It would be really sad if Dorje Yudon were leaving under difficult circumstances. But she is leaving to go to her husband's place, and she will be consort of the governor of eastern Tibet, so why are you all crying?

She will be enjoying all the splendor of their new position and she will be meeting her husband after a long time." On hearing this my mother and I started to laugh. Then I bade them a final good-bye and left for the Yuthok house to prepare for an early departure the next morning. Little did any of us guess the trouble I would face in Chamdo.

Finally I left Lhasa. At that time, late in 1944, my younger brother Lhawang Topgyal and his wife Dekyi Lhaze were posted at Nagchu, which is also in northeastern Tibet. My brother was serving as the general of Drabchi Gyajong Garrison in Nagchu, commanding about five hundred soldiers. There were three main routes leading to Chamdo: through Janglam, through Janglam Barma, and through Shunglam. I wanted to meet my brother on the way, so I had chosen the Janglam route, which would take me past his garrison. Our traveling party consisted of fourteen people: our two sons, two maidservants, a cook, five servants, and two stewards. Besides our party there were two traders from Sera Ngakpa Monastery, Tenzin Dakpa and Chakdor-la, who had arranged to travel with us. My youngest brother Wangchuk Dorje came to see us off. He came with us as far as the Drabchi Lingka park about half a mile from Lhasa where he had arranged some refreshments for us in a tent. After relaxing there for a while, my brother and his servants returned to Lhasa. That day, although the weather was cloudy and flakes of snow were falling, we did not delay our journey.

We were all thinking of our loved ones back in Lhasa, and with heavy hearts we headed north where we were to scale the famous Phenpo Gola mountain. All along this mountain trail we could get a clear view of Lhasa. Because we were very sad, we turned our heads back after every few steps to look at the Lhasa we were leaving behind. We kept going on like this until Lhasa was lost from our view. We had crossed over the mountain to reach Phenpo.

The first night we lodged in a house that had been arranged for us by an old man who was the head of Lhundup Dzong (fortress) in Phenpo. Shortly after we arrived, two persons came to serve us tea and chang. These were the representatives of the nearby village. They also gave us presents of fodder for the animals, about fifty eggs, and a full loin of lamb. It is the custom in Tibet to extend this kind of hospitality to all government officials. In return for their courtesy and hospitality, we gave them two bricks of tea and a length of white and blue cotton cloth. We also gave some money to those who were to take care of our horses and help us in cooking. We always wanted to give more than we had received. We always appreciated the trouble taken by strangers to make us comfortable and did not want them to suffer a loss. Since this was our first overnight stop, it took some time for us to get settled down to rest.

The next day we resumed our journey. Phenpo is an area where good crops are planted and harvested, but the route we took that second day took us through a countryside that was red and barren. It was a completely arid region with red rocky mountains all around. On the following day again our route followed the same kind of terrain, but by the fourth day the long road leading to Nagchu brought another change. It took us through a vast expanse of high pasture land, beyond which there were small mountains appearing on the eastern horizon. The small rivulets and streams falling on the slopes seemed to be dwindling away. The landscape would have been very beautiful with everything in green had the season been summer. During the warm season the nomads used to stay on these pasture lands with their livestock—yaks, sheep, and goats. Since it was winter we did not see a single nomad, and the whole place looked cold and forbidding. No doubt the nomads had shifted to lower altitudes to find food for their animals.

It took about eight long days to reach Nagchu from the Phenpo Lhundup fortress. All along the way we passed through small villages of twenty families or less, sometimes stopping to spend the night in the house of one of these villagers. Even though we were strangers all these people received us with great courtesy and hospitality.

The town of Nagchu itself had a total population of about

one hundred fifty families whose only occupation was trading. The land was not suitable for cultivation and we were told that only a few vegetables could be grown in this area. In Nagchu we stayed in the house of my younger brother Lhawang Topgyal. The residence of our cousin Phala Thupten Woeden,[3] who was a monk official, was also quite near to my brother's so we met him as well. At this time our cousin was acting as the governor of Jang or northern Tibet. We stayed in Nagchu for five days and occasionally went to the governor's residence to see our cousin. Sometimes he came to see us. We spent much time during the day playing mahjong and talking since the weather was cold and there was much snow.

Even in such faraway places one can expect to meet new and interesting people. At that time the daughter of Orong Sichod also happened to be in Nagchu on her way to Sok district where she was to join her husband Sonam Gangpa who was serving there as a district officer. She was invited to join our company by my sister-in-law Dekyi Lhaze. She told many jokes and also sang beautifully. Above all she had such a good sense of humor that she kept us laughing all the time. In every way the time in Nagchu passed very quickly and pleasantly.

After five restful and happy days in Nagchu we again resumed our journey via Riwoche. On the fourth day we came to Sok where we stayed an extra day with an old monk official friend who was the *dzongpon* or district head. On the ninth day at Kyungpo Thengchin we spent another extra day with people that we had known from Lhasa. Our route took us twenty-three days through the same sort of landscape as before, but in order to reach Riwoche we had to climb a very high mountain called Shawala.

The night before reaching Riwoche we could not find any accommodation, so we had to pitch our four tents on the cold mountainside. My sons I stayed together in one tent. The weather was very bad, and on that night I had an attack of nausea which I think was due to bad food. All night I was vomiting and feeling giddy. Early the next morning when I opened the tent to look out, the whole mountainside seemed to be moving. It had been a very bad night for me, and even though I had taken some medicines that I had brought from Lhasa, by morning I felt that I could not continue the journey. I stayed an extra day hoping to feel better.

After a day in Doshu Tremonlung, we finally arrived at Riwoche. This was a very beautiful place with vegetation growing all around. The mountains were covered with highland evergreen pine and juniper trees. To add to the beauty a river was flowing down the mountainside. That night we stayed in a monastery in the private chamber of Phakchok Rinpoche, who was the chief lama of the Riwoche monastery. Rinpoche was a close friend of my father. At that time Phakchok Rinpoche was not at the monastery but even so his attendants treated us very warmly. Although there were many shrines and holy places to visit in the area, we stayed there only for a few days. Unhappily I could not go to see any of them because I still had not fully recovered from my illness. However my two boys had the good fortune to visit these places of worship.

The beauty of the landscape gradually diminished after we left Riwoche so that by the time we neared Chamdo itself the scenery was not very attractive. As we approached our destination, at every halting place some horsemen came to welcome us, since we were family members of the dochi. At the larger places there were eight or nine horsemen. At smaller places there were always at least two local chiefs to greet us. As soon as they saw us, they would dismount from their horses and each pass us scarves. The servant leading the caravan would return the scarf by draping it over their necks. I also made a gesture of gratitude by waving my hand because usually there was such a distance between us that if I had tried to thank them verbally, I could not have been heard. I had made other journeys into the interior of Tibet before, but purely as a private citizen. This time, being the wife of the dochi, my journey was a matter of high government concern. I never had had this experience before, and I felt very uneasy that we were giving a lot of trouble to so many people. The day before reaching Chamdo, we were met by two servants and one cook sent by my husband. They had prepared special accomodations for us. My younger sister Lhawang Dolma and her husband Rongtrak Tsering Dorje also had come to meet us in that place. We spent the night together there.

All along the journey I had worn a hat, but not any jewelry. Since the next morning was the day we were to reach Chamdo, we all put on our best clothes and I wore the patruk as well as other ornaments. After some time we reached Karthang where the office of the dochi had arranged a reception party for us in a big tent. The personnel who came to receive us included the colleagues of my husband with their servants, a number of monks representing the various monasteries in the region, several army officers, and some of our own trader friends. All of these people came to greet me, but I was not anxious to talk to them. My mind was filled with the happiness of meeting my husband again, but mixed with this happiness were many doubts as to how he would receive me.

By this time our group consisted of about one hundred horsemen. All the persons who had come to receive us along the way were now leading our long procession. My sons, the servants from Lhasa, and I followed directly behind. Soon we reached the gateway of the Chamdo Khorchen monastery, which was also the residence of the dochi. It was situated on a hill, and was protected by a bodyguard of about forty soldiers. A military band was waiting at the gateway to play in our honor while the bodyguard saluted us. Still I had not seen my husband. According to the custom we would meet first in his private room.

By that time most of the people who had come to receive us had begun to return to their homes. We met some servants of my husband on the top of the staircase leading to his chamber. When I first met my husband at the doorway of his room, I noticed at once that there were some changes in his facial expression. According to Tibetan custom, whenever one meets one's parents, relatives, elders, or any people of higher rank, including one's own husband, one greets them by bowing. I also paid respect to my husband in this way when I first met him, which is called chambul.

Finally when we settled down, we talked about Lhasa and Chamdo and then had dinner together. Later that night I told my husband that while I was in Lhasa, I had heard many times that he was having an affair with one lady. I told him straight out that this was not proper and would not result in good for anyone. When I sought his clarification on this, he replied frankly that he had had such an affair with Dhemon Yungdrung when he first came to Chamdo. It had started at a party and he himself had initiated this. After that he had not had any other affairs, nor was Dhemon acting as his wife. Moreover he told me not to listen to any talk about such things, as it would only create misunderstanding between us.

Even at that time I knew he was not telling me the whole truth since I had already heard too many details of his meetings with Dhemon Yungdrung from reliable sources. But anyhow on that night I pretended to agree with him. I thought it best not to pursue the matter any further, because if I did, there would be every probability of generating a quarrel. Since I was again with my husband, I hoped that this type of affair with other women would naturally come to an end. I told him that I was very happy with what he had said and would not review the past. I reminded him that our relationship as husband and wife would be strained if he still kept on behaving in this way. He responded quickly that he did not have any thought of doing so. I implored him to be more considerate in the future. For a while we enjoyed the relationship of husband and wife.

Tibetans have a custom of going to greet their friends whenever they have come from a distant place, taking with them various refreshments such as chang and tea. So on the very next day after our arrival at Chamdo and for some days thereafter, I was busy greeting the people who kept pouring into our house. They were both the colleagues of my husband as well as some of our own personal friends.

Even Dhemon Yungdrung came to see me. When the servant first announced that she had come, my thoughts were filled with anger at the impudence of the woman. Yet at the same time I felt an uneasiness in confronting her, the woman who was my husband's mistress. She had come alone and made a special effort to meet me since at that time her husband, Dhemon Drungkhor, was away. She had brought a tray full of dried yak meat and about one hundred eggs. At first she seemed very embarrassed and could not look straight into my face when she talked to me. But afterwards her mood became easier and I too felt more comfortable talking to her. We made small talk, but never discussed my husband. After a period of time my anger subsided and I was able to think much more rationally. After all, I could not blame her for the affair when my husband had admitted that it had been his fault. Husbands are expected to love their wives and try not to hurt them, which of course includes being faithful. It was my husband's own duty to fulfill these moral obligations towards me. Nevertheless it was his weakness to seduce other women and to have affairs with them. Since she had not tried to attract him, there seemed to me no ground to blame her for falling under his spell.

Khorchen Monastery in Chamdo had been the official residence of all the previous dochis who had been stationed there. Although the office of the dochi was situated in the monastery, the lower officials stayed in rented houses in the neighborhood of Marthang on the outskirts of Chamdo. As the dochi was responsible for the administration of the whole of eastern Tibet, everything regarding the administration of that part of the country had to be reported to him.

Chamdo is not a big town. Nevertheless it was a very active business center that attracted traders from all over the country. Most of them were Tibetans. The shops were full of goods imported from China as well as indigenous Tibetan products. All in all it was a busy and interesting community. To celebrate government functions including the Tibetan New Year, the dochi along with his colleagues used to have big parties just as they would have in Lhasa. They would pool contributions from the salaries and allowances paid to the dochi and his staff. This pay used to come from the taxes collected in the form of money and grains from all over Kham. These functions were also attended by everyone's children so all could enjoy them.

Naturally the routine of our sons in Chamdo was not at all the same as it had been in Lhasa. Both boys were missing out on their school work, and so I arranged for a monk official named Zeto Lhanyer to tutor them. Every day the boys went to his residence early in the morning. They also needed time to play. For over a year my husband had been asking Amchi (Doctor) Jangchub, one of his friends from Bathang, to procure two very small horses from China for our two sons. One day two small and lovely light brown horses with dark eyes and beautiful manes arrived through a traveler coming from Bathang. Of course the boys were very excited to see those two horses, and each selected one for himself. They loved those horses so much that when they returned to Lhasa they insisted on taking them along. The boys used to visit many children of their own age and play together. Sometimes my sons were both very naughty.

After I arrived in Chamdo, my husband and I had several unions, but after that he did not come to sleep with me at all. Before, he used to be exceptionally kind to me after he had gone to another woman. He would console me by saying that this habit of visiting other women did not arise out of attachment to them but was just like going to a toilet when you feel the urge to pass urine. He wanted me to think nothing more of it. In the past whenever he had visited other women he always tried to keep it a secret from me, but this was no longer the case. It seemed that his love for me was gone. He did not even try to console me anymore. He kept carrying on like this and gradually this habit became excessive. In desperation I sometimes had to fight with him. Many times I warned him that this kind of fighting was not good. There was the danger of losing our respect for each other, which was sure to happen if he still kept on. It was in desperation that I said all these things. I began to wonder what had happened to the love between us. Little by little I began to realize that there was no way to bring any change in his habits.

One day I finally decided that a showdown could no longer be avoided. Although I had come from a long distance to be with him, now he only seemed to be annoyed with my presence. It appeared as if he wanted to ignore me instead of giving me love. That day I told him plainly that I could not decide what I should do about all this. In reply he told me straight out that nothing could be done. The best and only thing for us was to separate. Although I told him that I would agree to this if he so wished, even so I urged him to think about our many children. Should we not try once more to find a better solution? Even on this matter he had already decided: since we had four sons and one daughter, he would look after the elder sons and I could look after the younger ones. Regarding the daughter we would look after her jointly. In addition we would have to divide the estates and property owned by the Yuthok family. Some agreement between us should be worked out.

I was shocked when I realized that he had already worked out every detail in his mind, but again I asked him if he really meant it. His reply was very firm. He had decided that we should each lead our own lives in whatever way pleased us. I would be free to decide whether I wanted a religious or a mundane life, and he also would be free. On hearing this last remark I became very angry. I told him straight out that I also agreed with what he was saying and asked him if there needed to be any witnesses. He told me that since the agreement was mutual there was no need for any witness. However, he said that he would give me a letter to confirm our separation and at once wrote this down and handed it over to me. I asked him if he was going to stand by that too. To all my queries he said that he meant it from his heart and he had no regret at all. He said he would not change his mind. Up until this time I had always tried to cultivate some understanding between us but now I realized all had been in vain. I was very disheartened to hear his firm decision but I tried to console myself that in the end my life would be happier if we were separate; to continue in a life like this was nothing but misery.

In our country people of every class whether rich or poor regarded the separation of a family as very unfortunate. Now our family was like a table with broken legs. I tried to think that there was a natural tendency for all things to fade away from the mind with the passage of time. This would be true not only regarding my feelings but one day all the gossip about us and criticism by others would also diminish. Since I had to talk to someone, I repeated all that happened between my husband and myself to my younger sister, who was very sad to hear these developments. She consoled me by saying that there was nothing I could do to change the situation.

Now that the separation had become a fact, there was nothing to do but to shift from my husband's room to another. The room I took used to be the chapel. I stayed there by myself all the time. Of the two personal maidservants traveling with me from Lhasa, Bhuti had remained to look after me even though the servants already in Chamdo could have managed. Yangchen Lhamo also had remained to take care of my two sons. At that time my elder son was nine years old and the younger son was only seven. They had not been told about our separation since I thought that they would be too small to understand. There was no need to upset them prematurely. Thus in the following days our two sons sometimes stayed with their father and sometimes they came to me. During the daytime I went to my husband's room only when necessary. I would ask what food he wanted to order or else I would consult him about some other household work. In this way I still supervised all the routine household duties as usual until I left for Lhasa.

I thought that now would be a good opportunity for me to do a retreat. I had received an initiation together with special instructions from Kyabje Trijang Rinpoche a few years before in Lhasa. Since that time I had longed to do this practice. Remembering this I made a plan to complete a White Tara retreat for longevity lasting four months. When all details were arranged, I went to see a visiting Rinpoche Jampa Thaye who was staying at the Tsenyid Monastery in Chamdo. I asked him to pray that the retreat I was about to undertake would be successful. He was a very learned and famous monk from Sera monastery whom the monks of the Tsenyid Monastery had invited to give religious teachings. Besides these he gave religious instructions to many people. He was very helpful to me as well as to others. He stayed in a separate room on the top floor of the monastery. Many laymen used to go there for his help and inspiration, and he gave me instructions for doing my retreat.

While I was in retreat, the officials gave a large party in a park near our house on the banks of the river at a spot called Tsetothang. Various officials and dignitaries from Chamdo were gathered for the usual five days of festivities. People stayed in tents, played mahjong, and enjoyed eating, drinking, and talking with friends. The military band played for the guests. My son Dondul thought that I must be sad and lonely while such a nice party was going on nearby, so he brought his children's regiment up to play their own version of military music to cheer me up. Dondul asked me to go out onto the balcony to look. When I went to see who was in the courtyard, I could already hear them playing their instruments. When they saw me, they saluted as if I was their general. I gave a little bit of money to each of the twenty-five or thirty boys in his play regiment.

Each of my sons had adopted one of the two regiments stationed in Chamdo. Seven-year-old Dondul felt that he was a member of Tathang while Gyalten liked the Dingri. Each regiment had about five hundred soldiers from among whose families there must have been twenty or thirty children the age of our boys. The children from these regiments formed separate bands that played pretend wars and went on parades. Our children had their own little horses and got completely carried away with their make-believe world. Their excitement spread to the other children to such an extent that before long even their parents got involved in their disputes. This interfered with the studying we expected them to do. The competition between our two boys grew intense since each had his own band of followers who got to be jealous of each other. The freedom they had made them get out of hand and create all sorts of mischief.

At that time there was a monk named Drayap Gangchung Trungnyig who used to be our secretary and storekeeper. He would come to my room to consult me about household matters and used to help me also by making various religious offerings. I appreciated what he did very much. During this retreat I never left the house nor met any outside people except my younger sister and a very few of our relatives. Although our secretary, the storekeeper, and all the household servants knew very well that my husband and I were not getting along well together, they never made me feel embarrassed by showing disrespect. They always prepared foods of my liking and everybody tried to keep me happy.

Living like this was very painful, so after finishing my retreat, I told my husband of my desire to return to Lhasa as soon as it could be arranged. He agreed that it would be good for me to do so and asked me to start making the preparations whenever I liked. He also said that he would procure the things I needed. Whenever we discussed my return to Lhasa, his mood was always very decisive so I realized there was no chance for a change of mind. Since I had a long journey to face, regardless of how much I wanted to leave this unhappy environment, it was not possible for me to leave immediately. My husband cooperated and helped very much, often asking me what I needed.

At that time a *gyapon* or commander of one hundred soldiers named Tseten Namgyal was also leaving for Lhasa. He was taking five soldiers and some horses with him to collect some uniforms and bring them back for the army stationed in Chamdo. I had known him before and asked him if we could join him, so that we would have a good escort to take us to Lhasa. I was very happy that he agreed to do so. This relieved me very much because not only would we be safe, but we would not have to take so many servants. Moreover he had had much experience in traveling. At last my mind was at ease and everything was properly arranged for us to accompany him. In order to manage our own personal needs I decided to take along six servants, plus two cooks, and four people to look after our horses. Of course we would need two maid servants to take care of my sons and myself. We also needed two muleteers because we would have to carry with us a total of twenty mule loads, which would include the provisions for the trip plus the many gifts I would need for family members and friends in Lhasa. Tseten Namgyal had suggested that we should return to Lhasa via the Janglam Barma route to which I gladly agreed. Every night he would tell me where we would stay the following night so that my stewards could go ahead with his servants to make the arrangements prior to our arrival.

When we were ready to leave Chamdo, as a special gesture my husband along with many of his colleagues accompanied us to a distance of a quarter day's journey, to see us off. My younger sister Lhawang Dolma and her husband had also come along and continued to accompany us until we came to Lhadha where we had planned to spend the first night. This was the same place where we had met the reception committee over a year ago when we first came to Chamdo. My sister and her husband departed the next morning to return to Chamdo leaving my sons and me to face the long journey which lay ahead of us. Now my feelings were mixed with anxieties on all sides. When would I meet my sister and her husband again? What about the long journey ahead? But the most pressing question was ringing every moment in my mind: how would I spend my days now that the relationship with my husband was completely changed?

12 Table with Broken Legs

The first twelve days of the long journey back to Lhasa took us through many places that were new to us. Sometimes we made our night halts in small towns and sometimes in very small villages with fewer than ten families. The guidance of Commander Tseten Namgyal made our return journey to Lhasa considerably easier.[1] Just as in the previous year when we were coming to Chamdo, the heads of each village or town through which we passed would make very nice preparations for us and the officials would greet us with much ceremony.

The terrain we crossed for the next fifteen days was quite different from that of the first two weeks. We traveled over vast plains passing only field after field. In the middle of some of these plains there might be a lone house built especially for travelers who wanted to halt for the night. Such houses were made from marshy clay that had been cut into bricks, dried and then stacked together to make a shelter. We sometimes had to stay in those simple houses. Usually the kitchen was so close to the room in which we were sleeping that we were nearly smothered by the smoke. It was while staying in one of these places where the ventilation was so poor that I suffered a terrible eye irritation. All night long the smoke from the kitchen kept getting into my eyes. The next morning the trouble seemed to be only in my left eye, but by the second day both eyes were affected. Unfortunately there was no eye ointment among the medicines we carried. Only the black snow goggles I had brought helped me a little to relieve the terrible pain.

To add to my discomfort the weather conditions the next day made the going very difficult. Heavy snow was falling and in some places was already almost two feet deep. Sometimes we had to hire special guides to lead my sons' two little horses through the most hazardous places. The two horses had been very convenient when the road was clear, but wherever the snow was very deep these poor little creatures were unable to negotiate the path. Finally the snow became so deep that we had to put the boys on two of the larger horses brought along as extras. My own horse was guided in turn by servants, but in the most dangerous places, Commander Tseten Namgyal himself would do the leading. Sometimes the servants leading my horse had to let me hold the reins because the road was so dangerous. All this was more difficult for me because for three days I had hardly been able to see anything.

When I realized there were not many days before we would reach Lhasa, I became more and more troubled. I could not imagine what I would do if my eyes did not get better. When I was in Chamdo, Jampa Thaye Rinpoche had foretold that on the return journey I was likely to face some obstacles or misfortunes for a few days before our arrival in Lhasa. My confidence in him had increased tremendously when his prediction proved to be true, so I was encouraged when I remembered his instructions on how to bear these hardships. I was relieved to think that in this trouble the fruit of my previous bad deeds of a past life was ripening and, since this was destined to happen to me at some time or other, it was better to face it now and get it over with.

Gradually my eyes began to feel somewhat better and I could see a little again. By this time we had reached Drikungthil, a famous Kargyupa monastery still almost two days from Lhasa, where my brother Lhawang Topgyal had come to receive us. Even though I could not see his face clearly, I was able to recognize him since he was wearing the blue brocade robe with which I was so familiar. To be with him made me very happy. In Drikungthil overnight arrangements had been made in the house of a big trader named Dundul, and here we rested for one day to get the relaxation that we badly needed before starting life again in Lhasa. The happiness of seeing my brother had given me relief both in mind and body. The next day I noticed the condition of my eyes was slightly better. We traveled with my brother until we reached Gangtho where we stayed in our uncle Wangchen Norbu Chagtrak's house. Chagtrak was one of my mother's brothers; he had made very special arrangements to receive us warmly.

On the following day when we finally reached Lhasa, we went straight to the Yuthok house. My daughter Thupten Choden and my nieces Tashi Paldon and Norzin Dolkar all were waiting there for our arrival. My two little sons were also very happy to be home again because, even though they liked the adventure, the journey from Kham had been a great ordeal for them. In a very short time they forgot the hardships and began to tell their playmates and relatives all about their small horses and traveling experiences. In fact they started talking continuously like this from the time they first met my younger brother at Drikungthil and kept on telling their stories for days on end as long as anyone would listen.

On the first night we all went to the Surkhang house to meet my mother and brothers and spent the night there. By this time my eyes were getting much better but still I felt a little uneasiness. Since my condition had so improved, I went on the following day to seek the blessings of my root guru, Kyabje Trijang Rinpoche. After two days I went to the temples in Lhasa to pray.

In Lhasa there was a big school of medicine and astrology called the Tibetan Medical and Astrological Institute, which was founded around 1916. As soon as I could I went there for a consultation with the head of the center, Dr. Khyenrab Norbu. He was about sixty-five years of age and very learned in both medicine and astrology. He examined my eye very carefully by looking into it with an electric torch. He explained to me that there was a small cataract just beginning to form in my right eye to which the smoke had caused a painful irritation. He gave me some medicine and told me not to worry. He reassured me that no further complication would develop but there would be some limitation of sight in that eye. I was very thankful that my eyes were left with only minor defects. For some days I had been fearing the loss of sight in both eyes. I believed my recovery was due to my good karma, so I became calm and reassured. Naturally my mother and brothers were very concerned but I explained to them not to worry as the suffering was inevitable and nothing further could be done. After hearing the doctor's report and seeing that I myself was not too much bothered about it, they became less worried.

The first few weeks in Lhasa were very busy for me because of our custom of visiting friends with presents whenever someone leaves or returns from a journey. Following this practice people coming from Kham usually brought various products from that region to present to their relatives and friends. Gifts from this area typically included different varieties of tea leaves from Dartsendo for making special Tibetan tea, various animal skins from Kham and silk or other things from China. I brought presents such as these to my relatives and friends when I visited them on my return.

As soon as I reached Lhasa, I came to know that there was an official messenger leaving soon for Chamdo. Through him I sent a letter to my husband telling of our safe arrival in Lhasa and of the well-being of our family members. I also wrote him about the difficulties we had experienced on the way. He never responded to this letter. It was not long afterwards that I heard the rumor that my husband was having a new love affair, this time with Rigcho-la, the exceptionally beautiful eighteen-year-old daughter of Dhemon Yungdrung, with whom he had had an affair in Chamdo. Although they were living together like a husband and wife, they had never married officially. Later she even accompanied him to Lhasa. Hearing this last bit of news, whatever hope there was lingering in my heart melted away. I finally forced myself to be realistic and soon set about making positive plans to organize a new life for myself and my children. Now that the Chamdo part of my life was over and my marriage was finished, I had to face the future alone with my children.

I thought that the time had come to send my two sons to St. Joseph's School in Darjeeling, India. I asked my brother Lhawang Topgyal to accompany us to India since he knew English and could help us along the way. He agreed but had to request leave from the government. About two weeks later when his appeal was granted, we left for India along with my two sons, one maid, and a few other servants.

This was in 1946. We had to travel many days before finally reaching Kalimpong. There we stayed with our old friends Pomdatsang Rabga and his wife Jomo Tsedron, who had an adopted son also studying at the St. Joseph's Convent School in Kalimpong. The Pomdatsang family had come to Lhasa from Markham two generations before and had become wealthy merchants. Rabga had a good connection with the school authorities and did not hesitate to help us, so that we faced no problem in getting my two sons admitted. After making all the arrangements for their uniforms and settling them as boarders in the school, we stayed on in Kalimpong for some months. On holidays we used to bring them to Rabga-la's house to be with us. We also went several times to Darjeeling to meet my two stepsons who were happily studying in the St. Joseph School there.

At that same time my uncle Khemed Sonam Wangdu and his brother-in-law Khemed Tsewang Rinchen together with some other officials stopped for a short time in Calcutta on their way to China. As representatives of the Tibetan government, they were going to China to congratulate the Chinese government on its victory in the Second World War. When we got the news that they were soon to leave for China, my brother Lhawang Topgyal and I along with some servants hurried to Calcutta to see them before they left. My uncle was accompanied by his wife Dekyi Yangchen. We checked into the hotel where all the officials were staying and on the very next morning went to see them off at the Dum-Dum airport.

After they had gone and we were alone, my brother suggested that I see a good eye specialist. We consulted some of his Indian and Tibetan friends in an effort to find the best in the city. As a result we visited several different doctors who confirmed that there was no further treatment needed. Having done all I could, I accepted that there would be some limitation of my eyesight, and hoped the condition would not worsen. We then concentrated on going to the markets to shop for things that were needed back in Tibet as well as for the western-style clothing that my two sons would need for school.

Before leaving Calcutta for Kalimpong, we received a message from my elder brother Wangchen Gelek in Lhasa that he wanted us to stay at the house of Pomdatsang Yarphel when we returned to Kalimpong. Although I had been very comfortable with our friends at Pomdatsang Rabga's house, we decided to comply with our brother's request and stay this time with the Pomdatsang Yarphel family. At that time Pomda Yarphel was still in Lhasa so we were received by his wife Sonam. Although I had not known her before, I found her very informal and frank, so we never felt any uneasiness or shyness as her guests. The food in her house was always so fine that we thought the menu had been specially prepared for us. Later on we came to know that this was their usual fare. During the three months we stayed at the Pomdatsang Yarphel house, we often were able to meet with our old friends and relatives. When after some weeks Pomda Yarphel returned from Lhasa, we spent many happy hours playing mahjong with him and his wife and their friends. Pomdatsang Yarphel's younger brother was Pomdatsang Rabga. Although they seemed outwardly very affectionate, they did not follow the usual custom of staying together with their families in the same house. Since 1940 I had been a close friend with Jomo Tsedron, the wife of Pomdatsang Rabga, so while staying in the Pomdatsang Yarphel house I often used to walk the half hour it took to reach her house. She was especially fond of our children and always prepared foods to the liking of my sons. I was touched by her special affection for my younger son Dondul Wangchuk. Sometimes he would stay with her overnight. He called her Mother Jomo-la. It was finally time to leave my sons, so after making the final arrangements for their staying on in school, my brother and I returned to Lhasa.

Then in 1946 before my husband returned from Chamdo and directly upon my return from India, I was visited by Tsepon D. W. Shakabpa.[2] He came to Lhasa to ask me news about his younger brother who was also in India. On the following day he sent one of his servants to me bearing a letter telling me of his love and his desire to see me again. I had much earlier seen Shakabpa at parties and festivals but I had never really known him well. I had not even known that at one time his mother and mine had discussed him as a possible bridegroom for me. Now his approach coincided with my failed marriage. At the time our separation was common knowledge to most of my relatives and friends, so Shakabpa must have known. After several more letters from him, I finally gave in to his amorous approach and wrote back to say that I wished to see him too. Since I had been alone for a long time, this sudden attention had its desired effect. This was the beginning of our love affair, which lasted for several months.

Long before this I had taken the Yongdzog Genyen vows which forbid intimacy with any person other than one's own husband. Even though I was separating from my husband, I had every intention of maintaining my vows. But my relationship with Shakabpa made this impossible. Though I entered this liaison willingly, I knew from the start that it could not last. Shakabpa had a wife.

Our meeting place was arranged by the Surkhang's servant Tsedor. We met in a room above the shops run by some Tibetan Moslem traders. These buildings were attached to the main Surkhang house and were leased to them by us. Thus, it was very convenient for me to go into that upstairs room by a passageway from my mother's house unnoticed. Messages were exchanged through our servants.

Though I knew that this relationship was a negative act that could only bring negative results in this life or the life after, I was drawn into it. Gradually the friendship and affection turned to love. Although I could not check the love that began to grow in my heart, I did not want to disturb his family life so we tried to keep our affair a secret from all. I knew too that my children would not approve of my having an affair like this. It ended in 1947 when Shakabpa left with my younger brother Lhawang Topgyal and some other officials for Europe, the United States, and the Far East as a member of the Tibetan Trade Delegation. I missed very much not seeing him, but gradually my life returned to its normal routine.

Towards the end of this affair I received a letter from my husband mentioning that he was planning to return to Lhasa from Chamdo and asking me to send some special food provisions he would need while traveling. Soon afterwards I sent two servants and one muleteer with eight mules carrying, among other things, biscuits imported from India, tea, and fresh tsampa made in Lhasa. As he was very fond of beer, I included a good brand of beer from Germany. I felt it my duty to comply with his wishes even though our marriage was almost over.

I had been told that my husband was still living with Rigcho who was now expecting a baby. Furthermore, he was bringing her to Lhasa with him. Two weeks after I sent the provisions, two servants went to meet my husband at Maldro Gongkar, a village near Lhasa, with refreshments such as peaches and apples, and I asked one of them to return ahead of the others to confirm the story. The servant not only did this but he also told me that my husband had arranged for Rigcho to go on to Tengyeling to stay with her relatives. Their house was very near to the Yuthok house, and some of the Yuthok servants were to go to stay with her there. Across the Kyichu River of Lhasa there was another estate named Gungthang owned by my uncle Khemed Sonam Wangdu. I had sent our senior servant Tashi Tsering and one other servant there to receive my husband, and Uncle Khemed had arranged a reception for him. Altogether there were twenty people including our changtzod, some of my husband's colleagues from Chamdo, and his own servants.

It was in June of 1947 that my husband returned to Lhasa. Since it seemed difficult to predict just what was going to happen, I decided for the time being to stay on in the Yuthok house, even though Rigcho had come to Lhasa to be with my husband. The Yuthok house had been thoroughly cleaned and my husband's room pleasantly decorated. I instructed the servants as to what foods should be served to him. Extra arrangements for the servants and steward accompanying him were also made. Our first encounter was cordial, which made me suspect that he was pleased to see me. On the surface our relationship remained the same. At times we ate together but that was the extent of our togetherness. At night we slept in separate rooms and he never asked that we sleep together. Naturally I thought my husband might be inviting his mistress Rigcho to his room but I never actually saw her in our house. Perhaps he was visiting her in the house of her relatives, but I tried not to think of these things.

Soon I came to know that some people were addressing Rigcho as if she were my husband's new wife. In fact one day a man from Kham had left a big bundle addressed to Yuthok Lhacham at our house. Naturally I thought it was for me, but when I opened the bundle, I found inside a letter addressed to Rigcho from Yudon, the Queen (Tsunmo) of Nangchen.[3] The package contained a pair of three-eyed *gzi* (semi-precious stones) and some turquoise-colored material for a blouse. Since the bearer of the package had already left before I discovered that it was not meant for me, I sent a servant to deliver the packet to Rigcho.

Although my husband and I had already decided in Chamdo to separate, up to this time I had not raised the question of how the details of the divorce should be arranged. It was during his stay in Lhasa that one day he suddenly came to me and told me that he wanted to sleep with me that night. I replied that I would not mind if he wanted to, since I too had that desire, but I made sure he understood that even if he did, there would not be any changes in the decision to separate our family. Too much had happened for us to find happiness together.

My husband had probably heard some vague rumors about my affair when he returned from Chamdo in June. Once he even asked Geshe Jinpa Ngodup, the monk who lived with me and my children, if I had taken a lover. Geshe replied that he knew nothing about it and that, so far as he knew, there had been no men coming to the Yuthok house. My husband never asked me anything directly but it was evident from his behavior that, separated or not, he did not like the idea of my having another man. Often he visited my little house to sleep with me, and sometimes stayed for several days. But we could not recapture the love and compatibility we had once had as man and wife. Besides, he had taken another woman, Rigcho-la. We wanted to maintain a good relationship, friendly though impersonal, and even after the formal separation neither of us said anything unkind or disparaging about the other. In fact many people in Lhasa commended us on our ability to live together without too much friction.

Having given up all hope that our marriage could continue, I made the request that he finalize the division of the property. He replied that he too wished to do that. Our separation paper was to be based on the decisions that we had made previously in Chamdo. At that time we had discussed the final details of our separation between ourselves, but contrary to Tibetan custom, we had done all this without consulting either my relations or my husband's. We wanted to stand by the agreement that we had made peacefully and now needed to follow formal procedures for our separation. Since there were lots of details to work out, we put everything in a formal written agreement. The Yuthok family was a big estate holder, and there were many properties to divide.

It took us many days to settle all the matters and prepare the necessary documents. The two largest estates were Delek

Ling in Nyemo district and Tul in Kongpo, but besides these there were sixteen smaller estates. We divided all of them into two parts. Although there were nomads living and working on all the estates, there was no need to make special arrangements for them as they were automatically included in the respective properties. Almost forty miles to the east of Lhasa there was a big area called Chum, which included mountains with vast pasture lands extending up into the foothills. This place was difficult to divide so we kept it for our common use. Some nomads used to stay there from whom we would get butter and cheese in lieu of rent for the land they were using. During summer the Lhasa traders would let their horses and ponies graze on the pasture at Chum, for which service we used to receive some money from them. There was one person in charge whose main duty was to inspect and collect from both the nomads and the traders. He would keep track of all these activities and from time to time he would come to Lhasa to settle the accounts. Thus we decided that we each would receive the yearly benefit in turn.

We had to decide where I would live. To the east of the Yuthoks' main house there was a smaller one which had been built in 1930 for one of our good friends, Commander-in-Chief Kalsang Tsultrim. Soon afterward he had shifted to another location, so this house was now vacant. In the interest of all it was decided that my husband would stay in the Yuthoks' main house and I would move to the smaller one. We also decided to share equally the liabilities. Regarding movable assets, I took only those things that were most necessary for me. Both my husband and myself were by nature easy-going with money matters and neither of us was greedy to possess more than our share. In this mood we separated all our properties as best we could into two equal parts, and then allocated these by drawing lots. We did the drawing in front of Jowo Rinpoche, the main image worshipped in our family shrine. This was how Delekling and eight of the other estates came in the drawing to my husband and the Tul estate along with the remaining eight estates came to me. When the official agreement was finalized, witnesses were needed from both sides to verify the details of the separation. My elder brother Wangchen Gelek stood as witness from my side and Tsepon Ngapo Ngawang Jigme, who was a relative of my husband's, stood as witness for him. As I have already mentioned, the agreement was drawn on the basis of the decisions we had first discussed in Chamdo.

When both witnesses had affixed their seals as signatures at the bottom of the papers, they were submitted to the government. The agreement became final when the regent signed his approval. Henceforth we were separate in the eyes of the people and the law. My husband wanted it to be clear also that all of his children were to be treated equally. By this he demonstrated great foresight in settling the family's affairs.

While this agreement was being finalized all the sons were in India studying, and only our daughter Thupten Choden and my nieces Tashi Paldon and Norzin Dolkar were staying in Lhasa. Although the nieces were from my husband's side, we decided that it was best if I kept Tashi Paldon while Norzin Dolkar went to stay with my husband. When all these details had been worked out, my husband helped me to shift to the smaller house. The house was not only small but it was also empty of furniture and other household goods. However, this did not sadden or discourage me. I began planning to build a new house for my children when they grew up. Thus from the beginning I thought of this small house as temporary. Nevertheless, when my friends and relatives came to know of my move, they visited me bringing presents which included various household necessities. With this help, setting up the new house was not a burden.

There was a monk from Drepung Gomang Monastery named Geshe Jinpa Ngodup who was an attendant of Kyabje Khangsar Rinpoche and who we had known since about 1930. From the very first meeting he had developed a close relationship with our family. Sometimes he would come to visit the Yuthok house and spend a week's holiday with us. Whenever there was family trouble we consulted him, and he always gave us good advice. Everyone who was close to us knew about Geshe-la's wisdom, and whenever he visited us, friends and acquaintances flocked around him for advice. Gradually Geshe-la became more and more like a psychiatrist. Like a true renunciate, whatever he did was in the spirit of helping others with no thought of gaining anything for himself. It was my good fortune when in 1946 at my request Geshe-la came to stay permanently in the little house with us. He had a special room, and his presence helped my religious practice. He remained with us until 1958 when he died of the flu. Even though Geshe Jinpa Ngodup helped me spiritually, it was not easy for me to readjust to living without the affection of my husband. But things, I thought, would change.

In 1948 my husband took leave from government duties and left for India to meet his sons who were studying there. With him he took our daughter Thupten Choden and some other children who were related. All were to be enrolled in the St. Joseph's Convent School in Kalimpong. After several months I set out for India with some servants to meet my children. At Kalimpong I again stayed at Pomdatsang Rabga's house. My sister-in-law was also staying there awaiting the arrival of my younger brother. Though the school vacation had not yet started, I was able to meet my children frequently.

During this time Shakabpa and my brother Lhawang Topgyal returned from the United States. While staying with my friend, both my husband and Shakabpa paid frequent amorous visits. As before, I found opportunities to be intimate with Shakabpa. It could have been embarrassing if either of them had visited me unexpectedly. My younger brother Lhawang Topgyal, his wife Dekyi Lhaze and their son were planning to go on a pilgrimage. I decided to join them as it seemed a good opportunity to break the unfortunate pattern that had taken hold of my life. Taking with me my son Dondul Wangchuk I left Kalimpong to visit some of the Buddhist shrines in India. I was not only relieved to leave Kalimpong and the ways of worldly life, I knew that in these holy places I could be refreshed spiritually.

Bodh Gaya was the first place we visited, and we found accommodations at a guest house. As soon as I could manage, I made the usual circumambulations and prostrations at the holy sites, and as I did so a very strong feeling of the unreality of this world came over me. I was thinking that not only were temples impermanent, but people too. Sooner or later every one of us would have to leave the mortal body. Moreover, as I thought about the sufferings in this worldly life, and especially the ones which I myself had been experiencing, the reality of this world began to fade. I began to think that if only I could practice religion as preached by Buddha, it would not only help me, but perhaps I could help other people by teaching them to understand the workings of karma. As a result of this, I began to have a strong desire to become a nun and to practice Dharma. When I told him, my brother Lhawang Topgyal expressed his admiration for my courage.

Pema Choeling Rinpoche, a lama from the Shang Pema Choeling monastery in Tibet, was staying at that time at the Tibetan monastery in Bodh Gaya. With my new resolution in mind I asked him to guide me when I took my first vows as a nun. He very kindly agreed to ordain me. I felt it a special privilege and honor to be ordained in front of the very tree where Buddha had attained his enlightenment. After that I had my head shaved. When I could not get a complete set of nun's robes, I wore only simple red garments with a yellow belt and some shirts bought from the market. Later I bought a proper set of robes and wore only those. Now that I was a nun, I looked forward to the secluded life and the freedom to give myself to devotion, far from the problems of the secular world. With a mind full of bliss I continued to visit all the holy places in Bodh Gaya. My family members and I continued on our pilgrimage to other holy sites in other parts of India. The whole journey took us about two months. We returned to Kalimpong by way of Calcutta.

Again I stayed with Pomdatsang Rabga and his wife. I was very much surprised when she said that she did not like the idea of my having become a nun. Very seriously she explained that I was still young, and might find it hard to live up to my vows. She was older than me by twenty-two years, and in her eyes I was still in my youth. It did not take long for Jomo Tsedron's prediction to come true. My husband began to visit me again and sometimes he spent the night in my room. He still wanted me as before and since my mind was full of desire, I accepted him. I had no wish to turn him down nor could I control the passion that was overruling my judgement. I was leaping about blindly. In a rash moment all my resolutions were broken. At the same time I was full of remorse when I realized that in my heart I was not ready to be a nun. While the idea was still beautiful to me, I could not live up to the restrictions it put on me. My hair grew out and I began to wear regular clothes again. Since it took a long time for my hair to grow back again, I often used to wear a wig whenever I was visiting friends or attending parties. But deep inside my feelings for a religious life had not changed. My karmas were still too strong to enable me to fulfill this wish.

Shakabpa was still staying in Kalimpong and came to see me several times when I arrived. He was disappointed to learn that I had become a nun, but I told him that I had had to take this step as I was fed up with mundane activity. He was very understanding and recognized my problems. During his visits we had much time to talk as friends, not as lovers. Very soon afterwards he returned to Lhasa, at which time we broke our connection and did not see each other at all. That was not the case with my husband. I continued my relationship with him even after I returned to Lhasa.

When I returned from India in 1948 I did not feel like remaining in Lhasa long. As soon as I could make the necessary arrangements, I went to stay in Dujung Kyibuk, one of the estates in the Tsang province that had come to me from the Yuthok family. Dujung was about twenty miles from the town of Gyantse and was one of the district headquarters in the Tsang province. The government sent an official to Dujung to act as the district collector, gathering the taxes from about one hundred families in the district. About twenty families worked on our estate and owed their allegiance to the Yuthok family. Their taxes were collected by a family member who then turned over the revenue to the government collector. The Dujung estate had been owned by the family for many generations. Seven or eight years before, we had leased that estate to one of our servants named Tsewang Rabten. It was arranged that he pay us about one quarter of the wheat harvest once a year from the farm production. Every year he paid some of this amount in money and some in grain. Payment was made after the harvest in October or November. After paying the amount due us Tsewang Rabten always had enough to take care of his family.

He and his wife had thoroughly cleaned my residence in Dujung by the time I arrived. They had also arranged for all the foodstuffs that I would need. Sometimes meat was available in Dujung from the butcher; otherwise Tsewang Rabten would send his servant to the nearby town of Gyantse for this and other necessary things. I had brought about seven servants along with me, but I kept only my maid servant Tseten Dolma and the cook Kalsang Wangdu who had both gone with me to Kalimpong. The rest of the servants who had accompanied us on the journey were sent back to Lhasa to join their families there.

From one point of view Dujung was not a very pleasant place to stay. There were no rivers, and water was very scarce. The farmers always had to rely on rain to cultivate their lands. Since the rains were not heavy there were no trees or green grass growing around. The land seemed to me like a desert, but even though our Kyibuk house was not a very good one, I was contented with whatever was available because my mind was at peace due to my religious practices. Even though our servant Tsewang Rabten and some of the other people in the area suggested that I not stay in Dujung during the winter, I wanted to remain. However, after listening to all the warnings from them and others I did take some precautions against the severe cold. I ordered thick woolen blinds made for the doors and windows to block out the piercing cold wind and had additional carpets brought for the beds. There were fireplaces in some of the rooms, so I sent servants to distant places to buy firewood and dung so we could keep fires burning all day. Thus I spent the winter without too much difficulty.

While my husband was still in Kalimpong I had no doubt that he was watching over our children. Even so when it was time for school vacation I sent Tseten Dolma and one servant to Kalimpong to check on them. They took along with them ten loads of Tibetan foodstuffs like dried meat, cheese, barley flour, and so forth. In wintertime the people in Kalimpong appreciate Tibetan foodstuffs, but in the summer we did not dare to send such things because they would only spoil in the heat. In those days there were no refrigerators.

Since in Dujung I needed two maid servants, I asked for two girls both about sixteen years old. These girls, Kalsang Dolma and Tsering Yudon, were selected from the people on our estate. They were very helpful and stayed with me for many years. I was very sad in 1959 that Tsering Yudon could not join us when we had to flee Tibet. She had to stay back to take care of her ailing child, but the other maidservant Kalsang Dolma managed to escape with us. After I left India for the United States she went to the Mundgod Tibetan Settlement in South India.

In 1949 my husband's son Rinchen Tsetan[4] married the beautiful daughter of the Choegyal (King) of Sikkim. His bride was known as Kuku-la, and made a great impression on all who met her with her charming manner and graceful appearance. Since I was in Dujung, I was unable to attend the ceremony.

In 1950 the Dalai Lama fled from Lhasa to Yatung on the border of India, along with his two tutors and most of his senior officials and attendants, among whom was my older brother Wangchen Gelek. His Holiness stayed in Dhongkar Monastery, which belonged to Domo Geshe Rinpoche.[5] He stayed there for six months while waiting to see the full extent of the Chinese invasion then taking place in Amdo and Kham. When the main Chinese army stopped short of U-Tsang, the Tibetan government returned to Lhasa. The Chinese had in effect taken over approximately half of Tibet's land area and population. We never knew from that time onward what would happen next. Stories of the destruction of monasteries reached us from Kham. Soon both Lhasa and other areas in Tsang were visited by refugees from this invasion, many of whom became resistance fighters secretly supported by the government of His Holiness.

It was in 1950 that Geshe Gedun Tashi, a monk from Drepung Losaling, visited me at this estate. I had earlier requested him several times to pay us a visit. Formerly Geshe Gedun Tashi had stayed in Drepung Monastery to study and later on had moved to Drakna Lhugug near the Potala to do a retreat. Drakna Lhugug is a hermitage situated on a small rocky hill near the Potala Palace, with a few small houses nearby. He had rented one of these with many peach trees growing in the courtyard that produced much sweet fruit. He was both learned and famous, so many people flocked around him to receive religious teachings and to take lessons in the scriptures.

Now he stayed in one of the rooms on our estate. Every morning he used to give me lessons from the scripture *Jangchub Lamrim*. He had many things to tell about religious practices and what our duties were in worldly life. He was always happy and ready to answer questions on any point I asked. We always took our dinner together and whatever was served to him he accepted impartially.

I was gaining so much from him that I was glad to accept his suggestion to go with him on a pilgrimage. He had been in Dujung for three months before we started on this pilgrimage to the Tsang Province. Besides our riding horses we had to take about ten mules for carrying rations and bedding. We were nine in number including the servants. The first place of our pilgrimage was Sed Gyudpa Monastery, then Sakya, and afterwards Lhatse Monastery, Jonang Taranath Monastery, and Tashi Lhunpo Monastery, which were all near each other. In this way we went to most of the monasteries and holy places in Tsang, and I took advantage of this opportunity to pray and make offerings. It is normal practice to give alms to the poor whenever one undertakes such a journey. Sometimes we stayed as long as five days in one monastery. In other places we stayed only a couple of days.

The pilgrimage with Geshe Rinpoche was a totally new experience for me. He was so learned and knew the scriptures so extensively that he not only taught me about how to pray but at each monastery and every holy place we visited he also would tell us the history of its origin and its special significance from a religious point of view. My faith in the religious life increased. Seeing all these monasteries under his inspiration and guidance, I became very happy. In all, the pilgrimage took one month and fifteen days. We returned to Dujung, where Geshe Rinpoche stayed on for another month. When he was ready to return to Lhasa, we made arrangements for his return journey by providing him with horses and escorts. A few months later I also returned to Lhasa. It was 1951. I had passed two and a half years in Dujung, a period in many ways reminiscent of the time I spent at the Treshong estate in 1930.

I considered staying even longer in Dujung because I was so happy and contented there. I had no special responsibilities and could spend as much time as I wanted with my religious practices. Also, my youngest brother Wangchuk Dorje was stationed in Gyantse as the government tax collector. Since Dujung is only about twenty miles from Gyantse, we often used to visit each other. These were always enjoyable reunions that I looked forward to with great happiness. Nevertheless, I began to feel that I should go back to Lhasa to see my children who were returning that year for their school vacation. It had been a long time since I had seen them, and I missed them very much. When the Kalimpong school vacation was about to start I sent some servants along with horses to bring my daughter and nieces back to Lhasa. My two sons remained in India during the winter holidays.

In 1951 thousands of Chinese Communist soldiers armed with modern weapons had first started entering eastern and northern Tibet. Later when I was staying at the old Surkhang house in Lhasa, my mother and I watched from the window to see about five hundred of these Chinese soldiers marching four abreast just like an army on parade past our house. Most of them had come all the way across Tibet on foot. Only a few were riding on mules or horses. I think they must have been the officers. They were coming to Tibet not on business nor on any peaceful mission, but as military aggressors saying that they were going to "liberate" us. I saw them carrying huge photographs of Mao Tsetung and others, which made me feel very sad, angry, and afraid. With tears rolling down from my eyes, I saw that my mother also was crying. Everyone including the servants was shocked and frightened. Great numbers of the Chinese started camping in parks and open areas. Very soon they occupied all the important places in Lhasa. To lure the Tibetans the Chinese gave many feasts, inviting important persons like government officials, nobles and abbots of monasteries. But the Tibetan response to their hospitality was very cold.

In order to influence Tibetans the Chinese spent money lavishly in Lhasa. This resulted in a sudden heavy rise in the price of all commodities. The prices of foodgrains and dairy products jumped eight-fold. Naturally the Tibetans in Lhasa were badly affected by these price increases. In many ways the heavy influx of Chinese soldiers caused all sorts of problems. About this time the Chinese had opened a new school in Lhasa in the house of the Zeshim family. Tsemad Rinpoche of Ganden Shartse Monastery along with some other learned Tibetans and a few Chinese were appointed as teachers there. The Tibetan teachers taught the children Tibetan history and Tibetan religion and culture. The Chinese teachers taught the Chinese language and customs. At first I had intended to send both my daughter and niece back to Kalimpong after the holidays, but when I heard that Tibetan culture and religion were being taught, I didn't think there would be any harm for the girls to attend. What the girls and I wanted most of all was to remain together.

About that time I began to think of constructing a new house. On the east side of Lhasa there was a large plot of land that had remained until then unused, and it was on this plot that I wanted to build our new house. When I applied to the Sonam Lekhung, the land office in Lhasa, for four acres of land for this purpose, the plea was easily granted; I was only to pay a tax every year for the use of the land. This particular plot had remained vacant for a long time because it was said to be haunted. Since nothing happened to us when we built our house there, we did not worry about the talk of ghosts.

In 1953 I first built a wall around the four acres. On the northern side of the enclosure I constructed a long but not very large one-storied building. After finishing the construction my daughter and I along with the servants all shifted from the small Yuthok house to the even smaller newly constructed one. Although our new home was not as large as our former one, there were two advantages: first, it was planned according to our family requirements and second, it was only five minutes' walk from the Surkhang house.

By now the Chinese had already started buying houses from the Tibetans. Even my husband had sold the large Yuthok house to the Chinese. Since the smaller Yuthok house that belonged to me was lying unused I asked him to sell it also, which he arranged. A cousin of my husband named Taring owned several smaller houses surrounding his own in Lhasa. My husband had rented one of them since his family was now smaller. His house was only a twenty-minute walk from mine. The Surkhangs had sold their huge old house the year before and had built a new one in a private park that had been in the family for several generations. This park was on a river and near my new house.

About that time the Lhangsur family sought the hand of my niece Tashi Paldon for their sons' bride. The proposal was accepted and the engagement ceremony was held at my house. I also gave her the dowry when she went to her new husband. The Lhangsur family held the usual marriage party lasting for five days, and we all attended. It was a happy occasion but none could foretell the misfortune that was to befall them later.

In 1954 the Chinese had invited His Holiness together with some high religious and government officials including my brother Wangchen Gelek to attend the first Chinese National Assembly to be held in Peking. The Dalai Lama traveled with his two tutors, Kyabje Trijang Rinpoche and Kyabje Ling Rinpoche, several great lamas such as the Gyalwa Karmapa, Sakya Trizen and Dudjom Rinpoche, who were heads of the other three Buddhist sects in Tibet, as well as many important abbots. The mother, brothers, and sisters of His Holiness also attended, along with three prime ministers, of whom the senior was my elder brother; the Lhagyari Trichen and other government officials. The entourage totaled about fifty people, while the servants attending them numbered about one hundred. The procession began very formally from the Norbu Lingka Palace to the Kyichu River about a mile away, with everyone on foot except His Holiness' two tutors and all the government officials who were on horses. His Holiness was carried in a yellow curtained palanquin held by eight servants wearing green robes and special broad-brimmed red hats with long red fringe. The entire population of Lhasa lined the road holding incense at the time of this ceremonial departure. The procession passed by the new Surkhang house. My mother and I waited with our family and servants in front of the wall that stood between our property and the road to watch the procession pass. Preceding the palanquin were the monks and the monk officials. His Holiness' tutors and other great lamas and prime ministers clustered around the litter in which the nineteen-year-old Dalai Lama sat in the lotus position looking out happily at everyone. Beside the palanquin rode his two bodyguards, and they were followed by his mother, brother and sister, and then the lay officials.

When the procession reached the river the most important personages proceeded in private jeeps, but most of the entourage had to ride in large army trucks. His Holiness' jeep was driven by Tashi, a professional driver from Kalimpong.

The trip to the Chinese border was horrendously difficult and took about two weeks. Had they proceeded in a caravan on horseback as the Thirteenth Dalai Lama would have traveled, the journey to the Chinese border would have taken at least two months. However, that would have been more comfortable than the violent bouncing of the trucks on the rough roads.

This road from Lhasa to Kongpo Nangtre on the Chinese border was newly built by the Chinese with forced Tibetan labor. My son Gyalten drove the jeep for the two tutors and their attendants and became very worried because the road was so terribly rough. My son remained with His Holiness' official party during the five or six months of the visit, during which their hosts made every effort to present the new China in the most favorable light.

The Tibetan New Year happened to fall while the party was still in China. His Holiness wanted the festival celebrated in the same way that it was in Lhasa, which included the promotion of one monk and one layman to the position of full-fledged government officials. Therefore that year the promotion (*shabtod*) was announced in Peking during the Tibetan New Year celebration. Phala Ngawang Tseten was given the monk promotion and my son was given the elevation to a lay official. My son stayed behind in Peking for one year to study Chinese at the University.

By the time my brother returned from China in 1955 I had constructed a large two-storied house adjacent to the small house I had built for myself the year before. The smaller house was then turned into servants' quarters. Now each servant had his own room, but the housing of the monks was not so easily solved. According to the divorce agreement the support of the eight monks from Beser Monastery fell on my side, but I did not have sufficient room even in the new house to keep them. Although they would still do special prayers for us as before, I requested them to remain in their own monastery where I would send them the same amount for their maintenance that they had received in the past. After they had gone we all, servants and family alike, greatly missed the presence of the monks in our house.

When my relatives and friends came to visit us in our large new home, they liked it so much that they suggested I have a housewarming party. I did not agree to this because everyone had given me many presents at the time of my separation in 1947 when I moved to my own house on the grounds of my husband's estate near Yuthok Bridge on the eastern outskirts of Lhasa. I did not want to give them the extra trouble of presenting me with more gifts so soon.

At this time my husband used to visit me and stayed with the Tarings in order to be nearby. For a time it seemed we might reconcile and live together again. One day while he was with me a messenger from the Kashag (Cabinet) office came bearing a letter announcing that His Holiness the Dalai Lama had appointed my husband, Yuthok Dzasa Tashi Dhondup, to the rank of *katsab* (an office just under that of prime minister) and directed him to join that office as soon as possible. My husband then called his manager Jigme Wangdu to come at once to my house for a conference, and it was decided to give the promotion ceremony at my new house where I could help him as much as possible.

It was customary that whenever an official was given a new appointment the first thing he had to do was to go to His Holiness the Dalai Lama to offer *kagyur jaldar* (the acknowledgement scarf) and *mentral tendod* (the ceremonial offering of money). My husband did this through the chamberlain. The Dalai Lama then ordered my husband through the chamberlain to serve the government with a pure heart now that he had been appointed to the rank of Katsab. With this order the kagyur jaldar (acknowledgement scarf) ceremony came to an end. It so happened that at that time the chamberlain was our own cousin, Phala Thupten Woeden.

As was the custom, on the day of the ceremony early in the morning my husband circumambulated the Tsuglak Khang in Lhasa to pay homage and to make offerings. Following this he reported to the Kashag office and then returned to my home for the official celebration. He was to sit on a high throne while everybody else was to be seated around him according to status. Everyone including the servants then offered scarves to him. For the next two days there was an endless line of visitors with relatives and friends all coming with scarves and presents. Though I personally had not celebrated the opening of my new house, I was glad that from the very first day it had been useful in this special way. I always used to think that the value of having wealth was demonstrated at just such times, whenever something in our possession becomes useful to others in a time of need.

My younger son Dondul Wangchuk, when he was about seventeen years old, returned from the Bishop Cotton School in Simla in 1954. Since he was interested in sports, he became a member of the football player's club in Lhasa. Along with my half-brother Jigme and some Tibetan Moslem youths, he was among the sixteen Tibetan football players who went to China in 1956 to participate in a football tournament. When the tournament was over, he stayed on in Peking to study in the same Institute of Minorities where my older son had studied.

My half brother Ngawang Jigme was the son of our father and Dawa Dolma, the woman with whom he was living in Chamdo while posted there as an official. She bore him a son in 1929 and died about two years later. Since Father's head servant Tsetho-la and his wife were childless, Tsetho's wife became the mama for the baby boy and took very good care of him. Father then became the dochi or governor of Kham, so that they remained in Chamdo for several years. When Ngawang Jigme was eight, they returned to Lhasa, and he was sent to an English boarding school in India. Our father was not very close to him when he was young. In India, Ngawang Jigme became fond of athletics and modern customs. Then when the Chinese came into Tibet in 1951, he was very attracted to their doctrines. Whenever we got together, he talked constantly about how wonderful he thought the Chinese were. This was very upsetting to our family, so on one occasion I said to him, "If you like the Chinese ways, do what you wish.

I want to follow our Tibetan customs. Since we are brother and sister we should just love each other, and not discuss politics.'' Even though we agreed on this and he gave me his love as a brother, he and his wife went to China in 1957 without saying a word of this beforehand to anyone. Afterwards, we heard that he had gone to work for the Chinese, which disappointed us greatly. He did not return to Tibet until 1980. During all those years he became a physical education instructor and soccer coach at a college in Shayang near Peking. Although we heard news about him in 1975, we never received a letter from him until he returned to Lhasa.

In the same year I sought permission from the Dalai Lama to wear eyeglasses during His Holiness' teachings because my eyes were not well. Permission was necessary because in our society it was considered disrespectful for common people to wear eyeglasses when meeting with high lamas or any high officials unless absolutely necessary. Such requests had to be made through the chamberlain, and so through him I had requested an appointment. One day the chamberlain very suddenly sent me an order to come to an audience with His Holiness. As bad luck would have it, on the day before I was to have this audience, a very sad incident took place in my niece's life. Tashi Paldon, who had been sent to the Lhangsur house as a bride only a few years before, now had one son. That day she and her husband Lhuntub Dorje with their little boy and servants had gone on a picnic to Tsedrung Lingka park. Having taken with them a mattress and some refreshments, they were sitting together resting on the bank of the river Kyichu. While Tashi Paldon, her son Namgyal, and some servants were busy playing in the river, her husband with one of the servants went walking along the bank of the river out of sight. When after a long time they did not return, another servant went to look for them. He met some women who described what had happened. About half an hour before, they had seen a man drowning. A second man had tried to pull him out of the water; however, he too was caught in a whirlpool and drowned. Both bodies had gone under water and out of sight.

The witnesses to this tragedy were so frightened that they did not know what to do. Finally one of the men had gone to the caretaker of the park to report the incident. A little while later the news reached the ears of the manager of the park, who was a cousin of ours named Tsarana Chimi. One of his family members immediately went to Tashi Paldon to inform her of the tragedy as gently as possible. The manager himself also went to narrate the whole incident to her, which he did with great skill and sensitivity. About this time some Chinese soldiers happened to pass by, and with their help, they found the two bodies and pulled them out of the water. It was the custom for a drowned person to be left lying face down in the hope that the water would drain out through the mouth and he would gradually revive, so the bodies were laid out in this fashion on the riverbank. A servant came to our house to tell of this sad affair. Immediately on hearing this my younger brother left for the park in the family jeep with his driver and took the two bodies to the Lhangsur's house where all the customary religious rites were performed. That night we brought Tashi Paldon and her son Namgyal to our house to stay with us for a few days.

The next morning was the day I was to go for the audience with the Dalai Lama, but because of what had taken place on the previous day, it would not have been proper to wear my best dress along with the usual jewelry as was the custom. I first prostrated before His Holiness three times and offered the scarf and mentral tendod. I told him about yesterday's tragedy and asked him to pray for Lhangsur's soul. Then he very kindly told me that I had his permission always to wear the eyeglasses if my eyes were not seeing well. Never before in my life had I had a personal audience with His Holiness. He offered me tea. I still remember how much joy I felt to be in his presence. The audience lasted about fifteen minutes.

My son Gyalten Wangchuk who had been attending the Peking Institute of Minorities had returned to Lhasa in 1956. Because there was beginning to be more tension with the Chinese, he stayed with me only a short time before leaving for

India. In Kalimpong he lived with my youngest brother, Wangchuk Dorje, until my husband's arrival, when he moved to his father's house.

Throughout all of this time, my interest in religion continued to grow. Since 1953 I had had a great desire to receive the blessings of the full teachings on *Jangchub Lamrim*, the text that describes the stages of the path to enlightenment and entering into the career of the Bodhisattva. These teachings included how to practice religion and generate the Bodhimind and the thought of enlightenment, not only for oneself but in order to relieve all sentient beings of pain and suffering. I had repeatedly requested my root guru to give this teaching and he finally consented in 1957. Early that year in Shidey Gompa Monastery in Lhasa, Kyabje Trijang Rinpoche gave the full teachings of *Jangchub Lamrim*, as well as the commentary on it, *Namdrol Lhakchang*, which was composed by his guru, Pabongka Rinpoche. These teachings were attended by about two thousand monks, fifty high incarnate lamas, and some lay persons including myself and my mother. Giving teachings day after day was a great ordeal and lasted for one full month and four days. Sponsoring such an undertaking was extremely expensive for a private person. In addition to elaborate preparations and large monetary offerings, all those attending had to be fed at the benefactor's expense. I felt very fortunate to be the sponsor. Looking back to those days, I remember with great pride and joy that I was able to please my guru. During this time my mother and I went to listen to the teachings every day, and sometimes when there were no classes in her school, my daughter Thupten Choden accompanied us. All during that time arrangements had been made for Kyabje Trijang Rinpoche to stay at Shidey Gompa. Since I was the sponsor, I was all the more eager to share Kyabje Trijang Rinpoche's blessings and urged all the family members and the servants to attend whenever they could.

Up to the year 1957 our family activities and experiences more or less had followed the customs and traditions of the Tibetan nobility. Most important of all and central to everything that we experienced was the teaching of Lord Buddha.

I have described the happy events of my life and the traumatic experiences, including the separation and divorce from my husband, and how even after the divorce from time to time conditions were such that I again temporarily assumed the role of a wife. But this was not all that was destined to occur.

In the wake of all this uncertainty the increasing involvement of the Chinese in the official affairs of the government was worrying us and causing us grief. Even before 1957 various Chinese offices were being established in Lhasa. The Chinese contacted those who owned buildings in an effort to purchase them for their own use.

I was not attached to the house I had just built two years ago and in fact thought it might be wiser to sell it since very bad times appeared imminent. I had told friends that I might sell if I could get a good price. Soon afterwards a Tibetan official named Sumdowa Gyaltsen Yonten, who was working for the Chinese, approached me on their behalf to ask if I would sell. If I would, he assured me that I could get a good price. Although I wanted to sell, I decided to discuss the idea first with my daughter who said to do whatever I wished. Later I approached my mother and older brother who told me that I should make up my own mind. Then I went to pray before our image of Tara and performed a divination, which told me not to sell. To do the divination I wrote on two pieces of paper "sell" and "not sell", rolled each small piece up and placed them in balls of dough that had been weighed very carefully beforehand to make sure they were perfectly equal. Then I placed the balls of dough in a bowl and rotated it faster and faster until one jumped out. I sent Sumdowa a message that I would not be selling. Later when I arrived in India, I never felt any regret about this, since it seemed to me that it was not my karma to receive that money. Many other people whom I knew well, both friends and relatives, sold their houses to the Chinese. No one felt secure anymore, and we must have begun to realize that the Chinese would soon take our houses without payment if they wanted to do so.

Since our uncle Surkhang Pema Wangchen had accompanied His Holiness the Thirteenth Dalai Lama into exile in India in 1910 where he stayed with him for two years, our family was quite aware that something similar could happen again. When the Chinese and Tibetans were fighting in Lhasa in 1912, not too many buildings were damaged, but as fate would have it, both the Yuthok and Surkhang houses were almost completely destroyed. The Yuthok house was gutted by fire and the Surkhang house demolished by dynamite set off by Tibetan soldiers in underground tunnels below when it was being occupied by Chinese officers. After the war, both houses were rebuilt.

Clearly remembering these not-too-distant events, we were afraid of what might happen now since there were many Chinese soldiers in Lhasa once again. When the Dalai Lama attended the Buddhajayanti festival (the 2,500th anniversary of the birth of the Buddha) in India in 1956-57, my husband, who had accompanied him, remained there and never returned to Tibet. His son Rinchen Tseten had married the daughter of the Choegyal of Sikkim and had been living in Sikkim and Calcutta since 1949.

After the Surkhang family sold their house, our younger brother was sent to Kalimpong to help prepare the way for the rest of our family to depart Tibet. At that time our older brother Wangchen Gelek was the senior cabinet minister and was well known to be a strong opponent of the occupying Chinese.

All the happenings of my personal life that I have been describing tell something of the life inside Tibet. Looking backward I can now see how gradually the life and culture of my country were showing definite signs of eroding and breaking down, but none of us could imagine the tragic circumstances that would inevitably follow in a very short time. No one had understood or heeded the warning given by the Thirteenth Dalai Lama during the last days of his life:

> Unless the people of Tibet eliminate corruption and again embrace the substance of the teaching of the Buddha, there will be great suffering for all the people.

13 Escape

From 1951 until 1959 the Chinese had carefully planned to topple the existing system in Tibet and consistently tried to trick Tibetan leaders into believing that their intentions were harmless. At last in March, 1959, the Chinese made demands which threatened the safety of His Holiness the Dalai Lama. This triggered the beginning of the organized revolt by the Tibetans in Lhasa against Chinese aggression. Since the Chinese had finally gone too far, the people were at last frightened into action. Tibetans, men and women, rich and poor, poured into Lhasa from all the surrounding areas. With much difficulty they left their villages to hurry on foot or horseback along the dangerous mountains roads leading into Lhasa. We did not yet know that early in the morning of March 10th so many people had gathered together to shout their protests in a demonstration against the tyranny that had invaded their peaceful life. Marching continuously in a long procession around the Norbu Lingka summer palace, they bravely demonstrated against the Chinese Communists. This was the beginning of big trouble.

I did not know that this was also the end of the first part of my old life and the beginning of a new one. Only my daughter, aged twenty, and myself were living in our new home in

Lhasa at that time. My husband and our two sons were living in India. Although our house was only a twenty minute walk from the center of Lhasa, neither my daughter nor I nor any of the servants knew what was happening there. There were so many unconfirmed rumors that we did not know what to believe. We were not in ignorance for long. About nine A.M. on that day my mother sent us a message about the gathering revolt. By now everyone in Lhasa knew that His Holiness the Dalai Lama had been ordered to come unaccompanied by his regular entourage to attend a theatrical show given by the Chinese. In addition to being an insult to the position of His Holiness, the people very much feared for his safety. When this news reached the villages in nearby areas, thousands of people quickly joined the residents of Lhasa to surround the palace. In this way they hoped to prevent His Holiness from falling into what looked to them like a trap. With a mass of humanity around the palace how could the Chinese use force?

Rumors were falling like hailstones. I was very shocked and my mind was flying in every direction. I could not concentrate. We had heard that my elder brother and three other shapeys (cabinet ministers) had gone to the Chinese barracks as representatives of the Tibetan people. They went with the intention of informing the Chinese that it would not be possible for His Holiness the Dalai Lama to attend the Chinese show even though the Chinese had issued an order demanding his presence there. Finally around five P.M. we heard that the shapeys including my brother had been released from the Chinese barracks and had returned to the palace.

We were happy and relieved that they were safe for the time being, but at the same time we were very sad and frightened thinking about what might happen next in Lhasa and in Tibet. Lhasa had become a deserted city overnight. We heard that there were no people around the Barkhor market place where all the shops were closed. I remembered how my brother was one of the foremost persons who had all along flatly opposed the Chinese. He had been very bold and straightforward without caring for his own safety. The Chinese had many times directly and indirectly warned him of dire consequences if he did not reform his views. For about six months the Chinese had been giving him that warning. Once my brother was even summoned before Chinese authorities in the middle of the night. So remembering all this I naturally felt very afraid and worried about his fate.

Besides that, when the Chinese troops first came into Tibet, they had offered me the job of administrative secretary in their main office. I had each time flatly refused on the pretext that I could not see well. In my heart I was determined never to work for them at any time, whatever the consequences. I was never interested in politics. But now I had to face the reality of the moment. There was no doubt left in my mind that the Chinese had started a new and vicious campaign. I felt it was no longer safe to stay alone with my daughter and servants in our house. Leaving our loyal servants in charge of the house, around nine-thirty A.M. I walked with my daughter and one maid servant to my mother's, which was not far away. All we could do there was to wait for further developments but at least we family members were together in one place.

On the following day my mother, my younger brother Lhawang Topgyal and my sister-in-law Dekyi Lhaze, together with my daughter and me, discussed the danger from all sides until we decided that the only wise thing to do was to leave Lhasa, the sooner the better. At that time we called our younger sister Lhawang Dolma Rongtrak, who was living nearby, and begged her to come along with us but she refused. She did not want to leave without her five children, not to mention her eldest son Palden Gyaltsen and daughter Norzin Dolkar who were away studying in Peking, China. She thought that after the Chinese had established their military power, they would not be so ruthless and the situation might change for the better. Thus she remained in Tibet waiting for her children to return.

Since we suspected that something like this might happen, we had been sending some of our belongings little by little whenever we could in our truck to Phari on the border of India for nearly a year. We owned a large truck with which we used to carry on our shipping business between Tibet and India. Our driver was from Ladakh, which became a part of India in the early nineteenth century. He was named Gyaltsen and had worked for us for many years. He had a wonderful sense of humor and was always joking with everyone. For several years he went back and forth from Phari to Lhasa for us about twice a month, transporting products such as wool and yak hair to sell in India and bringing back Indian goods ordered by merchants to sell in Lhasa. When he arrived in Phari, he used to stay with our Surkhang business agent Tsedor for a few days. These trips were very profitable so we gave Gyaltsen excellent wages. He had a servant of ours who attended him as a helper. Through this business we had slowly been sending our own valuables out of Tibet on the regular trading trips for at least a year. When our personal goods arrived in Phari, they were sent on by Tsedor to our younger brother Wangchuk Dorje in Kalimpong. We sent such things as clothes, furniture, silver articles and other personal items. Although it was helpful to us later that we had done this, we never thought to purchase a house in Kalimpong or elsewhere but only rented one. Other families had also started to send some valuables to India for their future use in a similar way.

The driver had completed another trip and was now back in Lhasa. We could not now consider using the truck or our own jeep because only a few people in Lhasa had their own vehicles and it would be too conspicuous. There was another detail that presented a real problem. There were many priceless images, thangkas, and other religious objects in our family chapel which we would have to leave behind. The idea of taking these things with us did not enter my mind. They were so sacred I did not dare even to touch them. I could only pray for their safety with deep sorrow in my heart. Among them there was a very ancient two-foot statue of the goddess Tara exquisitely fashioned of copper, bronze, and gold. I always used to pray to this image. My heart is full of remorse even to this day because I had to leave her behind. I will never know what happened to her.

For the moment there was no time to think about these things. We had to plan our escape carefully. Since the locality around the Surkhang house was full of Chinese, we had to find an inconspicuous way to leave. After much talk, we decided that since it was too dangerous for us all to leave together, my mother, daughter and myself would first go to a friend's house located below the Potala. A few hours later my brother Lhawang Topgyal and his wife Dekyi Lhaze would join us there. Because His Holiness was in residence at the Norbu Lingka, the Potala area was almost deserted. A day or two later, as soon as we could finish our planning, we left the Surkhang house dressed in our most ordinary clothes. My mother, daughter and I left first on foot taking with us some servants and later that day my brother and his wife joined us at our friend's house outside of town.

On the third day in the morning we were finally ready to depart. We were wearing simple dresses borrowed from our friends. We carried our jewelry concealed around our waists. Setting out on foot, my mother, daughter, and I left first, followed a few hours later by my brother and his wife. We had planned to meet that night at our estate at Phupo Cheh, which was not too far away. My servants had been instructed to bring three horses from the Yuthok house, and my brother's servants were to bring four horses from the Surkhang house to Phupo Cheh. We had tried to plan every detail as carefully as we could but still the danger was great.

The day I left my home, I gave all the keys to our senior servant Tashi Tsering. At that time I told all the servants to stay there happily, hoping and expecting that I would be able to return when the danger was over. Little did I guess that many of them would join me in a few days or weeks. None of us could really believe the magnitude of the tragedy but by now all of us were feeling that the danger was real.

With all of these worries running through my mind, I was quite lost. Instead I found myself walking along the road with my mother and daughter and some servants. After going only a short distance, we met a mule-cart with a nice driver. When we asked him to take us to Phupo Cheh, he agreed and of course it was much easier and faster for us to ride in the mule-cart with him. This village was our first destination but the mule-cart driver explained that he could not take us all the way because his house was in another direction. On parting we gave him a few *gnulsangs* (Tibetan money) in appreciation for his kind help and climbed on foot the hill trail which would take us to Phupo Cheh where we expected to meet my brother and his wife. They came in time along with the four horses sent from the Surkhang house and my three horses brought by my servants. The next morning we could continue our journey to Darkhang; however, this was not on the main route to India. We needed more horses and some mules together with supplies for the long journey so we had to take a detour from our escape route. This is why we went to Darkhang, which was one of the estates of the Yuthok family under the ownership of my husband. Now that we were some distance from Lhasa, we could attend to the details for our travel. The servants in charge of the estate were very helpful and did not hesitate to assist us in our escape. In addition to the eighteen horses and mules we needed, they even gave us other necessities for travel such as tea, chang, eggs and two loads of fodder for the animals. During the two days it took to arrange all these details, nine more servants came from Lhasa to join us.

Some of the villagers from Darkhang and Phupo Cheh wanted to help us in another way. When they learned of our plans to leave Tibet for India, about fifteen of them came to us and requested that we not leave. They told us that we could stay hidden right at the top of the hills in the caves and they would bring us our meals every day. They did not have any idea of the dangers of a modern sophisticated war. They never thought that bombs could be dropped from the air. They were remembering how in olden times whenever there was a war, people used to go to hide in caves. This had happened in 1912 during the war between Tibet and China. They remembered that at that time members of the Yuthok family, including my husband with his mother, two little brothers and a sister, had remained hidden in those caves for several months near the village until the war ended. Nothing further had happened to them, so they thought that the Communists could not harm us if we hid there too.

We had to explain to these villagers that now we would go to India to meet my husband, sons, and brothers and then when it was safe, we would return to Tibet. Thus early in the morning of March 17th, 1959, we left Darkhang to start the long journey to India. Our party consisted of twelve people with eleven mules carrying food and bedding. Our next destination was Nethang Village where we planned to lodge at the Dolma Lhakhang temple. The road we followed most of the way was the main one which led to India, so it was usually one of the busiest routes in Tibet. Due to the threat of the movement of the Chinese troops that day, we did not meet a single soul along the way except a group of four traveling in a mule-cart. Seeing them in the distance we naturally became alarmed, but on approaching nearer we recognized those four persons. They were the Rato Khyongla Rinpoche and his entourage. Like us they were also fleeing.[1]

Just before reaching Nethang's Dolma Lhakhang temple, our next halting place, we saw about two hundred Tibetan volunteer guerrillas near the north side of the Tsangpo River. All of them had dismounted from their horses and seemed to be waiting for someone. We never expected to come across such an organized Tibetan force and were very relieved to see them. When they asked us where we were going, we replied that we were running away to India. The guerrilla captain and my brother Lhawang Topgyal talked for sometime. The captain explained to him that a permit card would be necessary for us to leave the country.

My brother then went with the guerrillas to their headquarters in Tashigang nearby for the necessary permission so that we ladies had to go on alone to Dolma Lhakhang. On arriving, first we took a little rest while the servants prepared tea.

When my brother caught up with us, he had in his hand the necessary permit card. Then he told us that he had seen the guerrilla forces crossing the river heading towards the south. That meant that we must not remain in that place for the night. Since the guerrillas had already left, there were no forces to protect us. We thought also that the Chinese would be coming any moment to look for them. When my mother heard this news, she agreed that we must leave right away. So although we were already weary from the day's travel, we started on our journey again going towards the south. We followed the route of the Khampa guerrillas, but before starting we took time to eat hurriedly our lunch of tsampa, dried meat and dried cheese. We also gave fodder to the horses and mules. Even then we delayed further, long enough to visit the Dolma Lhakhang where there was a very holy image of the goddess Tara. Our hearts were relieved as we made our prayers to her.

Danger seemed to come from every direction. A little later when we were crossing the river, the mule I was riding slipped on some stones and went down on its knees. Fortunately one of the Khampa guerrillas was passing by and came to pull up the mule. I was then able to complete the crossing safely. After making the crossing, the Khampa soldiers traveled in an easterly direction and were soon out of sight. As we continued westward we remembered how helpful they had been to us.

After crossing the river and traveling onwards alone for about eight more miles, we decided to stop overnight at a monastery named Ushang Do Lhakhang, which was famous for its very ancient historical monuments. We knew this place very well because we had gone there on pilgrimage. It was the only safe place we could find to lodge for that night, and we had to divert from the main road to reach this monastery hidden in the corner of a valley. We slept in the courtyard there.

The villagers in that area had not heard anything about the disturbances in Lhasa, but when we told our story, they gave us what help they could. On the next day, the 18th of March, they helped us prepare to leave about six A.M. Just when we were about to resume our journey we met the Senior Tutor

of the Dalai Lama, Kyabje Ling Rinpoche, who was also fleeing to India with four attendants. He purposely had come
that way to see the famous monastery. We were very fortunate
to get his blessing for our onward journey.

We had not gone far when we met two Tibetan officials
who had dismounted from their ponies and were leading them
along. Naturally we hoped to hear some news from them.
They told us how the previous night about eleven o'clock the
Dalai Lama, his family, two tutors and some other officials
had escaped from Lhasa. Included in the escape party was
Wangchen Gelek, my elder brother. The Dalai Lama's party
had crossed the Tsangpo River safely. We were all very happy
and relieved when we heard that my brother Wangchen Gelek
was among those who had escaped with the Dalai Lama's
party. We knew that he had been with him in the Norbu Lingka
Palace but we had had no further news. After talking with
these two officials, we were a bit more optimistic as we continued our journey by climbing the Je-la pass between Jethang
and Lumpa.

Then we met with good luck. While making the difficult
climb, we met Kyabje Trijang Rinpoche, who was traveling
with about six attendants. He was also fleeing to India and
had dismounted from his horse on the top of the hill to take
rest. Since he is my root guru, meeting him in this way gave
me special courage to face the unknown. Before we parted he
blessed us by placing his hand on each of our heads.

Our good luck continued. Higher up we met my brother
Wangchen Gelek who was traveling with two servants a short
distance behind His Holiness, together with a group of about
thirty other officials and their servants. We had not seen my
brother since the tenth of March. That was nine long days ago
so we were happy and excited to find each other safe. First he
told us that His Holiness was a short distance ahead and if we
traveled quickly, we might get a chance to see him. He then
arranged for us to stay that night at the village of Ramay
Kyishong with a friend of his.

The Dalai Lama already had crossed through the pass. Accompanying His Holiness was a large group spread out over the trail, totaling eight hundred people. The group of officials, the family of His Holiness, and all of their servants perhaps came to one hundred. Then there were about three hundred Khampa guerrillas and two hundred regular soldiers. Another two hundred monks followed accompanying the abbots of Drepung, Sera, and Ganden. Our brother was the only official who had any family members with him. He had stayed the previous night at Ramay Monastery. Although we had missed him, we were greatly relieved to know that he was safe. We doubled our journey on that day but still did not have the luck to meet His Holiness until we arrived inside India. His Holiness and his party including my elder brother had taken the short-cut to Yarlung but we went instead to Kalung. My brother had an estate there and wanted us to check on it for him.

After traveling two days from Ramay Kyishong, we reached a place called Chide Shol. One of the relatives of my neice Tashi Paldon's family, named Namgyal Sholme, lived there. We stayed in his house only for one day. During the whole time we were treated so well that we felt as if we were back in our own home. Like our house, theirs was very beautiful and spacious. On the following day when we bade them goodbye, they gave us much advice about the difficulties of the terrain lying ahead. They also warned us to be very careful about the Chinese. To our utter surprise three days later we heard that they also had had to flee from their house leaving everything behind. However, we did not meet them anywhere on the way as they went by another route.

It took us seven days to arrive at Kalong from the village of Ramay Kyishong. We had to cross a vast plain since we were not following the main route. There were only a few people living in this empty area in tiny village houses, and few if any lodging places where travelers could stay at night. Villagers here were usually very reluctant to give unknown travelers any shelter, but since we were a party of women with only one man, they were more sympathetic and less hesitant to accommodate us. They could not suspect us of being bandits.

Sometimes we were fortunate to pass near a friend's house where we could stay. At other times we stayed with nomads in caves. In any case we soon discovered that the people in that part of Tibet did not yet know of the trouble going on in Lhasa. Until then their way of life had been undisturbed. Naturally they asked us many questions as to what had happened, but they found it hard to believe the Chinese aggression could actually happen this way. At last we arrived at Kalung, a village situated in a vast and beautiful valley with many fields of barley and other crops. In Kalung we found the precious images and the ancient religious articles in my brother's estate undisturbed. We did not think to take any of these things with us from there. All we could think of was our own safety and how to continue our journey. Of course we did take whatever foods the villagers gave us because we had much further to go to reach India. Although it seemed peaceful there, we stayed for only one night as we were told the Chinese Communists were quickly coming nearer.

We went next to Diku. Here the news was frightening. One of the government officials whom my brother Lhawang Topgyal knew had come there. We heard from him that the Chinese Communists had dropped bombs on Lhasa on the 20th of March from two A.M. until six P.M. We learned that thousands of people were killed and more were injured. The summer palace with its vast grounds as well as other parts of Lhasa were the object of the attack. We were very shocked and my mother and all of us began to worry a lot about our younger sister Lhawang Dolma and her children who were left behind. All the time my mother was thinking about their fate, wondering whether they were still alive or not. When I heard all this, I was overcome with grief. To add to our sadness we learned that the scriptures and religious collections of art in the monasteries that had been blessed for centuries by the high lamas had been destroyed. However, I realized that we were not the only people that had suffered the destruction of their most sacred treasures. Throughout history it had happened to other nations too, and would probably happen again. In this way I tried to console myself. I remembered the religious images we had at our home and pictured them in front of my eyes, knowing I would never see them again.

We left Diku for Tsona as soon as we could. The distance was far and we arrived at midnight. Earlier on the same day the Dalai Lama had arrived there with his entourage, and was staying not far away. My brother Wangchen Gelek came to meet us. While the Dalai Lama and his party were moving on to Tsona, an airplane flew over them and returned toward Lhasa after circling above for some time. The Dalai Lama and his party decided it would be wise to leave post haste for the North East Frontier Agency (NEFA) in India. His Holiness had requested that my younger brother Lhawang Topgyal join his party because there was no one else in it who could speak English. Therefore Wangchen Gelek, Lhawang Topgyal and their wife also traveled in the group that departed for the border.

Since my mother, daughter and I were so exhausted, we remained in Tsona for two additional nights to rest. After that we also left Tsona for the NEFA. We heard later that the Chinese arrived in Tsona soon after we had left. However, by then we had arrived safely at Mon in India, near the Tibetan border. Although Mon is in the NEFA and the people of Mon are Tibetan, their dialect is different from ours and their customs strange to us. Even so, they were hospitable and wanted to help us. It took three days from Mon to reach Chu Dongpo, which is also in the NEFA but a little further inside India. There were one hundred Indian soldiers stationed in Chu Dongpo to protect the border. We met a Sikkimese friend there whom I had known long ago when he was working for the Indian government in Kalimpong. His name was Dawa Babu and he invited us to stay with him for the night. He made us very comfortable but we dared not stay even this close to the border any longer.

After leaving, it took us four more days to arrive at Tawang Monastery, as the roads were very tedious. Once we reached it, we rested there for seven days. My maternal uncle Guru

Rinpoche had been a lama in the Tawang Monastery, and although he had died many years before, his retainers looked after us very well.

Now we had to face a new reality. We realized that there was no chance of our returning to Lhasa in the near future so we had to sell our horses and mules. Since there was no good market there for these animals, we had to sell them at a very low price. The onward journey was by jeep and trucks provided by the Indian government, and from the monastery it took another four days to reach Bomdila. There we had to wait fifteen days for the necessary permit cards to reside in India. After we received formal permission, the Indian government sent both a jeep and a van to take my mother, my daughter, myself and the servants onward to Tezpur. Even so we were very tired when we arrived there about midnight. The Indian government had done a great deal to help us refugees.

By this time my mother had become ill but our journey had not ended. Our escape route took us quite far east of Sikkim to the Darjeeling-Kalimpong area where we had our children in school. The mountain roads from Mon only passed due south to the Indian plains from which we would have to travel north again back into the Himalayas. We therefore passed through many Indian villages to come to Siliguri on the plains of Bengal from where we took the mountain road north again to Kalimpong. My younger brother Wangchuk Dorje was living there. We stayed with him in a beautiful little house called Odling House. In Tibet he had been a monk official holding the rank of Khenchung. Later he was deputed to Gyantse district in southern Tibet as a Monk Trade Officer. In 1956 he anticipated the tragedy which was to happen in Tibet and left for India with his nephew Nuchin Thinley. Since then he had remained in Kalimpong and had forsaken his monk's vows to live with a beautiful Bhutanese lady named Pema Yangzom. Since my mother was disappointed that Wangchuk Dorje was no longer a monk, he was somewhat ashamed in front of her and had arranged for Pema Yangzom to stay in a separate house so that we would not meet her. However, they continued to live together after we left and had two children, a daughter Dechen Pedon and a son Jigme Wangchuk who was recognized as the reincarnation of Decho Yongzin Tulku, a Kargyupa lama. There were many Tibetan refugees in Kalimpong who all told the same horrible stories we had heard in Diku a few days back of the bombing in Lhasa. Naturally all our hearts were burdened with grief. None of us could guess whether or not we would ever be able to return to Tibet.

From 1940 onwards I had been coming from time to time to Kalimpong—once with my husband, once with my brother and several times with our children and the servants. Our children had attended the English boarding school in Kalimpong. Sometimes after settling them in their hostels, we went to Calcutta for sightseeing and shopping. Other times we went on pilgrimage to the Buddhist holy places in India and Nepal. There was no shortage of funds, so we went wherever we liked. Now it was 1959. We had come to Kalimpong once more, but this time as refugees, although we still did not realize it. Our friends and relatives in Kalimpong were still as nice to us as before, in particular the Banyak Athing family who to this day still remain good friends. Although there had been hardly any changes in the Kalimpong I had known before except for a few new houses, the happiness and peace of mind that I had experienced when Tibet was an independent country were not there. With the future that was so uncertain, my heart was heavy.

My husband had moved to India in 1957. He was followed a few months later by Tsering Dolkar, daughter of the Sholkhang family. My husband's elder brother's first wife had also been from this family. I had heard rumors on several occasions in Lhasa about my husband and her. Until I reached India I was not sure whether these stories were true or not. To my dismay, it was common knowledge amongst the Tibetan community in India that they were living together in Calcutta. I was saddened by this turn of events, but since I knew my husband well, it did not surprise me. I had hoped so much to see him on my arrival in India and was hurt not to find him waiting when I finally got there. When he heard of the revolt and the flight of His Holiness along with the exodus of thousands of Tibetans and that we were among them, my husband sent my son Dondul to Tezpur to receive us. My brother Wangchuk Dorje in Kalimpong also sent my niece Choden Dolkar. But in the turmoil of passing through Tezpur in the middle of the night, we missed them. On receiving a message that we had safely arrived in Kalimpong, they rushed back to meet us here three days later.

We had been in Kalimpong for about a month when my husband came into my life again. He had written to me to say that he would visit. I received him with mixed feelings. I was happy to see him, but nothing seemed permanent in our relationship. He stayed at Rinchen Tsetan's[2] house, paying me frequent visits and at times sleeping with me. After staying for a while in Kalimpong, my husband, my son Dondul Wangchuk, my daughter Thupten Choden (Thupchu) and I with a few servants left for Mussoorie by rail, over one thousand miles to the west in northern India. At that time my elder son Gyalten Wangchuk was working in Buxa near Siliguri for the Tibetan government-in-exile. Thousands of Tibetan refugees were pouring into the Indian border town of Buxa, and he was one of the members of the reception committee deputed to receive them. As a result, he could not accompany us to Mussoorie. My husband had also been summoned to Mussoorie for some government business. There the Dalai Lama was forming his government-in-exile, which would later move permanently to Dharamsala.

My elder brother Wangchen Gelek had been asked to continue as shapey or cabinet minister in Mussoorie where he stayed in a house called Kildare with my other brother and Dekyi Lhaze. After staying with them for two days, my husband and I rented a house for ourselves. Since my mother was not at all well, she and my younger brother Wangchuk Dorje stayed on at Kildare House with the others. My husband was never happy in Mussoorie although he had been maintained in his same position with the Tibetan government-in-exile. Our

younger son Dondul Wangchuk had also been given a temporary position to serve under His Holiness. I requested my
husband to stay on a while longer and give Dondul a chance
to serve his country when everyone's help was crucial. Furthermore, I needed him to share in making the many decisions that we faced. I had great expectations that he would
listen to my plea and stay a little longer, but to my utter dis-
appointment, my request fell on deaf ears and he left for Calcutta with our younger son. Until that time I had always taken
the initiative, trying on some level to hold our family together,
but now I made the firm decision to face life alone with our
children.

My mother moved to Mussoorie a month after I did and was
never well. We consulted several doctors who examined her
carefully. Finally she was admitted to an American Christian
hospital. In spite of everything we could think to do we all
could see that her condition was not improving, so at last we
brought her back to Kildare House. During her final days my
mother was very lucky. Once His Holiness the Dalai Lama
happened to visit the hospital where she was staying so that
she had a special opportunity to receive his blessings and advice. A few weeks later on the very morning of her death, my
brother Wangchen Gelek brought our root guru Kyabje Trijang
Rinpoche to see Mother. In his presence she took the vows
of a nun that she had been longing for. A little later in his
presence she passed away in a very calm mood around six-
thirty in the morning. My three brothers and I were all present at her bedside at this time. She died at the end of 1959
at the age of sixty-seven from cancer. It gave us some comfort
that my brother had all the usual religious ceremonies performed in the same way that we used to do in Tibet.

Even though I felt Mother had been very much blessed during her last days, I never felt happy in Mussoorie after she
was gone. I missed her too much, so after a while I left with
my brother Wangchuk Dorje and daughter Thupchu for Sarnath and Bodh Gaya where we visited Buddhist shrines. At
each of these sites we offered lamps and religious rites in

Mother's name. This pilgrimage took us about six months. While in Sarnath, my brother Lhawang Topgyal wrote to say that an English couple, Major and Mrs. Knight, who were sponsoring my nephew Nuchin Thinley and niece Jampa Yangchen, had agreed to sponsor my daughter as well. She was to leave for London in 1961 to study nursing. At the end of this pilgrimage we returned to Kalimpong to stay with Rabga Pomdatsang for a few months. There we met our old friend, Mrs. Zeshim Sonam Yangkey. We were related by the marriage of her son Pema Singay to one of the Yuthok daughters, Tseten Dolkar. Since we had known each other very well, she introduced me to one of her friends, Chhoto Ram, a merchant who lived in the Kulu Valley.

Kulu Valley is the most beautiful hill station in India. Zeshim Sonam Yangkey was well acquainted with Kulu Valley and advised me to go there, so I left for that place with my daughter Thupchu and old friend Chonzed Gedun Lhawang, a monk from the Drepung Monastery. My maid servant Kalsang Dolma and her husband Lobsang Tsering accompanied us. These two were the only servants who had remained with me. Among the others, one of them had wanted to return to Tibet and the rest had preferred to stay in Gangtok or Kalimpong. For a few days we all stayed in Chhoto Ram's house in Kulu. Later we moved to Raison, a nearby village where Mr. Nirmal Chand Thakur, a friend of Chhoto Ram's, rented me a new Indian-style cottage some distance away overlooking the valley. The Kulu valley was so peaceful and so like Tibet, it began to give some rest to my heart. The climate of the valley is similar to Lhasa, and the area is well known for its apple orchards, which were the main source of trade and business there. Even though in some places the altitude of Tibet is very favorable for growing fruits such as apples, peaches and grapes, very few farmers planted these trees because it was too difficult to maintain the orchard. Our friend in Kulu told us the story of how apples had become popular there in the first place. During the First World War a few British soldiers had settled there, married Kulu women and planted apple trees.

The inhabitants of Kulu thereafter began to plant these trees also. The three or four families who had planted the first trees are still in Kulu and are prospering. During the two months that my daughter was with me in Kulu, we were able to visit various parts of the countryside. The weather was beautiful and we were able to go up to Rohtang Pass. Since my daughter spoke good English, we were able to make friends with some of the European families who were living near us.

After two months, my daughter and I left for Calcutta, where my brother Lhawang Topgyal was waiting for us. He assisted us in the application and the paperwork that were necessary for my daughter's departure for London. He was also in touch with Major and Mrs. Knight regarding her. My two sons, who were staying with their father, visited me frequently. My ex-husband called on us a few times. Since the whole process of my daughter's departure was going to take several months, I decided to return to Kulu and leave my daughter with my brother. My ex-husband could also watch out for her needs.

Since my return from Calcutta, there was little for me to do. I lived simply and although my expenses were few, since coming to India I had been selling my jewelry to meet them. Being back in Kulu gave me peace of mind and freed me from worries about money. It was during this time that my uncle Khemed Sonam Wangdu came to stay with me for fifteen days. This uncle together with his brother-in-law Khemed Tsewang Rinzin had managed to escape in 1959, but the rest of their family could not come with them. Both were government officials—my uncle was Commander-in-Chief and Tsewang Rinzin was Tsepon, an officer in the Revenue Department. One day we all went together by bus up a high mountain road to Manali. It resembled my birthplace Drak in Tibet so much that it took our hearts back to the mountain life we had known. We stayed there for several days.

After my uncle left, the monks of Spiti Monastery in nearby Lahaul invited Kyabje Trijang Rinpoche to bless them. Even though this area had been for a long time under Indian authority, the people there were mostly Buddhists. Since ancient times Lahaul Spiti had been a Tibetan kingdom. Although it had become an Indian territory in the nineteenth century, the Tibetan culture and religious practice there had not changed. The monastery in Lahaul Spiti where many Tibetan Buddhist monks live and meditate is the second largest monastery in the Indian Himalayas. Since Spiti Monastery was only two days' journey from Kulu, I invited Kyabje Trijang Rinpoche to pay a visit to my place on his way. He had come from Dharamsala in a jeep with two servants while four more attendants followed by bus. He blessed me with his presence in Kulu for two days, one day on the way to Spiti and one day on his return from the monastery where he gave teachings that lasted for a couple of weeks. The trip to Spiti was very tiring for him. The roads were so rough that he had to go on horseback. The monks had originally made special arrangements for him to rest elsewhere overnight in Kulu. Instead, he paid me the honor of staying at my house while his attendants and some monks from Spiti stayed at the place that had been prearranged.

Later I went into retreat for two months. During that time the Raja Mata Parik of Nalagarh, mother of the Raja of this princely state, had come to the Kulu valley to spend the summer. She was renting for the summer a lovely cottage belonging to an English family named Johnson, which was quite near ours. When going for a stroll one evening, she learned that a Tibetan lady was staying in a house nearby and came to see me out of curiosity with her younger sister. My landlady, Dolma Nirmal Chand, had told them that it would not be possible for them to see me since I was in retreat. After five days they came to see me again. My landlady refused to admit them, so they had to return home. Again after a week they came the third time to try to meet me. In desperation they urged our landlady to tell me that she was a mother of a Raja and that she had not come to seek any favors. My landlady then told me all this while the Raja Mata and her sister waited outside. Because there is an exception permitted for interrupting for a short time the study and prayers of a retreat provided it is not against the religious activities, I told her that they might come in to see me.

The Raja Mata stood little over five feet tall and was on the plump side, but in her beautiful sari one did not notice. She was bright and cheerful, and her hazel eyes sparkled. It was impossible to resist her charm. My landlady acted as interpreter. I knew a little Hindi, so I could speak a few words directly to her. Our talk began with our family backgrounds. I learned that she was the daughter of the Raja Ragunath Chand of Mehalog. She was the widow of the Raja of Nalagarh who had died at the early age of forty. She had one son. Nalagarh was a small but important kingdom in the Punjab, forty miles from Chandigarh. They were Sikhs. When India had gained her independence from the British, they had lost their titles and most of their lands. Now the Raja Mata occupied a small section of a palace and was subsidized by the Indian government. She told me that the house I was now living in was not very safe. She invited me to her palace in Nalagarh which was much safer because it was always protected by ten guards.

Raja Mata Parik was twelve years older than I while her younger sister Chand Kumari who lived with her was younger than Raja Mataji by six years. By our conversation I could see that Raja Mataji was a religious person so I started to think that it would be nice to stay with her. I thanked her for her kind invitation but told her of my inability to join her right away. I had heard that His Holiness would be coming to Kulu to give a sermon in early winter, which I wanted to attend. She appreciated my decision and a few days later left for Nalagarh after giving me her address. We kept in contact through correspondence until I was able to visit her. Though Raja Mataji had invited me to live with her, before I made a decision I wanted to see her place first since I knew that I would not want to stay there if it was not conducive for prayers. I made the journey to Nalagarh with a monk named Namgyal Chophel, an old acquaintance from Lhasa, who knew Hindi well and had been living in Kulu for some time.

Leaving for Nalagarh by bus, the journey took us almost

twenty hours. Raja Mata did, indeed, live in a palace. After a steep climb we reached the place where it stood overlooking Nalagarh. The huge gate at the entrance was guarded by police. The palace itself was built along three sides of a square with a large courtyard in the middle. Raja Mata occupied a few of the fifty rooms in the main section, while the guards and servants lived in the wings. There was a small household staff consisting of only three servants and a cook. The palace grounds were lovely and secluded. There were trees all around; it was like being in a woodland. I liked the trees, which gave me the good feeling of being close to nature. In the middle of the courtyard grew a large guava tree. Raja Mataji thought that we had come to stay permanently with her and asked me to choose the room I liked. I chose one adjoining her room. At that time we stayed for only two days but when we left to return to Kulu I told her that I would be returning soon. It was not until December, 1962, that I was finally free to return to Nalagarh after living in Kulu for two years. Accompanied by my maid Kalsang Dolma and her husband Lobsang Tsering I took all my belongings with me, which were few.

Life at the palace was very pleasant. At six o'clock in the morning the servant brought a glass of tea. For two hours after that I meditated and attended to my prayers and devotions. Then we had breakfast of toast and jam and Indian sweets. I spent the morning with my correspondence and working to improve my Hindi. The Raja Mataji and her sister and I used to have our meals together. Although they were vegetarians, I soon got used to their diet. Whenever I wanted meat, I could go to a restaurant in the town. I stayed with her for the next two and a half years until I went to the United States. I used to try to speak Hindi with her and her sister. I looked forward to their trips to Agra and Delhi, and I would always accompany them. Raja Mataji would go to Agra to visit her guru at the Radha Soami ashram there. Although she was a Sikh and I was Buddhist, we both got along well and respected each other's beliefs. In Delhi I met her son Raj Surinalas Singh Nalagarh who was working for the Indian government. She also introduced me to her niece, Mrs. Bikram Singh, with whom I became very good friends. I sometimes stayed with her at the Red Fort Military Camp where her husband was serving as a Colonel. In this way my circle of friends outside Tibet was continually growing.

For these first years as a refugee I had been going here and there seeing new places and meeting new friends. Although almost six years had passed since I had fled from Lhasa, I was still looking for a home away from home. Sometimes I thought about going to the U.S.A. My brothers and family, my niece Choden Dolkar and my son Gyalten Wangchuk had all settled in Seattle, Washington, where my brothers had received appointments at the Sino-Soviet Institute at the University of Washington. While I was thinking about this, I heard about Mrs. Freda Bedi in Dalhousie. She was doing some wonderful work there by arranging for the education of many young incarnate lamas who had been able to escape from Tibet. They were taught English while Tibetan scholars taught them scriptures and religious observance. I wrote to Freda Bedi who asked me to come to see her. I went to Dalhousie, which is a beautiful, cool hill station, and stayed at a guest house with an American girl, Jane Werner. With their help I began to learn a few words of English. Jane and I have been good friends ever since. In our guest house I also met Mr. and Mrs. Kenneth M. Ranney, who were concerned about the plight of the Tibetans. Mrs. Bedi asked them to sponsor me to go to the United States, which they agreed to do before leaving three or four days later. I then returned to Nalagarh to discuss my plans with Raja Mataji. I told her that I wanted to go to the States, and that I had found a sponsor. She reminded me that I was not young any more—I was fifty-three—and thought I might find it difficult to adjust to a country that was so different from my own. Furthermore, she said, I had no western educational background and did not know what to expect. She really wanted me to stay in Nalagarh with her. However, I was determined to go, in spite of her misgivings. My brother's family, son Gyalten Wangchuk and my niece Choden Dolkar were already in the States, where they seemed to be quite happy.

There was a good deal of red tape to be dealt with before I could get away. I had to go to Delhi to the Bureau of His Holiness the Dalai Lama, as well as to Indian government offices and the American Embassy. There were applications, interviews, and papers to be signed. I shall always be grateful to T. C. Tethong, an official in the Tibetan Bureau. Without his help I would never have gotten through the maze of rules and regulations. Before I left Delhi, I had a private audience with His Holiness the Dalai Lama at which I told him of my plans. He was very understanding and gave me his blessing, wishing me well on this start towards a new and different life.

In June, 1965, I left Delhi by Air France for Geneva. My younger son Dondul came to see me off at the airport. Since this was my first trip to the West, he asked one of the lady passengers to keep an eye on me since I knew so little English. Twice while we were in the air she came to check on me. When we made the stop in Israel, she came to say goodbye. Her thoughtfulness boosted my courage and morale. I had trouble in Frankfurt where I had to change planes. At the information desk I was given directions but I became confused. I said a silent prayer to my guru and it helped. Some ladies noticed my dilemma and asked me where I was going. When I showed them my ticket, they told me to come along with them as they were going to Geneva too. I was then able to relax and went to breakfast with them. My cousin T. W. Phala was then the representative of the Dalai Lama in Switzerland. In Tibet he had been the chief of protocol for His Holiness. He met me at the airport to help me through immigration and customs, and then drove me to his home in Geneva. I was amazed when I first saw a Swiss grocery store. There seemed to be an endless variety of canned as well as fresh meat, vegetables and fruits. I had never seen anything like it before.

I stayed with my cousin for a month. During that time I visited Trogen, a small town that is a center for refugee children. This center, the Pestalozzi Children's Village, contained nine or ten homes for children from various countries of the world. There were two homes for Tibetans with a total of fifty children where Tethong Rakra Rinpoche and his wife along with his sister Tethong Sopal, acted as foster parents. I stayed in Trogen for a week observing how the children were being treated and helped. The guardians were kind and the teachers patient. The children were being educated for life in the western world but at the same time were taught their own Tibetan religion and customs. I knew that children adapt easily to a new environment and learn a new language quickly, but it pleased me to know that they would not be allowed to forget their homeland and cultural heritage.

After my month in Geneva, I flew to London where my daughter Thupchu met me at the airport. She was studying nursing at the St. James Hospital in Brixton. Since she was living in the nurses' quarters, I could not stay with her. I was not, however, to be cast on my own resources. I stayed with my nephew Nuchin Thinley, the son of my brother Wangchen Gelek, who was also studying in London. He was generous with his time and took me sightseeing. After seeing most of the tourist attractions in London, I visited the Pestalozzi Children's Village in Sussex. In the Tibetan home there were thirty children. Geshe Tsultrim Gyaltsen, a religious teacher, and Mr. and Mrs. Drupok were taking care of them. The program in Sussex was similar to the one in Switzerland. Children were being prepared for life in a western world without losing knowledge of their background. For me, meeting other Tibetans made me feel less a stranger in a new country.

After I stayed ten days in England, my daughter saw me off for New York. It was a good thing my Tibetan and Mongolian friends were at Kennedy Airport to meet me. I could never have coped with the confusion by myself. Mr. T. T. Liushar, an old childhood friend and the New York representative of His Holiness the Dalai Lama, had arranged a hotel for me. I had thought that Geneva and London were overwhelming but New York left me speechless. I was dazzled by the skyscrapers, the thick crowds everywhere, the hundreds of theatres and shops. Then there were the subways, the au-

tomats and the incredible amount of traffic. I walked around
in a perpetual daze, wondering if I could ever adjust to the
activity of an American city. I stayed in New York for seven
days, then flew to meet my brother in Seattle.

I was eager to see all my relatives who had come to the United
States. My niece Choden Dolkar was the first of my immediate family to emigrate in 1960. She had been sponsored by
Mrs. A. L. Shelton of California. Mrs. Shelton and her late
husband had spent several years in eastern Tibet back in the
twenties. They spoke Tibetan and knew my country well. My
brother Lhawang Topgyal had met the Sheltons in the United
States in 1947 when he came as a member of the Tibetan Trade
Delegation. He had kept in touch over the years and asked
them to sponsor her.

I stayed in Seattle for a year with my brothers. While I was
there, Mrs. Ranney, the wife of my sponsor, came to Seattle
to visit me. I was sorry to learn that Mr. Ranney had died.
Although when I knew him in Dalhousie he had seemed in
perfect health, a few months later he died of cancer. She invited me to return with her to her home in California. As we
drove there it surprised me to travel such long distances without seeing anyone walking on the roads. It was so different
from my part of the world where almost everybody went on
foot. The fast highways were lined with restaurants and motels.
Accommodations were plentiful. It took us four days to reach
Garden Grove. I stayed for ten days during which time Mrs.
Ranney showed me her part of California, including the fascinating world of Disneyland. Her parents, son and many
friends came to visit. Communication was difficult as my English was limited, but somehow we managed to understand one
another. I was gratified at being made so welcome.

I flew back to Seattle, and enrolled in the Edison School
of English and Adult Education along with my sister-in-law
Dekyi Lhaze. There were other Tibetans in the class and for
all of us the first days were difficult. But I progressed with
added help from my brothers at home. I was learning other
things too in my brother's house. I was shocked to see him

helping his wife with the housework, drying dishes and helping to keep the place clean. It made me very uncomfortable.
In Tibet it was unheard of for a man to do any domestic chores.
But gradually I got used to it. I was beginning to adjust to
the American way. Also I felt that if America was to be my
home, I must prepare myself for citizenship, which I did, and
was naturalized in 1974.

Looking back, I think I have been very lucky, in spite of
the anxieties and difficulties I have been through. I have seen
many countries of the world, which has enriched my life. I
am comforted by having close family members near at hand.
While I look back nostalgically at the life I knew in Tibet,
a way of life that is probably gone forever, I am gratified to
know that displaced Tibetans are spreading their culture and
values in every country that has opened its doors to them. At
the same time we have added new values to our old ones. We
have been met with kindness and friendship. We have been
welcomed, and we owe new loyalties. But in our hearts will
always lie, undiminished, a love and loyalty to our roots and
the land of our birth.

14 My Heart Is My Home

The Tibetan life as it was in my day is no more. In Tibet itself the Chinese have imposed their order everywhere. The guiding and stabilizing influence given by His Holiness and the Tibetan Buddhist lamas, monks and nuns has been almost completely eliminated and in its place the law of the Chinese forcefully substituted. Tibetan refugees have gone to many different countries carrying with them the essential principles of Tibetan culture. Wherever we Tibetan refugees have found a new home, we have wanted to absorb the best qualities of that culture while at the same time retaining our own Buddhist values. We have kept as the cornerstone of our religion the principle of compassion.

In order to educate young Tibetans and help them cope with the modern world, the Dalai Lama with the help of the Indian government and other foreign relief agencies established many residential and day schools in various parts of India and Europe. As a result a new generation of Tibetan boys and girls are being educated in the modern way while keeping alive their native culture and religion. The two largest of these residential schools are the Tibetan Children's Village in Dharmsala, which with the assistance of the government of India and different international relief organizations houses several thousand orphans, and the Tibetan Homes Foundation in Mussoorie, similarly funded and organized.

Many cultural and religious institutions have also been established. In Dharamsala there are the Tibetan Medical and Astrological Institute, the Library of Tibetan Works and Archives, the Institute of Tibetan Performing Arts, and the Center for Tibetan Arts and Crafts. In New Delhi there is the Tibet House and in Sarnath the Institute of Tibetan Higher Studies, which has received world-wide recognition by university scholars. The main aim of these institutions is to keep our culture and traditions alive. For instance, the Center for Tibetan Arts and Crafts emphasizes the art of making images, religious objects, and jewelry. Wherever there is a settlement of Tibetans, centers of Tibetan handicrafts have offered training for the refugees, many of whom have become self-employed. Instead of becoming dependents, we have been able to manage our own support and at the same time retain our identity.

Most of the major monasteries of Tibet including the three big monasteries near Lhasa have been reestablished in India. This has made it possible for many young monks and nuns to receive both a religious and a modern education. Inside Tibet the Chinese have tried to eliminate the Buddhist religion in the life of Tibetans. Our ancient monasteries and priceless art works have been destroyed. However, outside Tibet, Tibetan lamas and learned monks have been active. They travel to places near and far, wherever there are Tibetans, to give teachings, vows and initiations and to give advice and consultation in both mundane and religious matters. They have established over five hundred religious centers in various parts of the world. Tibetan Buddhism is not a dying religion but a living force in the modern world. Because of its popularity among both Americans and Europeans, it may be one of the fastest growing religions today.

Nuns and nunneries formed an important part of Tibetan life and served both a religious and social purpose. When the Chinese destroyed all the nunneries and forced most of the nuns to marry, only a few were able to escape to India. Gradually the nuns who were in India organized themselves and sought to establish a nunnery. With the help of the Tibetan government-in-exile and some foreign agencies their dream became a reality when the first nunnery, called Ganden Choling, was built in Dharamsala. Some new members were admitted to their fold so that today there are about eighty resident nuns. When I visited this nunnery in 1983, I was glad to see that it had been built in the same pattern as the nunneries in Tibet and that the nuns are observing strict discipline as in the olden days. Now somewhere in the Kangra valley near Dharamsala there is another small nunnery at a place called Tilokpur which has about twenty nuns, and in other parts of India there are many new nunneries.

We Tibetans have spread all over the world. About one hundred thousand live in India and Nepal, perhaps another three thousand in Europe and approximately two thousand in the United States and Canada. His Holiness the Dalai Lama has not forgotten us wherever we are. At the request of the Tibetans living in the United States, he made his first visit there in 1979. We were very happy to see how he was received by both the government and the American people. Besides receiving private audiences, we had the opportunity of hearing religious teachings from him. His Holiness was even invited to give discourses in several Christian churches where he responded warmly to the interest Americans showed in our beliefs. Later in 1981 he came again, this time at the special invitation of Geshe Lhundup Sopa of Sera Monastery, the head of Evam Deer Park Buddhist Center and a professor at the University of Wisconsin. Geshe Sopa had requested him to give the Kalachakra Initiation in Wisconsin. Many of my Tibetan and American friends attended the ceremony. In fact the Americans who came from all over the United States outnumbered the Tibetans by several thousand.

This ceremony is an introduction for the participants into a perfected vision of the universe. The Kalachakra is believed by Tibetans to be the most esoteric and openly powerful form of the Buddha. His depiction in a body that is both male and female with many faces and arms represents his expanded ability to help all living beings. Those trying to attain Buddhahood imitate this mentally through visualization and meditation to develop the ability to help sentient beings. In order to practice this meditation, one must be taught by someone who has himself attained these abilities and who can visualize himself and the universe in this highly developed and perfect form. Therefore the Dalai Lama is the ideal teacher. The rituals include the actual reconstruction in the form of a sand mandala of this model of the universe, which was Buddha's highest vision. Hundreds of thousands attend for the blessing it confers and so that they will be enabled to practice this meditation in the next life, if not in this one. For the Dalai Lama to give this initiation in a foreign country is considered by Tibetans to be a great historical event. Kalachakra, which literally means "the wheel of time," is the Tibetan culture's perfected vision of the evolution of the whole planet that shows history in a positive light.

The members of my family who were in America did not miss this wonderful opportunity. My daughter and I went together from New York where we were living to Cleveland to join my niece Choden. Our friend Michael Harlin drove us in his car from New York. Because the weather was so hot and his old car was not air conditioned, we decided to fly for the remainder of the trip from Cleveland to Wisconsin. My son and his family along with the wife of my late brother and their son Nuchin came from Seattle. For the first time since 1959 my daughter, my son with his wife and children, and my niece with her son were all together. But the pleasure of being together was secondary to receiving the Kalachakra Initiation for which we had come.

His Holiness has always encouraged us wherever we might be in both secular and religious matters. For example, at the end of his sermon at the Kalachakra ceremony, he advised us about how to live in a foreign country. He has urged us to follow the law of the country in which we live and to pay special attention to our health since the climate is far different from

that of Tibet. He has encouraged us not to give up the hope
that one day our country will be free again and in the interim
to do our utmost to be self-sufficient wherever we might be.
Most Tibetans have been successful in this. But most impor-
tantly, he has encouraged our faith in Tibetan Buddhism by
showing us how to keep our own religious practices wherever
we are.

Even the practice of finding the new incarnations of great
lamas has been continued. The sad news that my root guru
Kyabje Trijang Rinpoche had passed away in Dharamsala in
1981 reached me in New York less than twelve hours later by
telephone. At first I felt very depressed to think that I would
never see him again. For me it was like falling into a deep dun-
geon. Then I reminded myself that he would be taking another birth, and if my karma was very good, I might see him
in his new body.

In India Palden Tsering, Rinpoche's private secretary, arranged for all the necessary funeral rites. At the same time,
he was looking for some auspicious signs which would indicate where the reincarnation would take place. When the cremation pyre was lit, white smoke rose in a north-easterly direction. During the ceremony everyone present witnessed a
remarkable phenomenon: some sacred relics (*ringsel*) appeared
in the form of one large and many tiny crystal-like balls in the
metal plate on which a Buddha-statue was standing. The altar was outside and in front of the cremation pavilion. Yet towards the end of the service the relics had disappeared, which
was taken to mean that the followers of Rinpoche were not
supposed to inherit them.

After the fire had died down, the presiding lamas opened
the entrance to the cremation pavilion in order to remove the
ashes. At the base of the pavilion they saw what appeared to
be the footprint of an infant and another one of a child of about
four. Then to their great joy they found a solid form about
one foot high amidst the ashes which had apparently been
created from Rinpoche's heart, tongue and eyes. The form,
which looked like the body of Rinpoche, was seated in the

same left-leaning posture in which he used to sit. It even had some protrusions resembling hands and legs. This extraordinary relic was then placed on the altar for the disciples and the public to see and pay homage. Some time later, a silver stupa with gold ornaments was constructed to contain the sacred relic, as required by tradition. The stupa is now inside the great hall of Kyabje Trijang Rinpoche's monastery in South India.

Next the most important task was to search for the new incarnation. Palden Tsering was looking for information about any unusual child born to Tibetan parents. A few months later he received news of a six-month-old baby born in the hill town of Dalhousie. Palden Tsering, accompanied by the late Rinpoche's attendant Jamyang Tashi, visited that family on the pretext of some business matter and saw the child. The baby showed signs of great joy and uttered sounds of happiness while reaching out to the two strangers. He sat in the lap of Jamyang Tashi and clung to him as if afraid that he would leave. He also showed great delight in witnessing religious offerings. Thus the search began in earnest.

A search party comprised of Palden Tsering, Lati Rinpoche (one of the late Rinpoche's close disciples) and an official of Ganden Shartse Monastery went to a number of Tibetan settlements in India and Nepal, all of them located to the northeast of Dharamsala. They inquired about all recently born boys who showed any kind of special qualities. Following that they visited places in other directions and inquired about extraordinary children. The search party compiled the names of five hundred forty-four male children and, through careful examination of their data, reduced the list of candidates to ninety-nine.

Following the established rule, the search party conducted the crucial personal test for the candidates by letting each one look at an assortment of sacred objects, including several used by the late Rinpoche. Some children were simply frightened by these objects while others showed a keen interest in them. Under the guidance of some high lamas the list of possible choices was then reduced to eight through this kind of examination.

This search continued until the end of 1984 when His Holiness the Dalai Lama visited the Tibetan settlement at Mundgod, South India, where Trijang Rinpoche's permanent residence had been newly located at Ganden Monastery. By this time there were eight candidates, one of which was expected to be the incarnation of Trijang Rinpoche. There His Holiness carefully performed special prayers and a special method of divination in front of the sacred stupa housing the relics of the late Rinpoche. As a result two names were left, one of which would be determined to be his new incarnation. His Holiness then foretold that the final decision would be revealed in a few months. One candidate had taken birth in Ladakh and the other was the one from the Dalhousie Tibetan Handicraft Center, the son of Sonam Topgyal and Lobsang Dolma.

In 1985 at the request of Palden Tsering, the Dalai Lama agreed to make the final decision. This time the prayers and divination were done in Dharamsala before the private altar of His Holiness with Palden Tsering and Lati Rinpoche. It was then revealed that the true reincarnation of Trijang Rinpoche was the candidate from Dalhousie. Although by this time the child was only two years and five months, he was already showing extraordinary intelligence and in many ways he was different from other children.

Within a few months the little reincarnated Rinpoche together with his family were brought to Dharamsala amidst traditional pageantry and ceremony. At that time I was in Calcutta. I watched a video tape brought to me by Jamyang Tashi, one of Rinpoche's attendants, showing his welcome to Dharamsala and the beautiful sight of the arrival of the little reincarnated lama in a special car. I could easily see the same dignity in the infant Rinpoche which I had many times observed in my root guru. The roads for several miles leading to Dharamsala were lined with Tibetans who had come to pay their respects to the new incarnation. The little Rinpoche acknowledged their greetings with a bow of his head. Every once in a while he showed the fatigue of a child, but only for a moment. Two months later I myself went to see him in Dharamsala, and upon seeing my face, the little Rinpoche greeted me as if he were recognizing me. On meeting this small child, immediately the image of my root guru came into my vision. My heart was extremely happy and full of faith in knowing that I was seeing him in a new body.

In 1985 at the request of many Tibetans His Holiness again gave the Kalachakra Initiation in India at Bodh Gaya, the place where Buddha himself achieved enlightenment over two thousand years ago. This time it was attended by about two hundred fifty thousand people, mostly Tibetans from all over the world, including a large number who had come from Tibet. There were also many Westerners who had come for the initiation. It was very hard to fit such a large number of people in the small sleepy village of Bodh Gaya, and accommodation became a big problem. To solve this a Tibetan welfare association was organized. The Indian government loaned a large number of huge tents, each of which was given a number. All around Bodh Gaya wherever there was space these tents were pitched. The Tibetans had to pay only a small amount of money to stay in one. The state government had taken great initiative to provide water, electricity, and rations to all at a controlled price as well as medical care. I was more fortunate than most because many months before, on my request, a monk friend had rented a house for me and my relatives. Whatever the accommodations, there was a spirit of cooperation and togetherness everywhere. Some had come from Tibet only for this occasion and would return there. Others were refugees like me whom I had not seen for many years. I also met some distant cousins who had come from Tibet, from whom I had not heard since 1959.

In Bodh Gaya while I was inside the huge tent that had been erected on the bare ground for the Dalai Lama to perform the Kalachakra ceremony, my eyes rested on the dais where soon he would be seated. My memory went back to the year 1954 when His Holiness gave his first Kalachakra Initiation in the Norbu Lingka summer palace just outside Lhasa. I remembered how in the midst of beautiful trees and flowering bushes there was a big tent like this one erected near the palace for the initiation ceremony. Inside at one end there was a dais with a throne for him, and around this were seated many important lamas, monks, and laymen who had come from all over Tibet to receive the initiation. They were waiting as we were waiting now for His Holiness to appear. For seven days we sat together in that tent to receive this important and lengthy initiation ceremony. But we never guessed how much this experience would give us the courage and wisdom to endure the perils lying ahead of us.

Now it was 1985 and I was one among the quarter million people gathered for another Kalachakra Initiation. In my heart I could feel that we were still one people with one religion living under the inspiration and guidance of His Holiness. For two weeks we sat with focused attention to absorb the teachings that preceded the initiation. In the evening when the ceremony had finished for the day, we would meet together, relatives and both old and new friends, to talk and laugh as before. We told each other about our present lives, and the many who had come at great sacrifice and risk from Tibet also told their stories.

When the last day of the ceremony had finished, the time had come for parting. We all took with us the inspiration which His Holiness the Dalai Lama had planted in our hearts. Along with this we found that the brotherhood of our people, both those living in Tibet and those living as refugees, has endured and that the ideals of Tibetan Buddhism and culture have profound meaning even today.

Postscript
by Michael Harlin

I first met Mrs. Yuthok accidentally when I was an under-graduate at the University of Pennsylvania in 1968 on the fourth floor of the old Hare Building. The oldest building on campus, it had been built of a rare soft green stone shortly after the Civil War, and housed the Smith Alchemy Library. I had be-gun to explore the vast Gothic structure, which was being emp-tied for demolition, climbing the immensely steep staircases to the upper floors where collections mouldered in gloomy high-ceilinged rooms. Each week more was removed to stor-age in the new library, which made the rooms seem larger but wilder looking, with endless tall oak cabinets standing haphaz-ardly open. Following an obscure back passageway which con-nected to adjoining Logan Hall, I noticed an Oriental woman sitting alone in an empty room. I was worried for her safety in such an isolated place, and asked if I could help. She spoke virtually no English, but indicated she would like some tea. I went back down the huge dark stairs to the student union building next door to get tea, and returned with it to the woman who told me to call her Amala, which means Mother in Tibe-tan. There were to be many, many more trips up and down those long stairs for tea in the coming year.

I found out that Mrs. Yuthok had been hired as a Tibetan

tutor for one of the graduate students in the South Asian Studies Department. Evidently the student changed his mind and never appeared. However, Mrs. Yuthok immediately assumed that I was her student, and my instruction began. Our lessons proceeded according to what was then called the "Peace Corps Method," which meant one was supposed to learn a language by conversing directly with native speakers who knew little or no English. Thus without the use of texts, we began. The following term I registered officially for her course and continued for seven years, more often than not as her sole student.

More profoundly affecting than the experience of a new technique for learning a language and the discovery of a new culture was the process of becoming the adopted son of my new Tibetan mother. Fairly rapidly I became a part of her extended family. Since I was an only child, this was a bit of a shock, but always an enjoyable one. What struck me most about my new family was the absence of concern for personal privacy combined with extraordinarily fine manners and lack of curiosity about others' personal affairs. Although certain qualities of refinement and noblesse oblige were probably peculiar to my new family's aristocratic background, I found later that most Tibetans have a similar combination of natural poise and relaxed warmth. They always seem to know how to take things easy and enjoy themselves.

I was astonished at the Tibetans' utter lack of resentment for their sufferings or hatred for the Chinese for having invaded their beloved homeland. I never heard anything worse about the Chinese than remarks such as "They are really quite bad," spoken in tones one might use to criticize a terribly naughty pet dog when one knew it was hopeless to expect otherwise. I enjoyed tremendously the medieval simplicity of belief in the miraculous along with the most subtle psychological insight, and above all, their exquisite but absolutely informal manners, ever considerate for others and unconcerned for oneself.

It was not until Amala took me with her to India in 1973

that I began to realize that her position in Tibetan society was unique. Her guru Kyabje Trijang Rinpoche, the Junior Tutor of His Holiness the Dalai Lama, was very sick, and Amala wished to receive his blessings. She had not been to India since her departure in 1965; it was my first trip.

It is difficult for a Westerner to conceive of the awe and love Tibetans have for the Dalai Lama, and of the absolute faith they have in him. His prestige among his own people is greater than that of the Queen in England, or the Pope in the Catholic world. His presence is believed to be a supernatural window through which divine energy radiates. A number of other great lamas in Tibet are revered almost as much—the heads of the major sects such as the Gyalwa Karmapa, the Sakya Trizen, and Dudjom Rinpoche; the personal tutors of H.H. the Dalai Lama, Trijang Rinpoche and Ling Rinpoche; and others such as the Panchen Lama, and various great living saints and meditation masters.

I was slow to realize what a privilege it was to be living under the roof of Trijang Rinpoche when we arrived in India. There was no formality, just an immense quiet of profound reverence which surrounded his tiny monastery. Amala was a very close disciple of his. Over the ensuing months, I was told by countless monks both high and low from all sects what great good she had done for them in Tibet. The monks adored her. The idea of taking a trip just to dispense charity was also new for me. Her intention in visiting her guru was not for the purpose of receiving something from him, but to have the happiness of giving to him and to as many as possible in a very concrete way. From what had grown to be a very intimate knowledge of her life in New York, it appeared to me that Amala's means were quite modest. Therefore the extent of her generosity absolutely astounded me.

I began to realize that Amala was not just a wonderful Tibetan mother, but a sort of super Amala. Although her title in Tibetan, "Lhacham Kusho," denotes the highest respect, people kept finding themselves calling her Amala instead, which was quite uncustomary. She is in many respects like her grandmother Lhagyari, very heavy, very religious, and in a way very powerful. Remarkably few Tibetans are heavy, and I was struck on the trip that the only other fat women I met were the Gyal Yum, mother of the Dalai Lama, and the Queen Mother of Sikkim, noted for her piety. I had read that the great woman saint Jetsun, who lived to one hundred and fourteen years, was fat. Perhaps it was from sitting so much in prayer. In any case, Amala's girth made going very slow when on foot. Tibetans may consider these comments disrespectful and odd; but to my Western mind these observations seemed to hold more than mere coincidence.

The following year when I returned to India alone on a Fulbright scholarship, settling in was made much easier because of the contacts arranged by Amala. After I returned to America, I worked for the John D. Rockefeller III Fund for several years, implementing programs to support traditional arts in the Tibetan refugee community in India. While in New York, I often made Amala's home my own. Although not particularly small by New York apartment standards, it always overflowed with both Tibetan and Western visitors from all over the world. A changing crowd of six to twelve people might be living in two rooms, all seemingly on different sleeping schedules because of jet lag or time zone differences. Wonderful food, endless tea and delightful hospitality were always forthcoming. There would of course be room for another without any tension or irritability; and although privacy was lacking, Amala always did her meditation, never bothered or upset at all if she were disturbed. Sometimes during certain portions of her visualizations she was not supposed to speak, and if interrupted would communicate with hand signals, apologizing for her inability to help just when needed. Her apartment was a nerve center for the Tibetan community in exile to which Tibetans, often total strangers without introduction, flocked for hospitality. Inside her door and away from the harsh world, it was always serene, an oasis of Tibetan culture.

Her daughter Thupchu-la with whom Amala lived was an indispensable part of this unique home they created. Bustling joyfully back and forth from her nursing job, always busy with many friends, events, and helping Amala with visitors, she and Amala were a team. When she passed away unexpectedly in 1982 in her early forties, it signalled the end of an era for the entire Tibetan community in New York and abroad. Amala was too old to remain in a New York apartment alone, so she left immediately to live with her niece Choden and the Surkhangs in Cleveland, both of whom had nice homes in the suburbs. I had already returned to the University of Pennsylvania two years before to work on my doctoral dissertation. Providentially Amala's long lost half-brother Jigme, from whom she had not heard for many years, had come to visit her from Tibet and was staying for six months when Thupchula died. He had the privilege of doing all that a brother could be asked to do, and went with Amala to Cleveland to help her make the transition while extending his visa from China another six months. Almost as soon as he returned to Lhasa, he died suddenly of a heart attack, in his early fifties. The circle had been completed and the wound of separation healed when his life ended, I am sure with new insight and a sense of fulfillment regarding his identity as a Tibetan.

Amala then began spending about half the year in India with the new incarnation of her guru, and the other six months of the year in Cleveland, with lengthy side trips to the beautiful residence in upstate New York of her friend Domo Geshe Rinpoche, to Seattle where her son Dondul lives with his family, or to Philadelphia to confer with me on the manuscript of her book. She began working on the book only a year after we first met. The first version, which I translated from her Tibetan, read almost like a fairy tale and was very enigmatic, too short for publication. Year by year a little more was added as I requested her to explain more, fill in details, and provide clearer visual descriptions.

After Thupchu-la died, she burned all of the original Tibetan manuscript, thereby frustrating the hopes of many that this book would have a Tibetan language edition for use in Tibetan schools in India. About the same time she also burned the contents of a large yak hair covered trunk full of original deeds and grants of honors and titles from various Dalai Lamas for her family's many estates. This was a great loss to scholars. These lengthy documents were written in exquisite formal calligraphy, stamped with many seals and wrapped in silk, and had been treasured for centuries. She also burned hundreds of letters from her guru, Kyabje Trijang Rinpoche. The yak hair trunk was sold to a museum.

Henceforth the translation of the book became more difficult, since there was no longer an official text from which to work. The manuscript went through several revisions with the help of many people, both Tibetans and Westerners, whose dedication to the project is a tribute both to the charisma of its author and to the uniqueness of the document. Through efforts such as these it is hoped that something of the values and world-view of old Tibet will be preserved as a legacy for future generations.

Appendix I
List of Tibetan Noble Families

I. YABSHI (6)
  * Samdup Photrang (family of the 7th and 9th Dalai Lamas) (bSam grub pho brang)
  * Lhalu (family of the 8th and 12th Dalai Lamas) (lHa klu)
  * Yuthok (family of the 10th Dalai Lama) (gYu thog)
  * Phunkhang (family of the 11th Dalai Lama) (Phun khang)
  * Langdun (family of the 13th Dalai Lama) (gLang mdun)
    Taklha (family of the 14th Dalai Lama (sTag lha)

II. DEPON (4)
    Gashi (Ga' bzhi) or Doring (rDo ring)
  * Thonpa (Thon pa) or Labrang Nyingpa (Bla brang rnying pa)
  * Lhagyari (lHa rgya ri)
    Dhokhar (mDo mkhar) or Ragashar (Ra ga shar)

III. MIDRAK (18)
  * Phalha (Pha lha)
  * Shatra (bShad sgra)
    Rampa (Ram pa)
  * Surkhang (Zur khang)

* Horkhang (Hor khang)
* Changlochen (lCang lo cen)
* Tethong (bKras mthong)
  Taring (Phreng ring)
* Shasur (bShad zur)
* Kunsang Tse (Gun bzang rtse)
  Namse Ling (rNam sras gling)
* Ngabo (Nga phod)
* Sholkhang (Zhol khang)
* Tsarong (Tsha rong)
  Drumpa (Brum pa)
  Lhating (lHa sding)
  Sarjung (gSar byung)
  Shekarlingpa (Shel dkar gling pa)

IV.   GERBA (150)

1.   **Lhasa Nyelkhor** (21)
     Gangtod Chagtrak (sGang stod lcag sprag)
     Chagri Shar (lCag ri shar)
   * Chagrong Chichag (lCag rong spyi lcag)
     Tsesum Phunkang (Tshes gsum phun khang)
     Sonam Gangpa (bSod nam sgang pa)
     Rasa Gyagen (Ra sa rgya rgan)
     Sumdo (gSum mdo)
     Shakabpa (Zha sgab pa)
   * Lhalung Surchi (lHa lung zur pyi)
     Dodrung (rDo grong)
     Tana (sTag rna)
     Taradopa (rTa ra mdo pa)
     Mondrong (monk official) (sMon krong)
     Liushar (monk official) (sNe'u shar)
     Jangthang Teling (monk official) (Byang thang bkras
         gling)
     Barshi (Bar gzhis)
     Thangnang (Thang nang)
     Dhenjatsang (sDan bya tshang)
     Gonshampa (dGon gsham pa)
     Kharab Shenkha (mKhar rab bshan kha)
     Gyaldak   (rGyal stag)

2.   **Phenpo District** (3) ('Phan po rdzong)
     Gyaldong Nangso (rGyal grong nang bzo)

Dokhar Nangso (bDo mkhar nang bzo)
Chang Gyaba (lCang rgyab pa)

3. **Yamdrog District** (2) (Yar 'brog rdzong)
Ling Onpo (gLing dbon po)
Gokhar (sGog mkhar)

4. **Yarlung District** (6) (Yar lung rdzong)
Dathang (mDa' thang)
Ragtsiba (Rag tsib pa)
Deshinpa (bDe zhim pa)
Gongthang (dGon thang)
Karchung (dKar chung)
Nangchung (gNang byung)

5. **Chonggye District** (9) ('Phyongs rgyas rdzong)
Phunrab (Phun rab)
Poshod Phunkhang (sPo shod phun khang)
Phulung (Phu lung)
Dumkhang (sDum khang)
Kharden (mKhar ldan)
Changkhyim (Chang khyim)
Dhumrak (lDum rag)
Bumthang ('Bum thang)
Tashi Perak (bKra shis pad rag)

6. **Drachi Dranang District** (6) (Gra phyi gra nang rdzong)
Drachi Phunrab (Gra phyi phun rab)
Drachi Jhingpa (Gra phyi byings pa)
Dranang Dhumbu (Gra nang ldum bu)
Dranang Chede (Gra nang lce bde)
Dranang Gomo (Gra nang sgo mo)
Dranang Gomo Shontsang (Gra nang sgo ma gzhon tshang)

7. **E District** (3) (E rdzong)
Shakjang (Shag byang)
Gongpo Khangsar (Gong po khang gsar)
Dengyon (sDing yon)

8. **Ölkha District** (2) ('Ol dga' rdzong)
Kharney (mKhar sne)
Drilung ('Bri lung)

9. **Ön District** (1) ('On rdzong)
Trimon (Khri smon)

10. **Nyemo District** (5) (sNye mo rdzong)
    Treshong (bKras gshongs)
    Junpa ('Jun pa)
    Marlampa (rMar lam pa)
    Dogon (rDo dgon)
    Nyemo Dokhar (sNye mo mdo mkhar)

11. **Shang District** (14) (Zhangs rdzong)
    Mon Kyid Ling (sMon skyid gling)
    Nyelung (sNe lung)
    Khonang (Kho nang)
    Kyar Sipa (sKyar srib pa)
    Muja (Mu bya)
    Layajari (Gla a bya ris)
    Drakar (Brag dkar)
    Salung (Sa lung)
    Sikshing (Sreg shing)
    Thangpon (Thang dpon)
    Chumdre (Chum bkras)
    Chapel (Cha spel)
    Driyul ('Bri yul)
    Migyabapa (Mi rgyab pa)

12. **Shigatse District** (11) (gZhis ka rtse rdzongs)
    Samdrupling (bSam grub gling)
    Drakthong Treling (Brag mthong bkras gling)
    Dhingja (sDing by)
    Lholing (lHo gling)
    Palhun (dPal lhun)
    Drekhupa ('Brad khud pa)
    Tshati Dechen (Tsha rdi bde chen)
    Ngapo Tshati (rNga po tsha rdi)
    Thangnang (Thang nang)
    * Tresur (bKras zur)
    Dhosur (mDo zur)

13. **Tanag District** (2) (rTa nag rdzong)
    Lungshar (Lung shar)
    Shukhupa (Shud khud pa)

14. **Panam District** (4) (sPa snam rdzong)
    Patsel (sPa tshal)
    Pishi (sPe gzhi)

Khyungram (Khyung ram)
Nornang (Nor nang)

15. **Gyangtse District** (18) (rGyal rtse rdzong)
Langthong (Glang mthong)
Langsur (Glang zur)
Neshaba (Ne zhab pa)
Netod (sNe stod)
Jiped (Bye phad)
Choktrey (lCog bkras)
Dode (mDo sde)
Numa (Nu ma)
Bonshod (Bon shod)
Drangjun (Grang 'jun)
Drakthon (Brag thon)
Nangkar (sNang dkar) or Changra (lCang rag)
Thangpe (Thang spe)
Nampon (gNam dpon)
Trogawo (Khro dga' bo)
Kyibug (sKyid sbug)
Kyisur (sKyid zur)
Nyendrong (sNyan grong)

16. **Kharkha District** (7) (mKhar kha rdzong)
Kharkha Gyatso (mKhar kha rgya mtsho)
Tarak (rTa rag)
Nangkhor (Nang 'khor)
Kashod (Ka shod)
Thangme (Thang smad)
Maja (rMa bya)
Drangtod ('Brang stod)

17. **Rong District** (10) (Rong rdzong)
Rong Drakpa (Rong brag pa)
Kyimed (sKyid smad)
Kyitod (sKyid stod)
Nara Kyishong (rNa ra skyid gshong)
Rangjon (Rang byon)
Dhemon (bDe smon)
Gadhe (dGa' bde)
Namse (rNam sras)
Gyama Khartsok (rGya ma mkhar tshog)
Nyamon (Nya mon)

18. **Dhojung District** (2) ('Dud byung rdzong)
    Dhojung Kyibug ('Dud byung skyid sbug)
    Drum Phola (Brum pho la)

19. **Wangden District** (5) (dBang ldan rdzong)
    Bartso (Bar mtsho)
    Goyang (sGo yang)
    Chalu (Cha lu)
    Chokpe (lCog spe)
    Kashi (Ka bzhi)

20. **Tod District** (7) (sTod rdzong)
    Tsogo (mTsho sgo)
    Gyelkhar Nangpa (rGyal mkhar nang pa)
    Shekarlingpa (Shel dkar gling pa)
    Lhamdun (lHa mdun)
    Ruthok Gyalbo (Ru thok rgyal po)
    Mentod (sMan stod)
    Omalung (rNgu ma lung)

21. **Dakpo District** (1) (Dwags po rdzong)
    Lathok Surkhar (La thog zur mkhar)

22. **Kongbo District** (1) (Kong po rdzong)
    Changdrong (lCang grong)

23. **Jhar District** (1)(sByar yul)
    Shagpa (bZhag pa)

24. **Jayul District** (1) (Ja yul)
    Drokhawag (Gro mkhar 'og)

25. **Lhuntse District** (2) (lHun rtse rdzong)
    Sonphu (Zom phud)
    Shaywo (Zhe 'o)

26. **Tholung Dechen District** (3) (rDo lung bde chen
       rdzong)
    Jhangopa (Bya ngos pa)
    Ringang (Rin sgang)
    Seshim (Zas zhim)

27. **Gongkar District** (4) (Gong dkar rdzong)
    Worbug Gyatso ('Or sbug rgya mtsho)
    Mongong (sMon gong)
    Gegyapa (dGe rgyas pa)
    Thonsur (Thon zur)

Appendix II
Yuthok and Surkhang Family Trees

Key: capitalized names indicate aristocratic surnames.

    m. = marriage

    x. = liaison outside of formal marriage

YUTHOK FAMILY TREE

YUTHOK Shapey (senior) and wife

I. YUTHOK Shapey (junior) Phuntsok Palden m. SHUDKHUDPA (GOSHIS PELING) Tsering Yudon
- A. YUTHOK Tsering Wangdu
  - m.1 SHOLKHANG Kunsang
    1. YUTHOK Yangzom m. LHALUNG SURCHI
       - 4 sons, 3 dau.
    2. YUTHOK Tsering Dorje [makpa]
       - m.1 RONGTRAK Dekyi
         - 2 sons, 2 dau. [RONGTRAK]
       - m.2 SURKHANG Lhawang Dolma
         - (author's younger sister who had divorced SHEKARLINGPA)
         - 2 sons, 3 dau. [RONGTRAK]
    3. YUTHOK Rigden Wangmo m. MENTOD
       - 2 dau.
    4. YUTHOK Yangchen Pema m. TRESUR Palden Gyaltsen
       - 1 son, 2 dau.

    m.2 YABSHI LANGDUN Chime Yudon (13th Dalai
    Lama's niece)
        5. YUTHOK Tsering Dolkar m. TSATI Dechen
            no children
        6. YUTHOK Tseten Dolkar (elder) m. NGABO
            Ngawang Jigme
            5 sons, 7 dau.
        7. YUTHOK Dekyi Lhaze m. SURKHANG
            Wangchen Gelek and SURKHANG Lhawang
            Topgyal (author's brothers)
            1 son, 1 dau.
        8. YUTHOK Tseten Dolkar (younger)
            x. SURKHANG Lhawang Topgyal (same as g.
            m.1 above)
                1 dau.
            m.1 ZESHIM Pema Sengay
                1 dau.
        9. YUTHOK Tsering Paldon
            m.1 NANGCHUNG
                1 son
            m.2 SAMLING
                1 son, 1 dau.
        10. YUTHOK Mingyur Drolma m. MARLAMPA
            4 sons, 4 dau.
    B. YUTHOK Dorje Wangdu (makpa)
        m. YABSHI LANGDUN Tsetzin Palmo (13th Dalai
        Lama's niece) although adopted by Yabshi Langdun, he
        was known as Senang Se after one of their estates,
        Senang. He lived in the same house as Silon Yabshi
        Langdun Kunga Wangchuk, the head of the house and
        his brother-in-law)
        1. YABSHI LANGDUN Yeshe Wangmo m.
            CHAGTRONG CHICHAG
            1 son, 3 dau.
        2. YABSHI LANGDUN Wangchen Palmo
            m.1 GYALKAR NANGPA
            m.2 YABSHI LANGDUN Kalsang
                (13th Dalai Lama's niece)
        3. YABSHI LANGDUN Dechen m. PATSEL SURPA
        4. YABSHI LANGDUN Phuntsok Drakdul (makpa)
            m. the Tenma Oracle
        5. YABSHI LANGDUN Kalsang m. TSATI Dechen
            (see I.A.5)
                3 children
        6. Dhedruk Rinpoche (Drepung Monastery)
    C. YUTHOK Thupten Tsultrim (Geshe Lharampa at Ganden
    Monastery)

D. YUTHOK Palden Chokyi
   m.1 CHANGLOCHEN Sonam Gyalpo
      1. CHANGLOCHEN Wangdu Dorje
         x. Phudron
            2 sons, 2 dau.
   m.2 KYIBUG
      2. KYIBUG Rigzin Dorje (makpa) m.
         KHEMED (KUNSANGTSE) Kalsang Yangki
         (the daughter of the author's paternal uncle
         who went to Khemed as a makpa).
         4 sons, 5 dau.
      3. KYIBUG Phuntsok Tseten ⌐
                 m. PHALA Ngawang Palmo
      4. KYIBUG Dondrup Phuntsok ⌐   3 children
      5. KYIBUG Chime Dolkar m. KHARASEPA
         1 dau.
      6. KYIBUG Kunga
      7. KYIBUG Tsewang Dorje (m) SUMDO
E. YUTHOK Kalsang Yonten (separated and took estate of
Dathang)
   x.1 YABSHI PHUNKHANG Rinzin Dolkar
   x.2 Nepalese girl (Pema)
      1. DATHANG Jorning
F. YUTHOK Tashi Dondrup (author's husband)
   m.1 YABSHI LANGDUN Chime Yudon (see
   I.A.m.2—also married to the eldest brother)
      1. YUTHOK Rigzin Tsetan m. Princess of Sikkim
      Pema Chokyi
         2 sons, 1 dau.
      2. YUTHOK Jigme Dorje m. POMDATSANG Wangmo
         2 dau.
   m.2 SURKHANG Dorje Yudon (author)
      3. YUTHOK Sonam Paldon (died infancy)
      4. YUTHOK Gyalten Wangchuk x. Norbu Lhamo
         2 sons, Jigme and Namgyal Phuntsok
      5. YUTHOK Dondul Wangchuk m. CHAMATSANG
      Tsering Choden
         2 sons, Rinzin Paljor and Tsewang Topgyal
         1 dau., Tsering Yudon
      6. YUTHOK Thupten Choden
   x.3 LUNGSHAR Phurpo Dolma
      7. LUNGSHAR Jampa (makpa)
         m.1 PHORONG Jepon
            1 dau.
         m.2 Swiss girl
            2 dau.
   x.4 SHOLKHANG Tsering Dolkar
      8-10. 3 dau., Tsepal, Namla, Tsenzom

II. Jamyang Tenzin (monk official, Chikyab Khenpo)

III. YUTHOK Depon, lived with Bhutanese girl (1 son)

IV. First daughter lived with Tagtselag in Yamda (3 dau.)

V. Second daughter m. Shigatse Dhondup Khangsar (2 sons, 5 daughters)

VI. Third daughter m. THANGMAD (1 son)

SURKHANG FAMILY TREE

SURKHANG Shapey Tseten Dorje m. eldest sister of 9th Dalai Lama

I. SURKHANG Tsering Palden (makpa) m. TRESHONG
    A. TRESHONG Tsewang Topgyal
       no children

II. SURKHANG (makpa) m. SHATRA
    A. SHATRA Dekyi m. PHOKPON SHENKA's son Paljor
    Dorje (makpa) (became Prime Minister and went to India in
    1910 with the Dalai Lama)
       1. SHATRA Namgyal Wangmo
          m.1 YABSHI LHALU Kung
             no children
          m.2 Samye Oracle
       2. SHATRA (Depon of the Dalai Lama's bodyguard)
          m. KYIBUG
             children died young
       3. SHATRA Tsering Lhamo m. PHALA
             a. PHALA Thupten Woden, monk official,
                Chief of Protocol of Potala Palace
             b. PHALA Wangchuk
             c. PHALA Dorje Wangyal m. KUNSANG
                TSE
             d. PHALA Yangchen Dolkar
             e. PHALA Sonam Lhamo
             f. PHALA Ngawang Palmo
       4. SHATRA SURPA (SHASUR) Gyurme Sonam
          Topgyal (Cabinet Minister who went to India in
          1959 with the Dalai Lama)
          m. DAMBAK SIMKHANG Tsering Dolma
             1 son, 1 dau.
    B. SHATRA Norzin m. PHOKPON SHENKA's son Paljor
    Dorje (see Surkhang II.A)
       1. SHATRA Lhoden Wangmo m. THONBA
          3 sons, 3 dau.
       2. SHATRA Paljor m. GONKAR GYATSO
          1 son
       3. SHATRA Lhayon Dolma m. LUNGSHAR (makpa)
          2 sons, 1 dau.

4. Khongpo Sharpa Rinpoche at Sera Monastery
5. Jokpo Rinpoche at Sera Monastery
6. Shatra Dhondup Dolma m. SARCHUNG
    4 sons, 1 dau.

III. SURKHANG Tseten Yudon
  m.1 TRIMON
    A. TRIMON Tseten Gyalmo m. HORKHANG Shapey Sonam
    Topgyal (suicide 1903)
        1. HORKHANG Kunzang Zompa m. TETHONG
        SURPA Dorje Wangyal (makpa)
            2 dau.
        2. HORKHANG Dechen Champa x.
            1 son (HORKHANG Ngawang Jigme)
        3. HORKHANG Nima Lhamo m. LHAGYARI
        Topjor Wangchuk (author's paternal uncle)
            2 sons, 4 dau.
        4. HORKHANG Kalsang Dolma m. YABSHI
        SAMDRUP PHOTRANG Chakdor Tsering
                a. YABSHI SAMDRUP PHOTRANG
                Namdrol Sangmo
                    x. CHISO
                b. YABSHI SAMDRUP PHOTRANG
                Phuntsok Tsering
                    (makpa) m. TSOGO
                c. YABSHI SAMDRUP PHOTRANG
                Tsewang Rinzin (Prime Minister left
                behind when Dalai Lama escaped in 1959)
                    m. KUNSANG TSE Kalsang Yangki
                    (see Yuthok I.D.2)
                d. YABSHI SAMDRUP PHOTRANG
                Sonam Wangchen
        5. HORKHANG Tsering Dolma m. son of their
        steward
            3 children
        6. HORKHANG Dzasa Sonam Wangchuk m.
        TSARONG Tseten Dolkar
            1 son, 1 dau.
  m.2 CHANGLO Wangchen Norbu (makpa)
    B. SURKHANG Kalsang Choden (nun at "Kunzang Choling"
    in Drak)
    C. SURKHANG Sonam Wangchen m. RONGNARA
    KYISHONG Namgyal Dolma
        1. SURKHANG Samdup Tseten
            m.1 LHAGYARI Tseten Chozom (author's
            parents)
                a. SURKHANG Wangchen Gelek ⌐
                            m. YUTHOK Dekyi Lhaze
                b. SURKHANG Lhawang Topgyal ⌐

       i. SURKHANG Nuchin Tinlay
      ii. SURKHANG Jampa Yangchen
        m. LHAKATSANG Tingyal
        2 children
    x. YUTHOK Tseten Dolkar
       i. YUTHOK Tashi Paldon
        m. LANGSUR Lhundrup
        Dorje (drowned)
        2 children
  c. SURKHANG Dorje Yudon (author) m.
  YUTHOK Tashi Dondrup
    4 children (see Yuthok)
  d. SURKHANG Lhawang Dolma
      m.1 SHEKARLINGPA Sonam Topgyal
       i. SHEKARLINGPA Thundup
        Phuntsok (makpa) m.
        PHUNRAB Kalsang Wangmo
          a. PHUNRAB
       ii. SHEKARLINGPA Choden
        Dolkar
          m. Mel Goldstein
          1 son
      m.2 RONGTRAK Tsering Dorje
       iii. RONGTRAK Palden Gyaltsen
       iv. RONGTRAK Norzin Dolkar
         m. Ngargyal
         1 son, 2 dau.
       v. RONGTRAK Jampa Gyalpo &
       wife
         1 son
       vi. RONGTRAK Namgyal Yangki
        m. DHONBO Dhargyey
        2 sons, 1 dau.
       vii. RONGTRAK Tsering Yangki
  e. SURKHANG Wangchuk Dorje x. Pema
  Yangzon (Bhutanese)
       i. SURKHANG Dechen Paldon
      ii. Decho Yongzin Rinpoche at
       Rumtek Monastery
  f. SURKHANG Sonam Namgyal
    (died infancy)
x. Dawa Dolma
  g. SURKHANG Ngawang Jigme (author's
  half brother)
    x.1 Chunyi Wangden Pembar
      i. Tamdrin Dorje
      ii. Chimi

x.2 Dechen Chodron
   iii. Ngawang Gyurmey
   iv. Diki Palmo
2. SURKHANG Pema Wangchen m. SHAKJANG
   Tsering Yangchen
      1 son died infancy
3. SURKHANG Sonam Wangdu (makpa) m.
   KHEMED (KUNSANGTSE) Dekyi Yangchen,
   dau. of KHEMED Shapey Rinchen Wangyal
      a. KHEMED Yeshe Dolma m. DELEK
         RABTEN
            1 son, 1 dau.
      b. KHEMED Kalsang Yangki (makpa) m.
         KYIBUG Rinchen Dorje
            4 sons, 5 dau.
      c. KHEMED Jamyang Lhodro (monk
         official)
4. SURKHANG Norbu Tsering (makpa) m. YABSHI
   SAMDRUP PHOTRANG (Chakdor Tsering's
   sister—see Surkhang III.m.1.4)
      a. YABSHI SAMDRUP PHOTRANG
         Palden Chowang, Depon (not married)
      b. YABSHI SAMDRUP PHOTRANG
         Dechen Tsomo
            (died young)
      c. Lilung Chitrong Rinpoche at Drepung
         Monastery
5. SURKHANG Dorje Yangki m. CHANGLOCHEN
   Kung Namgyal Tseten
      a. CHANGLOCHEN Namgyal Tsewang
         x. Lakyil Kyimo
      b. CHANGLOCHEN Dekyong Wangmo
         x. Nendak of Dhidruk Dechang
            Labrang
            1 dau. Dekyi m. Wangdu of
               Dhidruk Dechang Labrang
            1 dau. Nyima Norzom
      c. CHANGLOCHEN Sonam Gyalpo
         m.1 YUTHOK Palden Chokyi
            (YUTHOK Tashi Dondrup's sister)
            i. CHANGLOCHEN Wangdu
               Dorje
                  m. Yeshe Wangmo (see Yuthok
                  I.D.m.1)
                     1 son, 2 dau.
                  x. Phudron
                     2 sons, 2 dau.

m.2 SHAKJANG Tsering Yangchen
(widow of SURKHANG Pema
Wangchen, author's paternal uncle)
  ii. CHANGLOCHEN Yangchen
  Dolkar
    x. Ngawang
  iii. CHANGLOCHEN Wangchuk
  Gyalpo
    m. TETHONG Tsering
    Wangmo
      a. Tsewang Gyurme
      b. Wangchuk Namgyal
      c. Phuntsok Namgyal
      d. Tsewang Dorje
      e. Tsering Yangchen
  iv. CHANGLOCHEN Ngondup
  Wangmo
    m. YABSHI PUNKHANG
    Lobsang Wangyal
    1 son, 2 dau.
6. SURKHANG Wangdu Dolma (nun at Tsering Jong
Nunnery)
7. SURKHANG Jigme Dorje
  x. Yeshe Tsomo
  2 sons, 3 dau.

IV. SURKHANG Tsering Dorje (separated from Surkhang with his mother
who was sister of 9th Dalai Lama and became DECHEN KHARAB
SHENKA) x. TRENGPO DHIRAB Chime
  A. DECHEN KHARAB SHENKHA Choje Phuntsok
    x. MINDRUBUG Yangchen
      1. DECHEN KHARAB SHENKA Jampa Chowang
      (monk official)
      2. DECHEN KHARAB SHENKA Dorje m. BOTHE
      PELING Tsering Dolma
        3 sons

Notes

Chapter 1. Drak: My Birthplace

1. She later was to marry my future husband and his elder brother.

2. One quintal is equal to 220 lbs.

Chapter 2. The Branched House of Surkhang

1. Shatra Kalon Wangchuk Gyalpo.

Chapter 3. Childhood in Lhasa

1. My older brother Wangchen Gelek was born in Lhasa in 1910; I was born in 1912 in Drak; my younger brother Lhawang Topgyal was born in Gyamda in Kongbo in 1914 while my father was posted there in government service; my sister Lhawang Dolma was born in 1918; my youngest brother Wangchuk Dorje was born in Lhasa in 1920; and another brother Sonam Namgyal was born in 1922 but only lived for one year.

2. Many years later as a refugee in India she wrote her life story in a book called *Daughter of Tibet* (London: John Murray, 1970).

Chapter 5. The Pilgrim's Life

1. Udantapuri was a great Buddhist monastery in Bihar, India, which flourished after Vikramashila and was destroyed under the order of Baktyar Khilji, a Moslem king, in 1203 A.D.

2. Queen Sa Hor Maghen built Khamsung Sangkhar Ling. Queen Phoyong Sa Gyanmo Tsun built Pho Tsal Serkhang Ling. Queen Changchuk Je built Geygae Lima Ling.

3. Grandmother had given birth to nine children: 1) Tsewang Yudon (daughter), 2) Topjor Wangchuk (son), 3) Guru Rinpoche of Mon Tawang Monastery (son), 4) Namgyal Wangchuk (son), 5) Urgyen Chozom, (daughter), 6) Yeshe Wangmo, (daughter), 7) Kunsang Dekyi (daughter), 8) Yondo Rinpoche of Yardok Monastery (son), and 9) Tseten Chozom (our mother). I had seen only three daughters: Urgyen Chozom, Yeshe Wangmo and Kunsang Dekyi. All of the rest of her children had died a long time back.

4. Trichen literally means "great enthroned one" and is a title of royalty. The Lhagyaris were the only family in Tibet to claim direct male descent from the early kings of our country.

Chapter 6. Mistress of Treshong, the Lucky Valley

1. Chime Yudon of the Yabshi Langdun family. She was the Thirteenth Dalai Lama's niece.

Chapter 7. Marriage

1. See Prince Peter of Greece and Denmark, *The Polyandry of Tibet*, Actes du IVe Congrès International des Sciences Anthropologiques et Ethnologiques (Vienna: 1955), in which he discusses the Surkhang marriages.

Chapter 8. Yuthok: House of the Turquoise Roof

1. Rimshi's first wife was the daughter of the Sholkhang family, and was named Kunzang Dolma. Rimshi and Kunzang Dolma had one son and two daughters. While she was carrying her fourth child, they experienced problems in their marriage and

she returned to her family. The three children stayed with the father. The son, Tsering Dorje, later went to the Rongtrak family as a bridegroom more than seven years before I married my husband. Chime Yudon was Rimshi's second wife by whom he had six more children, all girls.

2. One khel equals approximately 32 lbs.

3. Her husband was the brother of Rimshi Yuthok's second wife. Tsering Wangmo herself was the daughter of Rimshi's cousin, Mrs. Kharkha Gyatso. Mrs. Gyatso's mother was Rimshi's aunt on his father's side.

Chapter 9. Jewels and Finery

1. The sixteen different kinds of ornaments were:

(1) *Patruk*

In earlier periods this headdress was worn at all times by women, but later on during my mother's time it was worn only during special occasions. The form for this headdress was made by rolling a cotton cloth into the thickness of one inch in diameter. This roll was covered with a red woolen cloth, decorated with corals, turquoise, and sometimes pearls. There were two kinds of patruks. The *mutig patruk*, or pearl patruk, has fourteen red corals the size of a large hen's egg and eight turquoises the size of marbles, as well as many seed pearls. The *yukyang-churkyang*, or turquoise and coral headdress, had about thirty-six large corals and thirty-five turquoises of fine quality. But if it had smaller stones, there would be about sixty corals and fifty-nine turquoises. In earlier days a patruk was worn in everyday life. The form was sometimes worn without any jewels at all. Gradually after 1930 the wearing of the patruk and other ornaments decreased.

(2) *Lentse*

This piece was a little like a wig and was worn along with the patruk. First a strip of black cloth was made to fit on the head. From this cloth eight long thick strands of hair were attached, three on each side and two hanging down the back. The hair was braided and then decorated with jewels and binding string imported from China. These braids hung to the ankles and were connected with red silk string called *trap-shu* that almost touched the ground.

(3) *Tsigyu Thakpa*
This ornament was fastened to the top of the patruk on the crown of the head. It was made in an exquisite design out of many seed pearls and one special large turquoise mounted on gold. One of the most beautiful types of jewelry, it was regarded as very precious. It had to be worn by the bride in her marriage ceremony. Placing a turquoise on top of the bride's head is an ancient Tibetan custom.

(4) *Mutig Thugkog*
In the same way as the tsigyu thakpa, this ornament was worn on the top of the patruk. Sometimes we used a mutig thugkog and sometimes a tsigyu thakpa, but both could not be worn at the same time. This ornament was shaped just like a pot. A form was made by bending thin bamboo sticks into the shape of a bowl and covering it with white cotton, pearls and a few turquoises. This piece was worn only on rare occasions.

(5) *Trakey*
This was a string of small pearls with four red corals with only one turquoise. It was almost ten inches long and was used for holding two braids together in an especially beautiful design. These strings of pearls and red corals were woven into the braids. This ornament was normally worn with the lentse by being attached in two places to the lentse and hung down the back.

(6) *Trakey Norbu Gakyil*
This trakey was also used to hold the two braids together but was very elaborate. There were bunches of pearls with a locket-like golden flap at the center. The strings of these pearls were woven into the braids giving a very pretty effect. This piece was worn on very special occasions of great pomp and show, and was worn in the same fashion as the trakey.

(7) *Agor*
This earring type ornament was elongated in shape and made out of gold studded with turquoise. It was fastened

to the patruk by a hook. It was always worn in pairs which hung down on each side of the face hiding the ears from view, and was worn always.

(8) *Agor Drum-Zar*

This was also an agor, but more elaborate. It was made almost like the agor described above but a string of pearls, corals, and turquoises about six inches long hung from each agor. In olden days this was worn at most ceremonial affairs, but about 1850 the more simple agor was substituted because it was more convenient to wear.

(9) *Gau*

This was a pendant box about three inches square and one inch deep made out of gold in a geometric pattern. The top surface was almost completely covered by semi-precious and precious stones such as turquoise, rubies, blue sapphires, emeralds and sometimes a few diamonds. This ornament was put on a string of beads consisting of eight corals, six *gzi* (a costly stone somewhat like an onyx) along with some pearls strung in a pattern. There was a second string of beads made with pearls, semi-precious and precious stones attached to the pendant in such a way that it hung parallel with other strings, but was worn high up on the chest.

(10) *Gau Sum Drum*

These were worn three in number and, except being smaller, they were almost like a gau pendant. The three pieces were strung together with a string of corals, gzi, and pearls. The middle pendant was worn at the waist while the others were placed a little higher on either side and worn only for special occasions.

(11) *Kyetreng*

This was a kind of necklace reaching down to the abdomen. It was made with more than one hundred rounded jade stones, twenty pieces of coral and fourteen pieces of turquoise. All of these semi-precious stones were arranged in a special design and worn frequently.

(12) *Yar Then*

This piece of jewelry was made with many strings of small pearls and was always worn with kyetreng on the left breast. The main purpose of this ornament was to lift the kyetreng and hold it in the desired position. Three ornaments made out of gold mounted with turquoise and other precious stones were fixed to the many strings of pearls with one at the top, one in the middle and one at the bottom.

(13) *Karshal Marshal Gyushal*

This ornament was a long string of round beads each about the size of an American penny, made of amber, coral, and turquoise. There were more than one hundred of each kind of bead, some of which were specially decorated. The string of beads would reach below the knee, and it was worn only for marriage or special celebrations.

(14) *Dikra Longtreng*

This piece included seven gold or silver pieces, all flat and diamond-shaped, fastened together to make one ornament. In the center of each was a design made out of turquoise. The largest was worn over the abdomen. On each side there were two smaller pieces of the same shape, one smaller than the other. The smaller ones hooked on to each side of the dress. There were two short narrow pieces of cloth sewn at the waist that were put through the hooks and tied to hold the ornaments in place. Hanging from the largest ornament that rested on the abdomen would be two smaller ornaments graded in size. The lower one had a hook. Two very long strings of small beads of turquoise, coral, and pearls were fastened to this hook. The other end was fastened to the smaller ornaments at the waist. These long strings of beads hung to about six inches above the ankle.

(15) *Bakug* and *Khabshub*

Bakug literally means purse and *khabshub* means a needle case. In olden days the ladies would fasten a purse to a belt on the left side of the back. A needle case would hang from the belt down the right side of the back. By the time I was born, there was no purse and no needle case, but an elaborate non-functional ornament had been developed from the original design. For fixing this ornament a belt was worn at the waist. The ornament was worn in pairs, one hanging on the right side of the back and the other hanging from the left side of the back. A round silver disc with a hook in the center attached the piece onto the belt. A silver chain about four inches long fell from the center of the silver disc. At the end of this chain was an elaborate embossed silver ornament from which four long streamers made out of silver fell. Because they were worn at the back, one had to be careful not to sit on them. They were not used much in my day.

(16) *Nagyen*

Nagyen literally means earring. In my day the earrings were of simple design. When no special earrings were worn, ladies like my mother used to wear simple gold rings in their ears for keeping the holes in the ear from closing. When I was a young girl the fashion of wearing earrings became popular, and by the time I was a young woman the new fashion was pearl earrings, which I started to wear. Afterwards the taste of some changed to diamonds. I wanted to follow the sophisticated fashion, so I wore diamond earrings. Any style of earring was called a nagyen, and this is the only modern type of jewelry among the traditional ornaments of Tibetan women. In olden days women wore only small pieces of turquoise that were fastened on a thread pulled through the hole in the ears.

2. See Note 1, sections (3), (6), and (14) above.

Chapter 11. Wife of the Governor of Kham

1. Although Do-Med was the name used officially by the Tibetan government, I will use the synonymous term "Kham" which is more familiar to most readers.

2. My husband's niece and Rimshi's daughter, Tsering Paldon, was the daughter-in-law of Kalon Nangjung.

3. Phala Thupten Woeden (1910-1984) served as Chief of Protocol to H. H. the Dalai Lama from 1945 until 1959. Afterwards he served as Representative of the Dalai Lama in the Office of Tibet in Switzerland.

Chapter 12. Table with Broken Legs

1. He later became a close family friend and was killed in the fight against the Chinese at the Norbu Lingka in 1959.

2. Author of *A Political History of Tibet*, 2 vols. (Delhi: T. Tsepal Taikhang, 1976).

3. She was the daughter of the King (Gyalbo) of Derge; her sister was married to the King of Lingtsang. These small kingdoms were all located in Kham.

4. His mother was the niece of the Thirteenth Dalai Lama, married to both my husband and his brother Rimshi.

5. Subject of the book by Lama Govinda, *The Way of the White Clouds* (Berkeley: Shambala Publications, 1970).

Chapter 13. Escape

1. Author of *My Life and Lives* (New York: E. P. Dutton, 1977).

2. Rinchen Tsetan, the son of my husband by his first wife, the niece of the Thirteenth Dalai Lama.

Glossary

AMBAN: the Chinese ambassador in Lhasa.

BODHISATTVA: one who vows to attain enlightenment for the sake of liberating all suffering beings.

CELESTIAL BURIAL GROUNDS: also called sky burial grounds. Consecrated areas where human corpses were taken for disposal by being cut into pieces and left for the vultures.

CHAMBUL: a gesture of respect offered by bowing slightly or joining the hands together in front of the face and raising and lowering them briefly.

CHANG: Tibetan beer, brewed from barley.

CHANGTZOD: the head servant or treasurer of a household or estate.

CHEMAR: a ceremonial offering of tsampa, in which a pinch is tossed in the air as an auspicious sign.

CHENREZI: the Tibetan name for Avalokiteshvara, the Bodhisattva of Compassion, the patron deity of Tibet.

CHOGYALS: the early religious kings of Tibet.

DEPON: one of the three groups of noble families at the top of the aristocracy of old Tibet, consisting of four families all with enormous land holdings. Also a fourth-rank general or commander of the guards—pronounced the same, but spelled differently in Tibetan.

DHARMA PROTECTOR: mundane deities tamed by highly realized beings and pledged by them to protect the dharma.

DRI: the Tibetan name for the female yak.

DROMA: tiny dark brown sweet potatoes prepared for special occasions and served as a delicacy.

DZONGPON: a district head.

GERPA: the largest group of noble families in old Tibet ranking below the midrak; included 137 families.

INCARNATE LAMA: (Tib.: tulku) The reincarnation of a famous teacher, usually recognized in childhood and educated to fill that teacher's former position.

KASHAG: the Cabinet of the government of the Dalai Lama.

KATA: a white silk offering scarf presented in formal greeting.

KHABSEY: special deep-fried pastries made for the New Year.

LAMA: a religious teacher, the Tibetan equivalent of the term guru.

LONGCHANG: the engagement ceremony in the bride's house, during which a marriage contract would be signed by representatives of the two families. If the groom was going to join the bride's house as a makpa, then Longchang was held in the groom's house.

LOSAR: the Tibetan New Year, which occurs at the new moon during the Western months of February or March.

MAKPA: a bridegroom adopted into a noble family with no male heirs, to marry one of the daughters and take her family name. He inherited the estates and assumed the accompanying government duties. A makpa is also brought in at times when the male heir is too young or suffers some form of abnormality.

MAMA: literally *mother* in Tibetan. Refers to a governess or nursemaid who tended the children of wealthy families until they reached the age of six or seven.

MIDRAK: one of the four groups at the top of the aristocracy of old Tibet, consisting of sixteen families.

MOMOS: steamed dumplings usually filled with meat.

MONLAM: the great prayer festival in Lhasa held during the first fifteen days of the new year.

NYERPA: a storekeeper, one of the head servants of a household or estate who would oversee the allocation of supplies.

NYERTSANG: the municipal council overseeing both the religious and secular affairs of Lhasa.

PATRUK: the jeweled headdress worn by the women of Lhasa and central Tibet prior to 1959.

POTALA PALACE: the winter residence of the Dalai Lama in Lhasa and seat of his government, built by the Fifth Dalai Lama in the seventeenth century.

REGENT: the monk official heading the Tibetan government during the minority or absence of the Dalai Lama.

RINPOCHE: literally "Precious One," the title of address for incarnate lamas often used with great teachers as a term of respect.

ROOT GURU: one's most important personal spiritual guide and mentor.

SAWANG: a lay cabinet minister.

SHAPEY: same as sawang or kalon.

TRUNGNYIG: one of the head servants of a household or estate appointed as secretary. He has to be literate and possess accounting skills.

TSAMPA: roasted barley flour, the staple food of Tibet.

TSEDRUNG: a monk official in the Tibetan government.

TSOKPA: a religious, social, or trade association in old Lhasa, whose members would carry out religious or civic as well as social duties.

TSUGLAK KHANG: the great central cathedral of Lhasa and holiest temple in Tibet, built in the eighth century.

WONGKHOR: a harvest celebration which included a ceremony of circling the fields.

WRATHFUL DEITY: a wrathful manifestation of an enlightened being who uses vigorous and apparently wrathful methods to overcome negativities.

YABSHI: one of the highest ranking groups of families in the aristocracy of old Tibet, consisting of families into which a Dalai Lama had been born and their descendants.